D1478633

A Parent's Guide to Gifted Children

A Resource for Caregivers and Advocates

(second edition)

Edward R. Amend, Psy.D.
Emily Kircher-Morris, LPC
Janet L. Gore, M.Ed.

Foreword by Arlene DeVries, M.S.E.

Gifted
UNLIMITED

Edited by: William D. Beuscher
Interior design: The Printed Page
Cover design: Kelly Crimi

Published by
Gifted Unlimited, LLC
12340 U.S. Highway 42, No. 453
Goshen, KY 40026
www.giftedunlimitedllc.com

ISBN: 978-1-953360-17-5

Table of Contents

List of Tables

A Tribute to Those
Who Paved the Way

Many books are published every year. Some are memorable, others are not. In the early 1980s, one published book changed the conversation about gifted children. *Guiding the Gifted Child*, written by Elizabeth (Betty) Meckstroth, Stephanie Tolan, and Dr. James (Jim) Webb put forth a message that highlighted parents' concerns about their gifted children. More importantly, it provided parents and teachers with understanding and strategies to help gifted children grow and develop fully.

I first met Jim Webb in the fall of 1990 at Wright State University's School of Professional Psychology. Jim became my mentor and friend, which I have written about in many places. I met both Betty and Stephanie a few years later through gifted events, such as SENG Conferences and NAGC Conventions. While I did not know either anywhere near as well as I knew Jim, I always admired them and their work, and I appreciated their dedication to gifted children. Each of those three authors took a different path to serving gifted youth, and each did it with distinction. They directly influenced my life and my career.

Guiding the Gifted Child created awareness of the social and emotional needs of gifted children, and much has changed since. Through the work of many others' research and books, the knowledge base about gifted children grew, awareness extended, and better environments were created for gifted children. The list is too long to mention all the others who helped grow the field of gifted education and psychology, and I'll cite just a few who have had a tremendous and direct impact on me, my thinking, and my work. They include Jim Delisle, Sylvia Rimm, George Betts, Julia Roberts, Joy Lawson Davis, Thomas Hebert, Tracy Cross, Maureen Neihart, and Sharon Lind. Each has placed their mark on both the gifted world and me, and I thank them for that.

Twenty years ago, when Jim Webb asked me to co-author a book he wanted to write about the misdiagnosis of gifted children, I eagerly agreed. With four other scholars, we wrote *Misdiagnosis and Dual Diagnoses of Gifted Children and Adults* in 2005. Later, Jim, his wife Janet Gore, Arlene DeVries, and I set out to write a comprehensive resource for parents, caregivers, and other advocates. We published *A Parent's Guide to Gifted Children* in 2007. Now, more than 15 years later, it is time for a revision. Sadly, Jim died in 2018 and so he was not able to be part of this second edition, but I know he was with us in spirit. I can hear him in my ear saying, "What about this? Don't forget about that! You can't cut that!" It always makes me smile.

After dedicating much of her life to educating gifted children, my friend Arlene DeVries is enjoying her retirement and decided not to be part of this revision. Arlene provided much knowledge and insight to the first edition and in her authorship of the *SENG Model Parent Group* manual. She made a tremendous impact on gifted children and their families in her many years presenting internationally and working in schools.

For this 2023 revision, I partnered with Emily Kircher-Morris, a respected clinician, speaker, and author, and first edition co-author Janet Gore, who conceptualized much of the framework for the original version of this book with Jim. Together, we have tried to follow in the footsteps of the many others before us to provide an updated resource to guide those who care about gifted children and support them on their journey.

—Edward R. Amend, Psy.D.

Foreword

Through facilitating countless SENG (Supporting Emotional Needs of the Gifted) model parent discussion groups over several decades, I have discovered parents of gifted children are desperate to meet and learn from educators and other parents of gifted. While all parents want what is best for their children, parents of bright children often wonder if typical strategies will work for them. Because bright children process information differently, the usual parenting advice is often ineffective for them. Additionally, the fast pace and complexities of modern society demand new approaches to raising these children. Instead of the traditional two parent family, students may now grow up with a single parent, stepparents, same-sex parents, or blended families. Issues of sibling rivalry persist in families, especially those with intense, gifted children. School populations are more diverse and teaching approaches are ever changing. It can be difficult to keep up, and effective communication is challenging in our technology saturated era.

The current authors, with extensive experience with gifted and twice-exceptional children (those with high intellect and also a physical, mental, or emotional disability), provide guidance in navigating the challenges associated with supporting gifted children in today's complex world. They assure that giftedness is not overlooked in parenting and focus squarely on the needs of these unique individuals.

They recognize what I have seen countless times in my groups—quick learners, when not challenged, can become disillusioned or depressed.

Their uneven or asynchronous development can cause problems understanding themselves. Their idealism can lead to perfectionism when goals for themselves, others, or society are set so impossibly high or unattainable that they consider themselves failures. Their social difficulties can include finding peers and fitting in.

With the countless challenges gifted students present to parents and teachers, *A Parent's Guide to Gifted Children: A Resource for Caregivers and Advocates* is a "must read" for all the concerned adults in their lives. Readers of this book will discover ways to communicate with their gifted children, strategies for motivating and disciplining them, avenues for fostering healthy perfectionism, and methods to help them pursue their own ideals without giving up their true identity to be accepted.

Schooling is only one aspect of your child's education. It takes a "village" of parents, relatives, teachers, neighbors, community organizations, professionals, and other parents of gifted. This book will guide you through the maze of issues.

Arlene R. DeVries, M.S.E.
Parent
Co-author of the first edition
Retired Gifted Educator

Preface

Parenting a gifted child is like living in a theme park full of thrill rides. Sometimes you smile. Sometimes you gasp. Sometimes you scream. Sometimes you laugh. Sometimes you gaze in wonder and astonishment. Sometimes you're frozen in your seat. Sometimes you're proud. And sometimes the ride is so nerve-racking, you can't do anything but cry.[1]

~Carol Strip & Gretchen Hirsch

Being a parent of a gifted child is an experience that is often filled with joy and laughter. These children are exciting and exhilarating, and it is a true pleasure to see them do things that can take your breath away. In our society, however, many parents also find themselves uneasy and perhaps even apprehensive to think of their child as unusually smart, quick to learn, or gifted. They may have conflicting feelings because they experience a sense of pride that their child is blessed with a quick mind, but at the same time they feel concerned that they will now have new and different responsibilities if they are to raise her in a way that will develop her abilities to the fullest. They may feel pressure, fearing they'll somehow mess up because having a gifted child is more complicated than it seems. Giftedness can create challenges for children and their parents, making daily life more difficult.

Parents' uncertainty and ambivalence are often due to confusion about what "gifted" means. They may mistakenly think that a gifted child is a genius, a child prodigy, good at everything, or perhaps far brighter than others in *all* areas. If their child is unusually advanced in only one or two areas, they may not be aware that their child could still be gifted. Giftedness can be expressed in ways beyond general intellectual ability, including specific academic aptitude, visual or performing arts skills, leadership, creativity, and vocational or technical ability. However, an area of giftedness does not need to define an individual, and gifted children have the right to an identity beyond their unique talent.[2]

Are gifted children like all children? In many ways, they are. Like all children, they want friends, enjoy play, love their families, and like to learn new skills. But clearly, some children learn faster and more easily than others. Most children need a fair amount of repetition and practice to learn a new skill in school. A gifted child who has already acquired a skill, or does not need repetition to master it, can become quite discouraged, sometimes to the point of disliking or even hating school if there is nothing new or interesting to learn.

All children need adult guidance and encouragement to develop their potential. Children with high athletic ability are encouraged to develop that ability through instruction and participation in teams or clubs; similarly, children with musical ability are encouraged to take lessons or to join band or orchestra. It is the same for children who have high academic, creative, and intellectual potential. They too need opportunities to develop their areas of talent.

The reality is that gifted children's educational needs arise directly from their strengths. It is precisely because these children are quick learners that they need specialized learning opportunities. They are exceptional children, and they need exceptional services in the same way that children with learning difficulties are exceptional children and need special services and attention. Of course, some gifted children, those we call twice-exceptional, also have learning difficulties, and need specialized services to address both strengths and weaknesses.

We believe it is important for parents and educators to make modifications that will match the curriculum to the child's readiness and keep the child progressing rather than "standing still." Gifted children need academic guidance and support for their talents to ensure continuous educational progress. Unfortunately, there is increasing ambivalence about, and in some cases hostility toward, gifted children and gifted education, resulting in educational needs not being met.

In addition to academic modifications in school, gifted children also need support in social and emotional areas. While they want friends and acceptance from others, their differentness can create interpersonal difficulties that make finding friends hard. They may be impatient with children who are slower to catch on; they may find themselves ostracized by those same children for wanting to do more advanced activities that simply don't interest the others. Many gifted people tend to be introverted, making social connections more complicated, and leaving them feeling alone and isolated. [3]

Parents and teachers can help gifted children navigate the emotional ups and downs which are common for them every day. They can help them understand differences, and see how differences in people enrich the world because being unique and different, yet wanting to belong to a peer group and society, can be a difficult task.

The lens through which gifted children experience the world is fundamentally different than most of their peers. Giftedness is integral to the child; it affects everything he thinks, feels, says, and does. It is a key to who he is and cannot be separated and dealt with only when it's convenient for others. Giftedness cannot be overlooked or minimized; gifted children *are* fundamentally different. As a group, they hit developmental milestones earlier—sometimes much earlier—and more intensely than other children. They process more abstract ideas at an earlier age than other children[4] and they react to stimuli with more sensitivity.[5]

To help and support gifted children, we must first recognize that they are different. Next, we must understand how they are different, because not all gifted children are the same. As the important and influential adults in their life, we must guide them—not only in academic endeavors, but also in social, interpersonal, and self-development skills. Finally, we must help gifted individuals understand their neurodivergence—how and why they are different—and the implications of those differences as they navigate the world. We must do these things to help gifted individuals find their place in a world that does not always recognize or appreciate their talents.

For gifted children, finding a balance between fitting in and following their own path is an important task. Each person's balance will be different. Each path will have certain difficulties and costs. Understanding those costs is essential to self-understanding and, ultimately, to self-actualization. We hope this book will help you understand and support your gifted child in all ways—academically, socially, and emotionally.

*There is no job that is more difficult than being a parent.
There is also no job more important than being a parent!* [6]

Introduction

Gifted children are like other children in most respects. They need acceptance, guidance, support, respect, love, protection, and the opportunity to grow without artificial distortions of their innate needs.... They need to grow in an educational environment that prepares them to make sense of the world and gives them the tools to change it.[1]

–Annemarie Roeper

The Importance of Parents

In her work with hundreds of families, Kathryn Haydon has observed one common truth: "Parents are the experts on their own children."[2] Parents play an essential role, particularly in a gifted child's early education years. They can help children find commonalities among family members who share their abilities, concerns, and ways of viewing the world. They can also help gifted children develop an appreciation for many things and people, while helping them find their place in the world. Perhaps most importantly, parents can make their home a stimulating and safe harbor where gifted children know there are always people who love them, who understand their dilemmas, and who will guide them to experience life comfortably with their unique talents.

It is never too early to ignite passion for learning through exploration, creativity, and collaboration.[3] A solid home foundation is especially important when gifted children feel out of place with the surrounding world. Home can be a haven—a place to recharge one's batteries—where adults help the child untangle and comprehend the many perplexing behaviors in the world outside. When home is that kind of refuge, and when one or two other adults, such as teachers, neighbors or others, emotionally support a gifted child's self-concept, these children usually survive, and even thrive, despite sometimes difficult or even traumatic events. Support and encouragement at home not only guide the gifted child, but also give the child models of inner strength.

We believe that parents are particularly important in the long-term outcome of gifted children. Where there are insufficient educational opportunities, parents can provide enrichment and can negotiate with schools to help ensure that there is a match between the educational program and the child's interests, abilities, and motivation to learn. And good parenting—in which parents understand, nurture, guide, and advocate for their high potential child—*can overcome a year or more* of mediocre or even negative school experiences.

Parenting a Gifted Child Is a Lonely Experience

Parents of gifted children often notice unusual behaviors and abilities long before their children enter formal schooling. They may see intensity, sensitivity, or perfectionism and wonder if they are typical among gifted children. These parents know that their child is different from other children, but they may have difficulty finding support from others.

Parents of other children may be unsympathetic, thinking claims of a gifted child's accomplishments are exaggerated. They may think that these parents are putting pressure on the child to achieve. They could be jealous or resentful about a gifted child's accomplishments or concerned that their own child isn't reaching milestones as quickly. Parents of gifted children may become reluctant to discuss child-raising concerns with other parents, unless they, too, are parents of gifted children.

Pediatricians and other healthcare professionals are often unable to be supportive because they seldom receive training concerning the needs of gifted and talented children. Parents may find some good information online, but even that can be conflicting or, even worse, toxic.

While parents certainly appreciate and even enjoy the successes giftedness may bring their child and perhaps even the family, they may be concerned their children will receive extra scrutiny, and they worry about their children feeling "different" or "out of step" because of their abilities. Parents also worry about their child's extreme sensitivity, intensity, idealism, or concern with fairness, knowing that these traits can lead to difficulties for the child later in life.

Myths about Gifted Children

Why is there so little understanding of gifted children? The lack of information and support seems to come primarily from the many myths that exist about them. One myth common among educators is that gifted children do not need any special help—if they are so bright, surely they can develop their abilities on their own. Still another misconception is that gifted children are those children who do well academically or in a particular talent area, which doesn't consider those who are gifted but currently underachieving.

There are many types of gifted children and different levels of giftedness. Some are good in many areas; others are gifted in only one or two areas. Some gifted children also have another type of neurodivergence, such as ADHD, autism, or dyslexia. Still others succeed in traditional ways yet somehow feel disconnected and "different" their entire lives. Some may become seriously depressed. Following is a list of some common myths about giftedness:

- ○ *Gifted children will succeed in life no matter what.*
- ○ *Gifted children love school and get high grades.*
- ○ *Gifted children are good at everything they do.*
- ○ *Gifted children have trouble socially fitting in at school.*
- ○ *Gifted children tend to be more mature than other kids their age.*
- ○ *Gifted children are always well-behaved and compliant.*

○   *Gifted children's innate curiosity causes them to be self-directed.*
○   *Gifted children seldom have learning problems.*

These and other myths need to be disputed because they complicate the lives of gifted children and their families. The prevalence of these myths and the lack of accurate information about giftedness is a major reason that gifted children's needs are not recognized or given appropriate attention in our schools and our society. These negative messages can make accepting oneself more difficult. Helping parents challenge these myths will help gifted children avoid believing that their differences mean something is "wrong" with them.

Challenges for Gifted Children

Children with high intellectual potential have certain advantages over children who have less ability. For example, high IQ often facilitates resilience and improves coping abilities. However, some intellectually gifted youngsters experience underachievement, perfectionism, procrastination, and stress. They are often more emotionally sensitive than their peers. Many experience challenges relating to peers and siblings. Certain types of depression may be more common among gifted persons, and some experts suggest a higher risk of suicide, though research is unclear. While clinicians specializing in work with gifted and twice-exceptional children note that research on the prevalence of these children's mental health challenges is limited, there is no doubt that giftedness plays a role in not only how they experience mental health challenges but also the type of support they need.

For some children who have higher intellectual levels, learning patience is an important and often difficult task. Gifted children describe the frustration of waiting for others to understand things that are obvious to them. In addition, these children are often impatient with themselves. They can set very high standards, show perfectionist tendencies, and become profoundly disappointed, stressed, or upset if they fail to measure up to their own expectations.

Parents and educators have a challenge also. They must help the child understand that he is valued not only for his achievements, but because he is a worthwhile person. When we help gifted children understand how they are different from others, we foster tolerance, empathy and respect for differences. Giftedness does not mean that one is "better *than other people*," but can be explained as making one "a faster learner" or "better *at some things*". These distinctions will increase understanding and acceptance of others without being negative, condescending, or elitist.

We want gifted children to feel valued and to understand that, though they are exceptional, they do have a place in the world and have much in common with others. They are different in one or more *fundamental* ways from other children, but there are *many* ways in which they are similar. Because gifted children may feel these differences more keenly, they may want and need a sense of belonging, respect, and emotional satisfaction more intensely than other children. There are also strong pressures to belong. Parents can help gifted children gradually find the balance between being an individual and being a part of a group in a way that works best for them.

Practical Advice

Our goal in this book is to try to help gifted and talented youngsters flourish—not just survive—by sharing information we have learned over the years. Much of what we say is based on our personal experiences working with parents, teachers, and gifted people over several decades, though we have also incorporated suggestions from other parents and information based on available research.

Our experience has taught us that parents of gifted children usually are as intense—and sometimes as impatient—as their gifted children. Some parents will want to read this entire book and immediately attempt to implement all of the parenting suggestions. Whether you read the book in one sitting or chapter by chapter, *please do not try to take on everything at once!* Give yourself time to reflect upon the ideas or concepts before you try to implement them. Start with one new skill, accomplish it, and then go on to the next, building upon your success. It may be several days—sometimes several weeks—before you see results when you try something new within your family. You will need practice and time to consider whether further modifications and refinements of a strategy are needed.

Some of our suggestions are simply good general parenting tips that will work with many children. Good parenting is important whether a child is gifted or not. Other recommendations focus on specific traits and behaviors that are notably common to gifted children, and will help you encourage, rather than stifle, your child's abilities.

This book offers parents, teachers, and others who work with gifted children a framework for better understanding the emotional and interpersonal needs of these children. Our book emphasizes the family and the relationships within the family. Keep in mind that most of what we say about gifted children applies as well to gifted adults. "Apples don't fall far from the tree," and many reading this book were gifted children themselves who encountered some of the same issues we describe in the coming chapters. You may find yourself saying, "I wish someone had done this (or recognized that) when I was a child!" The good news is that it's never too late to gain self-awareness and insight, and it will be a relief to find that some of the difficulties you faced were related to your own giftedness.

We want to provide advice and guidance that is practical rather than theoretical—advice to help you nurture your relationship with your gifted child, and to help gifted children find understanding and satisfaction for themselves and others as they strive to reach their potential. We hope these strategies will cultivate caring, courage, and creativity along with your child's intellectual, academic, artistic, or leadership abilities.

CHAPTER 1

Defining Giftedness and its Characteristics

Ten-year-old Ethan contentedly solves another of a seemingly endless supply of math puzzles, which he enjoys doing to challenge himself and others. Six-year-old Brandon spends hours constructing an imaginary play world of stuffed animals, complete with political parties and a business. When asked how a train and a plane are alike, six-year-old Rosa says, "They're both vehicles for public transportation." Shamika, age nine, is enraptured by music and softly hums a complex melody. Sanjay, age four, intensely fingers the materials in his hand as he tries to construct the intricate design he sees in his mind's eye. He also knows the states and their capitals. Five-year-old Lamont insists he cannot read; "I just know what words the letters make!" Two-year-old Mika distinguishes between colors like gray and black, sings the alphabet song, and can identify most of the letters in the alphabet. Fifteen-year-old Rolando has mastered all of the math offered at his rural high school and wonders what he will do next year. His 11-year-old sister is intensely engaged in conversation with her playmates about how puzzling it is that when someone kills a person, he is a murderer, but when an army general orders the dropping of bombs and kills the enemy, he is a hero.

Children like these are thinking and behaving in ways that are advanced and different when compared with other children of the same age. We call these children "gifted," "talented," or "creative"—all inexact terms. No one disagrees that such children exist, but many people think that truly gifted children are quite rare. The reality is that gifted children are more common than most people think. Nearly every school and neighborhood has them. They may not know they have them, but they are there.

Why don't people know? Educators don't always know how to look for or recognize such children. Some disagree about how best to identify them, what to call them ("gifted," "talented," "high ability," "prodigy," etc.), or the extent to which these children truly have differing educational and other needs that require any sort of special services or accommodations from the school.

What Exactly Is Giftedness?

What defines a gifted child? What are the different kinds of gifted-ness? Do gifted children have high ability in all areas? How do schools identify gifted children? Are all gifted children creative? Can a child be both gifted and ADHD, autistic, or dyslexic? These are all important questions to parents who are new to the concept of gifted children.

Individual states have varying definitions and criteria for the identification of gifted children. Most definitions are calculated to identify the top 3-5% of the children and stem from the U.S. Department of Education Marland Report (1972). The Marland Report definition, shown here, is sometimes referred to as the "Federal Definition" and lists several areas in which an individual may be gifted.

> *Gifted and talented children are those identified by profession-ally qualified persons who by virtue of outstanding abilities are capable of high performance. These are children who require differentiated educational programs and services beyond those normally provided by the regular school program in order to realize their contribution to self and society. Children capable of high performance include those with demonstrated achievement and/or potential ability in any of the following areas: general intellectual ability, specific academic aptitude, creative or productive thinking, leadership ability, and visual, performing arts, and psychomotor ability.*

The National Association for Gifted Children provides an updated description, recognizing the varied needs of gifted and talented children.

> *Students with gifts and talents perform—or have the capability to perform—at higher levels compared to others of the same age, experience, and environment in one or more domains. They require modifications to their educational experience(s) to learn and realize their potential. Students with gifts and talents:*
>
> ○ *Come from all racial, ethnic, and cultural populations, as well as all economic strata.*
>
> ○ *Require sufficient access to appropriate learning opportunities to realize their potential.*
>
> ○ *Can have learning and processing disorders that require specialized intervention and accommodation.*
>
> ○ *Need support and guidance to develop socially and emotionally, as well as in their areas of talent.*
>
> ○ *Require varied services based on their changing needs.*[1]

The Marland definition encompasses a wide range of abilities that extend beyond simple academic intelligence and recognizes that a child might be gifted in one or more of the areas listed. Nevertheless, most schools have focused almost exclusively on the first two categories—intellectual ability and specific academic aptitude, as "giftedness" is typically treated as though it is synonymous with intelligence test scores, academic test scores, or educational achievements.

Nature versus Nurture

Parents often wonder if their child was simply born with unusual potential or whether the child's abilities are a result of their parenting. Studies from the 1960s to the present have compared identical twins who were separated in infancy and raised in widely different environments. Researchers in these twin studies found a high similarity in intelligence—at least as measured by IQ scores—indicating a strong heritability component, accounting for as much as 80% of the similarity in IQ by the time they reached adulthood, although environment has a more direct impact during the younger years.[2] Some of the twin studies also indicate that personality characteristics and temperament have a hereditary component, perhaps influencing the motivation and drive that often accompany high intelligence.[3] In some cases, twins who lived far apart and didn't know one another chose the same career and even the same type of marriage partner.

Environment plays an important role as well. Gifted children, like other children, thrive in supportive environments that understand and address their needs, and they fail to thrive in non-supportive environments that do not. Socioeconomic factors influence development of talent, likely associated with the opportunities provided. For example, children adopted from working-class to middle-class homes show an increase of IQ between 12 to 18 points. Socialization expectations for gender also influence the expression of intelligence. Additionally, stress and trauma are shown to have negative effects on overall IQ scores.[4]

Measuring Giftedness

The definitions above recognize that gifted children include those who *show* potential, leaving a clear possibility that underachieving or disadvantaged youth will not show their talents and be deprived of the help they need. Thus, giftedness is not limited to those who have already accomplished amazing things, but includes those who, if given the right training and opportunity, would perform at higher levels. Giftedness in some individuals might become more apparent as they mature or are provided with more opportunities to cultivate their giftedness. For example, a three-year-old who proclaims that she can read but is told by her preschool teacher, "That's silly. Three-year-olds can't read!", may never have the opportunity to show her giftedness.

Measuring giftedness, whether through intelligence testing, academic achievement measures, or other means, will always involve incomplete and imprecise techniques and instruments. Intelligence and giftedness are not simple concepts that lend themselves to precise definitions, and their meaning continues to evolve as we learn more. In the early 1900s, intelligence was defined primarily by Intelligence Quotient (IQ) as shown on a standardized test that measured mostly verbal and academic problem-solving skills. These days, the concept of intelligence has been broadened to include many more areas, such as processing speed, concentration, memory, and verbal and nonverbal reasoning. Psychologists continue to develop new tests to measure various mental abilities, and measures of intelligence and cognitive ability continue to be widely used by many professionals, such as educators, psychologists, and neuropsychologists.

Where professionals draw the defining line for giftedness based on these measures can certainly result in honest disagreement; in fact, criteria for estimating giftedness vary from state to state and from district to district. The inconsistencies in definitions of giftedness, the various types of giftedness, and the different techniques used all contribute to difficulties identifying gifted children and conducting the necessary research to explore these important issues.

Most tests of intelligence or cognitive ability measure IQ scores up to four standard deviations above the mean (IQ scores as high as 150 to 160), though some allow for extended scoring well beyond that. For states identifying intellectual giftedness, an IQ score of at least 125 (the top 5% on a test with an average score of 100 and a standard deviation of 15) is typically required for a child to be considered gifted. Although states or school systems use different tests, most use similar scores on standardized measures of ability or academic achievement. When used properly, cognitive ability tests provide valuable information about students' abilities, including both strengths and weaknesses, and IQ scores do provide a way to describe some basic aspects of gifted children.

The performance variability among gifted children on ability tests, however, calls attention to the imprecision of the term "gifted" and highlights that this single term describes a quite heterogeneous group and does not adequately capture the remarkable skills and diverse talents of individuals. Because of the substantial range of abilities within the category called "gifted," some educators and psychologists now talk about degrees of giftedness using terms such as "mild," "moderate," or "profound."

Test scores tell only part of the picture, however. Being gifted involves more than scores on an ability or intelligence test; the behaviors of gifted children are very significant and indicative of the child's high ability. Gifted children show an uneven pattern of development, with some skills outpacing others. For example, they may be excellent in reading but poor in math, or they may show precocious ability with puzzles or machines but show average ability in verbal development. Sometimes intellectual skills are quite advanced, while motor or social skills develop more typically. Or their knowledge is advanced, but their judgment in social areas—such as tact—lags far behind their knowledge. This uneven pattern is called *asynchronous development.* So prominent is this characteristic, some experts even define giftedness in terms of asynchronous development, rather than potential or ability. While all gifted children show asynchronous development, the asynchrony is greater for the highly and profoundly gifted than for individuals who are mildly or moderately gifted.

Asynchronous development makes gifted children, as a group, more heterogeneous and diverse than a group of average children. This should not be surprising. Most parents and professionals easily recognize the diversity among children at the lower end of the intellectual spectrum who are served with Special Education individual educational programs (IEPs) because of the individual nature of their needs. If we consider the wide areas of difference that exist among advanced children, as we do with developmentally delayed children, the internal asynchrony of the gifted child is easily understandable. The more highly gifted the child, the more out of sync she is likely to be within herself, with wide differences between areas of strength and areas of weakness relative to those strengths. Thus, it is not at all unusual, for example, to see a seven-year-old highly gifted child who is reading at sixth-grade level and performing math tasks at fourth-grade level, but showing fine-motor skills at her age-appropriate second-grade level. Such a wide span of abilities and skills, naturally, has major implications for this child's curriculum and grade placement. This type of asynchronous child, even though gifted, will need an individually differentiated curriculum.

Giftedness is ability, potential, and asynchrony. Both heredity and the environment play a role in its expression. Just as athletes develop with appropriate training and support, gifted children will develop with direction, support, and appropriate educational opportunities. However defined, measured, or identified, giftedness requires parents and teachers to use different approaches to help them thrive.

Characteristics of Gifted Children

Tests provide one way to identify a gifted child; behavioral characteristics provide another. Despite the heterogeneity of the gifted population, gifted children *do* have common characteristics, though not all gifted children will show all of these at all times. The traits in Table 1 are compiled from numerous books spanning many decades and can have a lifelong impact on the lives of gifted children and their families.

Table 1: Common Characteristics of Gifted Children

- ○ Rapid learner; able to put thoughts together quickly
- ○ Has a very good memory and retains much information
- ○ Unusually large vocabulary and complex sentence structure for age
- ○ Advanced comprehension of word nuances, metaphors, and abstract ideas
- ○ Enjoys solving problems that involve numbers and puzzles
- ○ Early development of reading and writing skills
- ○ Heightened awareness of emotions at an early age

○ Thinking is abstract, complex, logical, and insightful

○ Highly developed idealism and sense of justice; concern with social and political issues and injustices

○ Longer attention span and intense concentration when challenged and engaged

○ Impatient with self or others' inabilities or slowness

○ Ability to learn basic skills more quickly with less practice

○ Asks probing questions; goes beyond what is being taught

○ Highly developed curiosity; limitless questions

○ Interest in experimenting and doing things differently

○ Tendency to put ideas or things together in ways that are unusual or not obvious (divergent thinking)

○ Keen and sometimes unusual sense of humor, particularly with puns and word play

○ Desire to organize things and people through complex games or other schemas

○ Imaginary playmates (preschool age children); vivid imagination

Personality Characteristics, Overexcitabilities, and Gifted Individuals

How does personality impact giftedness? And how does giftedness impact how people interact with the world? Psychologists who study characteristics of people with high intelligence are often attempting to understand *how* these characteristics influence the development of gifted individuals. The study of personality development has provided some insight in the search for answers to those questions. One framework to understand how personality traits impact intelligence and vice versa is through the Big Five Model of Personality, while Dabrowski's Theory of Positive Disintegration and his concept of overexcitabilities provides another way to contextualize the gifted individual's experience.

Five Factor Model of Personality. One of the most widely understood and accepted models of personality in psychology is called the Big Five Factor Model of Personality. This model consists of five personality traits (or factors) which show cross-cultural universality; the Big Five is used frequently to describe how personality traits impact behaviors, relationships, and life outcomes in people. The five traits are organized on a continuum and represented with the acronym OCEAN: Openness, Conscientiousness, Extraversion, Agreeableness, and Neuroticism.

Big Five Personality Traits
Openness: Also referred to as "Openness to Experience," this personality trait includes characteristics of imagination, curiosity, and emotions. People with high scores in this area tend to be open to revising their former beliefs and biases and seek out challenges and new learning experiences.

Conscientiousness: Individuals with high scores in conscientiousness tend to be hardworking, organized, and thoughtful. Lower scorers in this area tend to be laidback, impulsive, or careless.

Extraversion: This personality trait measures someone's sociability and assertiveness. People with high scores are often outgoing and talkative; a lower score generally shows that someone tends to be quieter, withdrawn, or preferring alone time.

Agreeableness: People who are cooperative, empathetic, trusting, and helpful have high scores on this scale. Scores on the low end of the scale indicate someone who may be skeptical, indifferent, or jealous.

Neuroticism: This scale measures someone's tendency to worry or experience anxiety. Someone with heightened scores on this scale tends to have more negative emotions and experience a lot of emotional distress. A lower score on this scale indicates that someone is more calm, relaxed, and secure.

Research consistently shows that Openness to Experience has a positive correlation with intelligence levels.[5] There are six facets, or characteristics, measured within the Openness to Experience trait. They include openness to ideas/intellectual curiosity, facility for imagination/fantasy, sensitivity to aesthetics, attentiveness to emotions, preference for novelty and variety, and openness of values/challenging authority and conventions. Of these facets, openness to ideas/intellectual curiosity specifically reflects the tendency to explore abstract information through reasoning[6] and is most closely correlated with cognitive giftedness.

Dabrowski's Theory of Positive Disintegration. In the field of gifted education, the Theory of Positive Disintegration (TPD) developed by Kasimerz Dabrowski, is a developmental theory often used to conceptualize traits of giftedness. While Dabrowski's TPD is not as widely known or accepted in the larger psychological community as the Big Five, it is well-known and frequently cited within the gifted education community. Within this theory, Dabrowski identifies the concept of overexcitabilities. An 'overexcitability' (OE) is defined as "an enhanced and intensified mental activity distinguished by characteristic forms of expression, which are above common and average."[7] These heightened responses to or heightened experiences of stimuli are often colloquially referred to as "intensities." The five areas of overexcitabilities described by Dabrowski are: intellectual, emotional, imaginational, sensual, and psychomotor.

Dabrowski's Overexcitabilities

○ *Intellectual OE*: Characterized by a drive to pursue new ideas, excitement for learning, and concern for fairness and justice; curiosity about topics with uncommon depth or breadth.

○ *Emotional OE*: Characterized by subjective experiences of intense emotions or strong emotional reactions that may appear out of proportion to the event; intense connections with people or objects.

○ *Imaginational OE:* Characterized by vivid mental imagery, love and appreciation of fantasy, and creativity.

○ *Sensual OE:* Characterized by a heightened experience of sensory aspects of life, such as sensual pleasure, including appreciation for aesthetic arts or music, or discomfort or pain, including sensitivity to light, sound, touch.

○ *Psychomotor OE:* Characterized by a need for physical activity, a love of movement, and boundless energy that may include impulsivity.

Parents of gifted children describe these characteristics often, and clinicians report that a parent's or an individual's desire to understand, manage, or control behaviors related to an OE is a frequent reason gifted children are referred for therapy or evaluation. Research on overexcitabilities shows a moderate effect size for intellectual and imaginational overexcitabilities based on intelligence level, while emotional and sensual overexcitabilities show a small increased average in individuals who are cognitively gifted. There is currently no research evidence of heightened psychomotor OE related to intelligence level,[8] though there is significant clinical and observational evidence of its existence in gifted children.

Openness to Experience vs. Overexcitabilities. Some researchers believe that overexcitabilities are a construct that is similar to openness to experience, and several of the facets of openness within the Big Five Model and the various overexcitabilities appear to overlap. While both are described in gifted children, neither the personality trait of openness to experience nor the presence of overexcitabilities alone is justification that a child is cognitively gifted. Although openness to experience is correlated with intelligence, there are many individuals across the spectrum of ability who also show this personality trait. While many speculate that overexcitabilities are more prevalent in gifted children, they are not solely present among the gifted and children of all ability levels have varying degrees of overexcitabilities.

While an OE can be viewed or described negatively by some parents and clinicians (e.g., "too sensitive" or "asks too many questions"), they can also be used to explain the sensitivity, intensity, empathy, and curiosity of gifted individuals. They should not be ignored or minimized. While the impact of overexcitabilities can be frustrating, it should not be debilitating. An emotional OE does not lead a child to have significant and frequent emotional meltdowns; a psychomotor OE that causes significant difficulties in a school or home environment should not be dismissed; sensual OE should not manifest as extreme sensory sensitivities that disrupt daily life. Any of these situations warrants investigation into the causes and the possibility that a gifted child is twice-exceptional (exceptional ability and a disability, see chapter 2). While overexcitabilities might be an adequate explanation for a behavior, excusing an unacceptable behavior or minimizing the concern as "gifted overexcitabilities" can delay the opportunity to seek help and be proactive in developing strategies and coping skills necessary for success.

Potential Problems for Gifted Children

Specific potential problems can stem directly from the characteristics and strengths of a gifted child. Each of these possible difficulties can cause stress for gifted children, as well as for those around them. For example, their curiosity and wide range of interests may lead to feelings of being spread too thin or feeling scattered. Their accelerated thought processes and high expectations can lead to impatience with others, while their intensity can lead to difficulty in accepting criticism or in modulating their behaviors so that they do not overreact so frequently. Table 2 describes some of the possible problem areas associated with the characteristic strengths of being gifted.

Table 2: Problems Associated with Characteristic Strengths in Gifted Children[9]

Strengths	Possible Problems
Acquires and retains information quickly	Impatient with slowness of others; dislikes routine and drill
Inquisitive attitude; intellectual curiosity; intrinsic motivation	Asks embarrassing questions; strong-willed
Ability to conceptualize, abstract, synthesize; enjoys problem-solving and intellectual activity	Rejects or omits details; questions teaching procedures
Can see cause-effect relations	Difficulty accepting the illogical
Love of truth, equity, and fair play	Worries about humanitarian concerns
Enjoys organizing things and people into structure and order; seeks to systematize	Constructs complicated rules or systems; may be seen as bossy, rude, or domineering
Large vocabulary and facile verbal proficiency; broad information in advanced areas	May use words to escape or avoid situations; seen by others as a know-it-all
Thinks critically; has high expectations; is self- critical and evaluates others	Critical or intolerant toward others; perfectionistic
Creative and inventive; likes new ways of doing things	May disrupt plans or reject what is already known; seen by others as different and out-of-step
Intense concentration; long attention span in areas of interest; goal-directed behavior; persistent	Resists interruption; seen as stubborn
Diverse interests and abilities; versatile	Becomes frustrated over lack of time
Strong sense of humor	Sees absurdities of situations; humor may not be understood by peers; may become "class clown" to gain attention

Gifted Children Who Question Traditions

The openness and intensity of the gifted child sometimes combine and lead them to behave in ways that seem tactless, ill-mannered, and inappropriate. They may ask questions like, "Why are you bald?" or "How old are you?" or "How much do you weigh?" This kind of personal question is not considered polite in present-day society. And some gifted children have no qualms about correcting a teacher who says something they see as incorrect. They may say, "You're wrong. Columbus didn't discover America; it was actually the Vikings, and it was lots of years before 1492."

Some of the questioning behavior occurs because gifted children are curious, but their experience limits them; they simply haven't lived long enough to realize that personal questions about age or appearance are considered rude. They haven't yet learned social customs, and even when we explain these customs to them, they may think the rules are "stupid." Some of society's conventions, such as wearing formal clothes to some events and casual clothes to others, just don't seem logical to them. Gifted children, with their quick minds, logic, and ability to see more than one way to do things, can get into trouble for challenging tradition. They sometimes behave in nontraditional ways that are atypical or different from the norm. And some gifted children violate rules simply as an expression of rebellious independence.

Sometimes gifted children and adults confront customs in an accepted, appropriate manner. For example, a 10-year-old might write to the advertising department of a major company to discuss the accuracy of facts in a commercial. Other gifted children may attempt to remedy situations through inappropriate means, such as by arguing or creating animosity between individuals. As adults with more life experience, we can help gifted children understand the value of certain customs and traditions, and the reasons for them, and then offer examples of when and how it is appropriate to challenge and break a tradition.

Most children, especially teenagers, will at least occasionally question the need for various customs and traditions with comments like, "Why do I have to dress up for the birthday party?" But gifted children, because they can creatively see "better" alternatives and because they can spot inconsistencies and lack of logic, are much more likely to challenge rituals and traditions that seem to them to be illogical, foolish, or arbitrary. "Why do women carry purses and wear lipstick?" "Why do men traditionally do the yard work while women do the housework?" "Why does the fork always have to be on the left?" "Why can't children correct grown-ups when we know they are wrong?"

On the one hand, we want them to be open and creative, because that is where innovation and progress come from. On the other hand, we also want them to respect tradition sometimes. Gifted children can create discomfort by asking questions that are difficult for adults to answer. They are seldom satisfied with, "That's just the way we do it." They want to know reasons and then will often question those reasons. Helping gifted children learn how to effectively communicate their concerns without ruffling the feathers of those around them will serve them well as they get older and enter adulthood.

Is My Child Gifted?

Are you still uncertain whether there is a gifted child living in your home? Do you have more than one? Sometimes, even at an early age, it is easy to tell that a child is not only gifted, but is highly gifted. In other instances, it can be difficult for parents to ascertain whether their child is gifted, as it may not show in traditional ways.

It may be that a child has unusual abilities in areas other than language or mathematics, or perhaps she is intellectually strong in an area that can only become apparent as she matures. It can be difficult to see a child's potential until she has an opportunity to gain some experience in that area. Jaynelle's parents knew that she enjoyed music but didn't know she was talented until she began excelling at Suzuki violin at age four.

Parents are often the first to recognize a child's ability, though they may not identify it as giftedness. They usually have some idea quite early in the child's life that the child is advanced when compared with others of the same age. This becomes particularly clear during interactions with other children or adults. When their preschooler engages in behaviors that are precocious, others will act surprised and ask, "How old *is* he?"

The asynchronous development of gifted children, where their abilities grow at uneven rates, can make judging giftedness solely on observations a very difficult task. Parents may be concerned that they might overestimate their child's abilities because of natural pride, but they should also trust their own observations and judgments about their child's abilities, along with the possibility that they may be underestimating the child's potential. Bright parents who have limited experience with children frequently tend to downplay their child's abilities. Sometimes, even after their child has been formally identified as gifted by a school system or a private psychologist, parents begin to harbor the notion that their child is not really gifted and "just a hard worker," or in other words, somehow an "imposter" who just "got lucky" the day of the test. They may also think giftedness doesn't really mean anything and has few implications for schooling or for life. And some parents simply don't want their child to be gifted; "We just want him to be normal."

To help parents understand and accept their child's giftedness, Carol Strip and Gretchen Hirsch describe characteristics of gifted children and provide several examples of the depth and intensity of these traits in gifted children.

Questioning style. Gifted children are curious and ask questions about abstract ideas, concepts, and theories that may not have easy answers. They may ask, for example, why light travels faster than sound, and whether this is true even in outer space. Their curiosity may lead to interesting experiments, like the one described by a frustrated parent who told us of a six-year-old dancer who wondered how the acoustics of her tap-shoes would sound if she danced on the hood of their car.

Learning speed and application of concepts. Gifted children may jump directly from Step 2 to Step 10, because by the time they've completed

Step 2, they've already figured out the answer. Gifted children may not want to list the steps they used in solving a math problem, because they figured it out mentally and not on paper. This can frustrate teachers and can create problems when the gifted child is asked to tutor other children who need to use all of the steps to understand the problem.

Level of interest. Gifted children show intense curiosity about nearly everything or immerse themselves in a single area that interests them. They dive into topics, like the two-year-old who insisted that his parents read "'Twas the Night Before Christmas" to him over and over again for what seemed like hundreds of times. He would correct them if they omitted a single word. Then one day, much to the family's surprise, he stood in his highchair and recited the entire poem from beginning to end without error. Gifted children and adults sometimes pursue their passion with intensity over time, a type of persistence that was coined "grit" by researcher Angela Duckworth. Other times, these interests, while still intense, may change rapidly, which prompted one noted authority on giftedness, the late Dr. George Betts, to say, "That is why you *rent* the clarinet!"

Language ability. Gifted children often use extensive and advanced vocabularies, understand verbal nuances that escape others, enjoy wordplay and puns, and talk over the heads of their playmates (and sometimes adults, too). When adults try to talk in code by spelling words, gifted children quickly break the code. They understand abstract concepts and use words in different ways. When asked to define creativity, one highly gifted child replied, "It is the melding of dogma and karma."[10]

Concern with fairness. Gifted children will show concern about fairness and equity far more intensely and on a global scale. They grasp some of the subtleties of complex moral and ethical questions relating to war, environmental problems, and humanitarian issues, and they will defend their viewpoints fervently. Parents of gifted children feel like they are constantly responding to their children's questions and concerns.

The traits of gifted children can create both joys and pitfalls for them and their families. Although troublesome or frustrating to parents, teachers, and even the gifted child, these traits are an essential and unchanging part of a gifted child's being that must be accepted and respected. In the coming chapters, we hope to provide helpful information about common concerns for families with gifted children, as well as many strategies to help you address these concerns. There are few tasks more difficult than parenting a gifted child, and few that are more rewarding.

CHAPTER 2

Special Populations
of Gifted Children

The intersectionality of giftedness with disability, cultural and linguistic diversity, and LGBTQ+ identities are important factors to recognize when we consider supporting gifted children. The layering of these aspects of a gifted child's life can have significant implications on who they are and how they develop. Throughout this chapter, we examine how these various factors influence the gifted child and how parents can make sure they are advocating and supporting their children effectively.

Culturally and Linguistically Diverse Gifted Children

Colin Seale, founder of ThinkLaw, is an advocate for diversity in gifted education and he eloquently points out, "…genius is distributed equally, but opportunity is not."[1] Gifted programs have made strides in identifying and serving gifted learners from culturally and linguistically diverse backgrounds, but there is still work to be done. Gifted children exist in all racial and ethnic backgrounds, including African-American Asian-American and Pacific Islander, Hispanic and Latino, and Native American; they exist in rural and economically disadvantaged areas as well. However, the access to opportunities and support varies based on unique circumstances to each group.

Parents of bright children from minority populations often face different hurdles while advocating for their children to have the same constructive challenges and opportunities as other students. When educated by teachers outside of their cultural group, minority students may be hindered by the expectations of their teachers. Teachers with a lack of understanding about minority cultures may perceive their students with unrecognized biases in the classroom, thereby reducing access to challenging curriculum. For example, when relying solely on teacher recommendations to initiate a referral for gifted education services, underlying implicit bias can influence which children are given the chance to be identified for gifted services and which are not. A study by Grissom and Redding (2016) showed that Black students were three times more likely to be referred for gifted and talented programs if they were taught by a Black teacher.[2] Many schools have moved to universal screening (assessing all students within a grade level, regardless of teacher assessments/nominations) to reduce the influence of teacher biases and lack of awareness of the nontraditional characteristics of high-ability when trying to identify students who should receive gifted services.

Joy Lawson Davis (2022) noted that teachers who lack cultural awareness and offer a curriculum that is disconnected from a child's cultural background can exacerbate the already existing achievement gap.[3] Additionally, some students of color report experiencing negative peer pressure related to their cultural identity to avoid being labeled as "too smart" or "acting White."[4] Any of these barriers can prevent a gifted child from accessing the services they need and deserve to reach their potential.

Gifted children who's native or home language is not English comprise another group that may be missed when schools look for children who would benefit from gifted services. Academic settings are based on language, from giving instructions to assessing learning. The cognitive assessments of ability used for placement in gifted programs often rely on language-based reasoning and vocabulary. Children whose families speak a language other than English at home may appear to be fluent in conversational English, but have a difficult time explaining nuanced concepts, which can suppress their overall cognitive scores. Ensuring that the examiners are familiar with a child's linguistic background is important to make sure they interpret the scores with regard for the fact that the child is multi-lingual. Using a nonverbal measure of cognitive ability is another way to ensure these children aren't overlooked for gifted education services.

Tips for Parents of Culturally and Linguistically Diverse Learners

Focus on the future. Some parents of children of color may feel pressure from their communities *not* to advocate for their gifted child, assuming that doing so will separate their child from their community, traditions, and culture.[5] By focusing on the future of your gifted child, you can ensure the vital benefits of academic challenge, social and emotional support, and future opportunity.

Find ways for your child to blend their cultural and academic identities. Many students of color, especially from Black and Hispanic backgrounds, report feeling negative peer pressure about showing their abilities in the school setting.[6] Additionally, being a student of color in a predominantly White gifted program can lead to isolation.[7] Helping your child find a sense of belonging with peers who accept both their intelligence and cultural background can empower them to reach their potential.

Connect your child with mentors in your community. Helping your child find someone who can encourage and support them outside of family support at home can give them another source of connection and guidance. This person might be someone who was also identified as gifted and dealt with some of the same pressures your child is experiencing, or they might have a successful career and can help your child navigate the unique circumstances of being a minority student navigating the path to a successful and fulfilling career.

Reflect on your own experience as a student. Many gifted children also have gifted parents. What was school like for you? Did you feel supported and challenged? How did you navigate peer relationships? Sharing those reflections with your child can help normalize their experience. Additionally, honest reflection on those experiences—yours and your child's—can help contextualize the emotions you have about your child's pathway and how you feel about advocating for them.

Partner with supportive advocates in the school system. As your child progresses through their academic career, you will find people who not only understand the barriers faced by culturally and linguistically diverse gifted learners, but who are also willing to do the work to change the systems that hold children back. This person might be a school counselor, a teacher in the gifted education program, or an administrator. Connecting with that person and collaborating about how to best advocate for your child can provide opportunities to navigate a system that otherwise is frequently opaque.

Gifted LGBTQ+ Children

The intersection of identifying as a member of the LGBTQ+ community and also being gifted creates an additional layer of "different-ness" that can be hard for kids to reconcile. Many children feel the need to mask their giftedness to establish the peer relationships they are seeking. A child who is trying to determine whether or not to disclose the fact that they are a member of the LGBTQ+ community may also face fear of judgement from both their social circle and family members.

There is not a lot of research that specifically explores whether gifted individuals identify as members of the LGBTQ+ at different rates than the general population. However, two factors that are associated with giftedness may be connected with LGBTQ+ identities. First, the personality trait of Openness to Experience (from the Big Five factors discussed in chapter 1) is positively correlated with both cognitive giftedness and increased levels of same-sex attraction. [8] Additionally, research consistently shows that the rates of identifying as gender-diverse are increased in the autistic population; many twice-exceptional individuals are both gifted and autistic. [9]

The current dynamic surrounding issues related to understanding and supporting children who identify as LGBTQ+ is difficult, at best. Parents who are working to be supportive of their children may find this issue hard to navigate. As with everything in our gifted children, we can use their cognitive ability to explore identity issues in a safe environment. Ask probing questions and answer their questions to the best of your ability. Encourage some research if there are questions you aren't sure how to answer. Take the time to ask questions and hear what your child says about their experiences. Help them explore their identity and help them determine the best time and place to share information about it.

Some children and teens may "try on" different labels and identities, as all adolescents do through their formative ages. *Am I a jock or am I a nerd? Do I fit in with this group or that group? Am I a "tomboy" or am I transgender? Do I just like my new friend, or do I really like them with deeper feelings of closeness?* Parents can be supportive through this and let their children know that it is typical for adolescents to question these things. As with any parenting situation, when arbitrary lines are drawn in the sand (e.g., "I don't care if you think you are transgender, you're not allowed to wear those clothes/have that haircut/change your pronouns."), it is unlikely that you will convince your child to go along with your beliefs.

There are many stages that the gifted LGBTQ+ adolescent will face as they begin to understand their identity. Sedillo and Chandler describe the various tasks and stages that a gifted LGBTQ+ person must explore related to both their sexuality and their giftedness.[10] Early stages may include researching to find out more about themselves and choosing to either hide either their intelligence or aspects of their sexuality. Finding like-minded peers who understand and accept all aspects of their personality can be difficult, but it is ultimately a major factor in helping the gifted LGBTQ+ child or teen to learn to accept themselves and live authentically.

Twice-Exceptional Children

Twice-exceptional children are gifted *and* have another diagnosis— they show exceptional ability *and* disability. Twice-exceptional children lie outside the norms of the bell curve not just in their abilities, but also in one or more areas of disability. The term *twice-exceptional* is an informal educational label to identify gifted students who also have factors that inhibit their ability to learn. The challenges or disabilities interfere with some aspect of schooling or learning, and can be neurological (like ADHD, autism, dyslexia), psychological (such as anxiety or depression), or physical (such as cerebral palsy, deafness, and visual impairment). Not all diagnoses combined with giftedness equate to twice-exceptionality. For example, it would be uncommon to refer to a gifted student with a peanut allergy as twice-exceptional because although the peanut allergy is a medical diagnosis and can be considered a disability, it doesn't interact directly with the child's ability to think or learn. Twice-exceptional children have unique needs related to how we parent and educate them.

The zeitgeist surrounding giftedness and twice-exceptionality is uncertain and volatile right now. The process for identifying gifted students from culturally and linguistically diverse backgrounds is often unfair, and can exacerbate inequities, leading educators to debate the value of gifted programs.[11] The understanding of the broad concept of neurodiversity and the need for disability rights is growing, but not yet widely supported: advocates push for appropriate accommodations in schools, work, and other environments. This leaves twice-exceptional children and their families caught in a precarious balance of trying to find their path, juggling exceptional abilities and struggles without appropriate guidance. On top of this lack of focus related to gifted education, many educators don't understand how somebody who has a 'disability' diagnosis could also be gifted (or that a student identified as gifted could also have a disability).

Integrating the Framework of Neurodiversity into Twice-Exceptionality

The term neurodiversity is analogous to the idea of biodiversity. Just as biodiversity provides v species variations that are necessary for survival, so neurodiversity recognizes that the wide range of brain development in humans challenges the concept of 'normal' as derived from the overall population; having people who think and learn differently is beneficial for our survival. Attention deficits, autism, dyslexia, gifted-ness and other conditions fall under the umbrella of neurodiversity. Neurodiversity in its many forms has been pathologized for far too long, leading to stigmatization of certain diagnoses. Parents, educa-tors, and even clinicians are sometimes hesitant to "label" a child, due to fears about what others will think, the long-term impact of being labeled on the psyche of the child, and opportunities that may be lost based on a diagnosis.

The neurodiversity community is comprised of people who are reclaiming their identities and refusing to fear a label that accurately describes their needs. Twice-exceptional adults who grew up as gifted and ADHD, autistic, dyslexic, or something else, are coming to embrace a greater understanding of themselves, and working to untangle the trauma of growing up in a neglectful educational environment that constantly told them they were lazy, unmotivated, or not living up to their potential. Educators are beginning to get training to under-stand the nuances of meeting the needs of twice-exceptional students. Neurodivergent children are learning to understand their own needs and to self-advocate for accommodations when they are needed.

One shift influenced by this movement is related to the language used to talk about neurodiversity. Instead of person-first language, like *person with autism* or *student with dyslexia*, many neurodivergent people prefer identity-first language, like *autistic person* or *dyslexic student*. The reason for this is that they feel their diagnosis, i.e., what makes them stand out from the norm, is an inherent piece of who they are. It influences every part of their lives—how they learn, relate socially, think, and solve problems. Person-first language implies that a person's neurodivergence can be fixed or cured (it can't, it is not a question of being broken), and part of fighting the stigma has been reclaiming the terminology used to describe their needs. The Deaf community was one of the first to embrace identity-first language. Giftedness is also a type of neurodiversity, though you'll notice that nobody has a problem with using identity-first language to describe gifted children and adults (as opposed to children with giftedness). This exemplifies the stigma surrounding various diagnoses related to neurodiversity. Throughout this chapter, we default to using identity-first language (autistic, ADHDer, dyslexic, etc.) based on the current advocacy efforts within the neurodiversity community.

The neurodiversity movement is based on the social model of disability, which recognizes that people may have an *impairment* of some kind. But it is society's failure to provide accommodation that turns the impairment into a disability. For example, a person who is diagnosed with Central Auditory Processing Disorder may be impaired when attending a virtual meeting; however, they are only disabled when closed captioning is not provided. Providing closed captioning accommodates the needs related to auditory processing, and so the person is then able to access and participate in an event without barriers. Advocates for neurodiversity don't insist that a diagnosis is solely a strength or a "superpower" because that denies the reality of the support required. They do, however, recognize that some aspects of a diagnosis can provide a unique outlook, interest, or skill that others might not have.

Providing a neurodiversity-affirming home and school for twice-exceptional children means that they are empowered with self-awareness. Neurodiversity-affirming parents accept their child's differences, provide support when needed, and don't try to force them to become someone they aren't by hiding their neurodivergence. The book *Raising Twice-Exceptional Children: A Handbook for Parents of Neurodivergent Gifted Kids* provides in-depth information and strategies to help parents establish a neurodiversity-affirming relationship with their twice-exceptional child.[12]

While all twice-exceptional people are neurodivergent (giftedness is a type of neurodiversity) not all exceptionalities are considered neurodivergent because some are psychological diagnoses (like Generalized Anxiety Disorder and Major Depressive Disorder) rather than neurodevelopmental ones. Students with psychological diagnoses still fall under the category of twice-exceptionality because they may require accommodations or supports at home or school and because their giftedness influences how those diagnoses manifest.

Identifying Twice-Exceptional Children

Because of the unique strengths and struggles twice-exceptional children have, it can be a complicated process of sorting through their needs. Sometimes, a child's advanced abilities compensate for their areas of weakness, leading to a delayed identification or diagnosis of twice-exceptionality. For example, a gifted/ADHD child who struggles with organization, time management, and sustained attention may do "fine" in school and earn acceptable (or even excellent) grades when they are young. As they get older, however, expectations for executive functioning skills increase along with the level of difficulty of the tasks, and the gifted/ADHD student may no longer be able to compensate, and the symptoms of ADHD become clear. The reverse of this is also possible: A gifted/autistic child struggles greatly with emotional dysregulation when they are young and is placed on an Individualized Education Program to help with their difficulties. Once they are placed in the special education program, they are never identified as a candidate for gifted education screening or services, even when their academics clearly show they are an advanced learner who needs a rigorous curriculum.

When addressing the needs of the twice-exceptional youngster, it is important to make sure that the diagnosis is accurate. Behaviors associated with giftedness can be misinterpreted, and characteristics of neurodiversity may be misattributed to giftedness, leading to either misdiagnosis or missing a diagnosis, which both result in losing valuable time to provide supports. The level of impairment is an important consideration in accurate identification, and giftedness may allow some students to compensate well, hiding the impairment in some contexts. Some examples of possible misinterpretation of signs of concern leading to a misdiagnosis or missed diagnosis might include:

○ A gifted child in an under-stimulating environment may exhibit characteristics of inattention. An environmental accommodation that provides appropriate challenge can mitigate this inattention.

○ Gifted/autistic children may be misdiagnosed as ADHDers if their giftedness allows them to build compensatory skills related to social communication, but their executive functioning difficulties are evident. As social expectations outpace a child's ability to compensate, these difficulties will become more evident.

○ A gifted/dyslexic student may be labeled with an anxiety disorder because they seem to be able to comprehend what they are reading, but become extremely stressed when asked to read aloud in class.

○ A gifted/ADHD child may have characteristics of hyperactivity and impulsiveness, but have these characteristics explained away as signs of giftedness.

○ Both gifted children and autistic children can exhibit traits of *hyperlexia* (an interest in letters and numbers at an early age, often associated with an ability to read at a very early age).

All too often, well-meaning adults engage in informal diagnosis and confuse the signs of one type of neurodivergence with another, or professionals without training in giftedness misinterpret data on assessments. Finding a clinician who is knowledgeable about giftedness to provide a thorough assessment and tease out the nuances of diagnosis is necessary. The book *Misdiagnosis and Dual Diagnoses of Gifted Children and Adults* provides an in-depth look at these diagnostic issues, and *Twice Exceptional: Supporting and Educating Bright and Creative Students with Learning Difficulties* provides information about comprehensive assessments and interventions for twice-exceptional students.[13] Additionally, the Gifted Development Center has published the "Checklist for Recognizing Twice-Exceptional Children," which can be found online at no cost.[14]

Labels are important and need to be accurate to provide appropriate interventions. A Chinese proverb says, "The beginning of wisdom is calling things by their right name." Frequently with gifted children, a generic solution is attempted without the thorough evaluation that can yield more specific interventions. A correct diagnosis is a necessary starting point, not a solution or a treatment—and certainly is not a child's destiny.

The approach most often used in diagnosing learning disabilities is to compare some measures of the person's *ability* or *potential* (usually using a cognitive assessment or intelligence test) with other measures that reflect the person's *achievement* (usually a standardized academic test). If the academic achievement falls significantly below what would be expected—based on the estimate of ability—a learning disability can be identified, unless there are other factors, such as visual diffi-culties, emotional distress, or lack of educational opportunities, that could account for the discrepancy. This "discrepancy model" continues to be used to diagnose a learning disability in some educational settings. However, for a discrepancy to be relevant in some schools, the child must perform two or more grade levels below their same-grade peers. Gifted children may not meet the criteria under these parameters because their overall achievement is in the "average" range, or "on grade level." In obtaining diagnostic information, clinical psychologists and neuropsychologists also explore significant varia-tions and atypical patterns that suggest a possible learning disability. But, because of the considerable disparities in psychologists' training, such variations and patterns may suggest different things to different professionals, and issues for gifted children may be overlooked.

Identifying gifted children who qualify for special education services for a specific learning disability can be complicated, because asyn-chronous patterns are simply more common in gifted children.[15] A child with above-average reading abilities but math skills that are on par with same-age peers is not uncommon, and such differences do not necessarily suggest learning disabilities, because they can reflect learning strengths, weaknesses, or even increased educational exposure. Because gifted children's cognitive ability scores are statistical outliers, there is often more variance between the scores; large differences between verbal and nonverbal abilities are not uncommon among gifted children and should not cause concern in the absence of other evidence.[16] Both asynchronous development and varied levels of exposure to certain academic concepts influence a child's performance on academic tasks. One study showed that 92% of students with an IQ over 120 showed at least one area of learning disability when the standard discrepancy between a child's IQ and their achievement scores was applied. A discrepancy of 30-37.5 points may be a better indicator of a learning disability in gifted children.[17] Nonetheless, we should still expect a child's achievement in academic areas to approach their overall cognitive skills. Additionally, gifted children who perform "at grade level" may not meet state requirements when their skills are not far enough "below average" to qualify, and simply applying the same criteria of discrepancy between ability and achievement to a gifted student's profile isn't necessarily effective either. The books *Teaching Twice-Exceptional Learners in Today's Classroom* and *Twice Exceptional: Supporting and Educating Bright and Creative Students with Learning Difficulties* can provide guidance for educators in identifying specific learning disabilities in gifted students. [18]

Specific Learning Disabilities (Dyslexia, Dysgraphia, Dyscalculia)

Gifted children who struggle with reading, writing, or math may be exhibiting a learning disability in these areas. In general, it is expected that a gifted child's academic achievement in these areas will be commensurate with their ability. A child who expresses ideas eloquently when asked a question but then writes awkward, disorganized, and developmentally immature answers on the same topic is confusing for most educators. When a gifted child exhibits significant difficulty or very slow progress related to various academic skills, it may warrant investigation into the possibility of a specific learning disability. The terms dyslexia, dysgraphia, and dyscalculia are also used to describe these diagnoses.

As with any type of twice-exceptionality, it is common for gifted children with learning disabilities to mask them. Sometimes, their ability masks their difficulties, and they use their cognitive prowess to compensate for areas of weakness. For example, a gifted/dyslexic student may have extensive background knowledge and show above-average comprehension when reading, but a closer look at their ability to make a connection between the sounds represented by letters may show a discrepancy compared to their overall cognitive ability. Other times, their difficulties mask their strengths. A gifted/ dysgraphic student may never be identified as gifted because their writing is below average, making them unable to demonstrate their knowledge and skills. There is also the possibility that their weaknesses and giftedness mask each other, making it difficult to see evidence of either. The DSM-5 acknowledges the possibility of masking and delayed identification, describing that specific learning disorders can occur in gifted individuals but may not become evident until situational demands outpace their ability to compensate.

Dyslexia. Dyslexia is a common term for some types of reading disorder which can impact a person's ability to write, spell, and process language. Children with dyslexia struggle with connecting phonological sounds to the symbols we use to represent them in writing; it is not a *visual* processing disorder. Reversing letters in reading and writing is often cited as a sign of dyslexia, which may occur because a child is mixing up the sounds the letters make. For example, *p* and *b* might be flipped when writing or mistaken when sounding out a word because the mouth articulation used to create the sounds, *puh* and *buh*, is the same, though one is voiced and the other is silent. Dyslexia is often associated with difficulties in sequencing, spelling, telling time, or writing, to name only a few.

The term "stealth dyslexia" describes the all-too-common situation in which a gifted child's cognitive ability hides the presence of dyslexia. These students may score adequately on some measures of reading, leaving their dyslexia to go unnoticed. For example, a child's reading skills are frequently assessed based on how they answer comprehension questions after reading a passage; bright students with a strong background knowledge can often use context clues to fill in the gaps of the passage and accurately answer the comprehension questions. However, if you ask the same student to sound out or spell nonsense words, like *ip*, *bor*, or *grig*, their ability to decode the symbols and assign them the correct sound can be a surprising area of weakness.

Dyslexic students benefit from multisensory programs that rebuild the neural pathways of the sound-symbol connection required for reading fluently. The gold standard of these programs is Orton-Gillingham-based reading intervention, which systematically and explicitly teaches the basic building blocks of phonological awareness. One benefit of these programs for twice-exceptional students is that they do an excellent job of finding and filling gaps created when the gifted child was compensating with their ability.

Assistive technology is also available to support gifted/dyslexic students, offering a world of technological tools that can help. Learning to type at a young age, text-to-speech applications, audiobooks, and spellcheck provide accommodations for gifted/dyslexic students to support their difficulties.

Dysgraphia. Children who struggle with writing encounter various factors that influence their written language skills. Some struggle with fine motor skills, leading to poor handwriting and a preference to write as little as possible. Others have trouble finding the words to express their thoughts, which impedes written expression. Some students' writing ability is impacted by co-occurring dyslexia when the difficulty sounding out words creates difficulty with writing and spelling.

A gifted/dysgraphic child expresses themselves much more easily when speaking than writing. Parents and teachers will notice oversimplification of thoughts when putting them on paper because of difficulty with written expression. They can speak paragraphs but write short sentences, being careful to use only words they spell and write easily. Basic grammatical rules, like punctuation and capitalization, may be inconsistent or missing.

Accommodations can help children who struggle with writing. Gifted/dysgraphic students benefit from tools such as graphic organizers to manage their thoughts before beginning to write. A teacher or parent who can scribe for a child while they verbally brainstorm what they want to write can provide a foundation for completing longer assignments. Technological tools also provide excellent accommodations. Speech-to-text software helps students get their thoughts on paper; grammatical functions in word processing software can help a student avoid common writing errors. Allowing students to test or present information orally and turn in dictated audio files instead of written work can help the gifted/dysgraphic student demonstrate the full extent of their knowledge and skills, while lessening the impact of their disability.

Dyscalculia. Although not as well-known as dyslexia, dyscalculia is a similar diagnosis that impacts someone's ability to understand and manipulate numbers and reason quantitatively. Educators often talk about students developing "number sense"—a set of general skills that are related concepts like *more* and *less*, ordinal numbers (first, second, third, etc.), and recognizing the relationships between different quantifiable amounts. Children with dyscalculia struggle to develop this number sense. Other skills that may be difficult include telling time, developing math fluency (the ability to solve basic math problems quickly), remembering and following multiple step algorithms, and reading and solving word problems.

Students with characteristics of dyscalculia can benefit from supplemental math solving tools, such as number charts for multiplication and lists of steps for algorithms. Assistive technology helps students, including calculators and various apps available on tablets or phones. There are programs that help with dyscalculia, similar to Orton-Gillingham programs for dyslexic students. TouchMath, for example, helps students build the skills necessary for number sense to be able to complete mathematical problems.

Processing Difficulties

Sensory processing differences. There is some evidence that increased sensory sensitivity is common in gifted children.[19] For example, the taste of mint in regular toothpaste may be perceived as painfully intense, or the smell of cafeteria food may distract from the task at hand. When these sensitivities cause significant disruption to daily activities, it is time to investigate what options may be available to support them, such as occupational therapy. Sensory processing disorder is not a standalone diagnosis, and sensory processing differences may be a sign of another type of neurodivergence. ADHDers may be hyperaware or easily distracted by a variety of sensory experiences; hypo- and hyper-reactivity to sensory input are part of the diagnostic criteria for autism.

Sensory processing differences can impact any of our eight sensory systems: gustatory (taste), visual, auditory, olfactory (smell), tactile (touch), proprioceptive (where one's body is in space), vestibular (how one's body is moving), and interoceptive (how one interprets internal bodily sensations). While the first five are the familiar senses we learned about as children, you may not have heard about the last three. A child who appears clumsy and bumps into things frequently may be struggling with proprioception, while another may seek vestibular stimulation by rocking in a chair or pacing. A child who struggles to differentiate between a stomachache due to illness, hunger, or anxiety may have poor interoceptive awareness.

Individuals who struggle with sensory integration may fall into one of two categories: sensory avoidance (hyper-sensitive to stimuli) or sensory seeking (hypo-sensitive to stimuli). People who struggle with sensory processing and integration are not going to "get used to it." While there is some evidence that exposure will desensitize someone to a nonpreferred sensory experience, many neurodivergent people will tell you this isn't the case. The best plan for supporting a child with sensory processing difficulties is to provide alternatives that do not disrupt functioning and allow those with sensory processing challenges to participate fully in life. Occupational therapy can help find strategies to meet a child's sensory needs.

Central Auditory Processing Disorder (CAPD). Most of us have experienced the difficulty of trying to follow conversations against the background noise at a social event. After a while, the effort involved in listening becomes too fatiguing and we lose the thread of the conversation. This description is similar to the experience of children or adults with an auditory processing disorder. Children with auditory processing problems try to learn algebra in the "noise" of a classroom that is equivalent to the noise at a party for someone without this disorder. Focusing on and processing the incoming information can be such a chore that all meaning is lost.

Auditory processing is different from hearing. Children who pass basic hearing tests can still have auditory processing problems; for example, they may have difficulty tuning out background noise, understanding distorted speech, or adapting to unfamiliar speaking styles. When they fatigue from the effort, they become less attentive.

Children with an unrecognized auditory processing problems may appear to have some other impairment—hearing insufficiency, inattention, language delays, or learning disabilities. Intellectual skills and potential are likely to be overlooked. In his book *Ungifted*,[20] Scott Barry Kaufman describes his personal experience of being overlooked due to CAPD and resulting anxiety. Audiologists are the medical professionals who are trained to identify and diagnose CAPD.

Accommodations are helpful for the child with auditory processing problems. Simply seating the child near the speaker with a clear view of the speaker's face can be very effective. Schools should have access to hearing assistive technology, such as FM systems, which project the teacher's voice over speakers in the classroom. Providing instructions in writing, either on the board or at the student's desk, is also an excellent accommodation.

Attention-Deficit/Hyperactivity Disorder

Attention-Deficit/Hyperactivity Disorder (ADHD) is estimated to be present in about 1 out of 10 children.[21] During an assessment for ADHD, a clinician will determine if a child exhibits characteristics of the Predominantly Inattentive, Predominantly Hyperactive, or Combined presentation of ADHD. While past diagnostic terminology separated ADD (inattentive) and ADHD (hyperactive/impulsive) into individual diagnoses, all types of attention issues fall under the umbrella of ADHD in the current diagnostic terminology.

Attention-Deficit/Hyperactivity Disorder is in many ways a misnomer. Instead of a lack—or deficit—of attention, ADHD is much better described as a difficulty with *regulating* attention. Some people struggle to tune out stimuli (either environmental or internal), resulting in distraction and inattention; others get so focused on a particular task that they are unaware of things going on around them (hyperfocus).

ADHD or gifted? Some characteristics of ADHD and giftedness may mimic each other. In the past, the American Psychiatric Association suggested using caution when diagnosing ADHD in gifted children, recognizing the possibility that "Inattention in the classroom may also occur when children with high intelligence are placed in academically under-stimulating environments."[22] Gifted students who complete their work quickly may disrupt other students who are working, which can look like hyperactivity; students who process information quickly and blurt out answers in class before being called on may appear to exhibit ADHD traits. Difficulty adhering to rules and regulations is one of the generally accepted signs of possible ADHD,[23] *yet gifted children show similar behaviors, although for different reasons.* Starting in the early grades, exceptionally bright children begin to question rules, customs, and traditions, and their intensity makes them prone to engage in power struggles with authority.

While some characteristics associated with giftedness may mimic ADHD, it is also possible that gifted/ADHD individuals compensate for attention-related behaviors with their intelligence during assessments. One study showed that gifted/ADHD students had different profiles of strengths and struggles compared to typically-developing ADHDers, leading to confusion and missed diagnosis by clinicians untrained in giftedness and twice-exceptionality[24]; other studies have explored the possibilities of misdiagnosis or failure to diagnose.[25]

The diagnosis of ADD/ADHD is supposed to be a diagnosis of exclusion, to be made after ruling out other possible causes for the behavior. There are many problems that can cause symptoms of inattention, hyperactivity, and impulsivity: depression, anxiety, learning disabilities, preoccupation with personal problems, unrealistic expectations, situational difficulties, boredom due to a mismatch of abilities and expectations, auditory processing deficits, concussion or mild traumatic brain injury, ill health, substance abuse, fatigue from sleep disorders, lack of energy because of poor eating habits or an eating disorder, and even a reaction to medications. Because a psychologist must take the time to rule out many other possibilities, ADHD is a difficult diagnosis to make and should not be based solely on a 10-minute appointment with a family doctor who has looked at a questionnaire filled out by the parent and/or school personnel. Similarly, a parent should question a quick recommendation to place the child on medication when the suggestion is given as, "Let's just try him on this medication for a month or two and see if it helps." Medications do often help focus, but parents should carefully consider the need and possible side effects before starting.

"Hyperactive" is a word parents use to describe both gifted children and children with ADHD. The difference between the two can often be seen when one looks at the purpose of the hyperactivity. A gifted student who exhibits an extremely high energy level directed toward goals may not be showing signs of ADHD, while a disorganized, ill-directed flow of energy is often more characteristic of ADHD.

It should also be noted that ADHDers *can* focus—and quite well—when they are directing their attention to a preferred activity, such as building LEGO, playing Minecraft, or even reading, for some children. A better question to ask about whether a child can focus is how they focus on a *nonpreferred* activity. Can they initiate a task that is something they really don't want to do, like homework? Can they maintain their focus on an activity they perceive as "boring" if it needs to be done?

Twice-Exceptional Gifted/ADHDers. For gifted/ADHD children, it is important to insist that schools acknowledge both labels. Advanced intellectual abilities can obscure symptoms of ADHD and can delay the appropriate diagnosis.[26] Children with ADHD who are particularly bright can, in the earlier grades, pay attention to only a small portion of the class period, yet because of their advanced knowledge and high intellectual level, still perform well on the tests or other assignments when compared with age peers.

A diagnostic error that misses ADHD in a gifted child can be just as serious as an incorrect diagnosis that a gifted child suffers from ADHD when in fact he does not.[27] If ADHD is overlooked in a young child, that student may suddenly discover that the compensatory skills he used in elementary school are not sufficient to meet the demands of the middle school or high school curriculum. The child becomes very frustrated and doesn't know what to do or what to think. It can impact self-esteem, motivation, and social relationships. When a child's behavior causes academic, social, or self-concept impairments, it is important to have him clinically examined to rule out conditions that are potentially treatable.

Executive functioning. Executive function deficits are some of the primary areas of difficulty for ADHDers. These skills are primarily executed in the prefrontal cortex of the brain, which is located at the front of the brain beneath the forehead; because the brain develops from the brain stem (near the neck) upward and forward, this the is last part of the brain to develop fully.

Executive function skills can be divided into two main categories: decision-making skills and behavioral regulation skills. When supporting gifted/ADHDers, identifying the specific executive functioning difficulties can empower them to find the accommodations and supports they need for success. For example, rather than setting the vague goal of "doing better at school," parents and educators can guide students to focus on developing the skill of estimating the length of time a task will take (associated with time management). Table 3 describes different executive function skills.

Table 3: Executive Function Skills

Decision Making Skills
Planning/Prioritizing: Identifying the steps of a process and organizing them in a logical order
Time Management: Accurately estimating the time a task will take and arranging blocks of time to effectively accomplish the tasks needed
Organization: Developing and maintaining a system to keep supplies and resources accessible and easily found.
Working Memory: Maintaining information, such as multistep instructions, in one's short-term memory
Metacognition: Reflecting on and evaluating thought processes and actions
Behavioral Regulation Skills
Response Inhibition: Pausing before responding; withholding a response rather than reacting impulsively
Task Persistence: Following a multistep project through to completion
Task Initiation: Getting started on a task
Shifting Focus: Transitioning from one task to another
Sustained Attention: Maintaining focus on an activity for a continuous amount of time
Cognitive Flexibility: Adjusting expectations for situations; finding new ways to solve a problem

Autism Spectrum

Our understanding of autism has exploded within the last decade. Understanding how autism manifests as a spectrum and impacts individuals in many unique ways has allowed us to offer much better support and compassion. The neurodiversity movement has provided a powerful voice for autistic people; the move away from seeing autism solely as a deficit has normalized its strengths and differences, while also recognizing that some traits of autism can be disabling.

We are beginning to learn that there is a connection between cognitive giftedness and autism. Evidence that shows that, genetically speaking, the alleles that are present when a person is autistic have a broad overlap with the alleles that are present when a person is cognitively gifted.[28] In many cases, overall cognitive ability in autistic individuals falls within the range of intellectual disability; however, autistic people are also 1.5 times *more* likely to have a full scale intelligence score in the gifted range, compared to non-autistic peers.[29] Cognitive profiles of gifted/autistic individuals frequently show a pattern of ability with very high verbal comprehension scores alongside significantly lower processing speed.[30]

There are two main areas that are impacted for autistic individuals. The first relates to communication; the second relates to comfort with routine and consistency. It is important to note that each of these characteristics manifests differently for each autistic person. The social communication habits of autistic individuals include:

○ Differences in engaging in neurotypical, back-and-forth communication, such as less frequent sharing of emotions or uncertainty
   about how to respond to or initiate social interactions.

○ Differences in receptive and expressive use of nonverbal
   communication, such as tone of voice, eye contact, or facial
   expressions.

○ Differences in expectations associated with relationships and
   preferred types of play.

Autistic people often find comfort in routine and consistency (worded as "restricted, repetitive patterns of behavior" in diagnostic manuals). Typically, autistic individuals exhibit at least two of the following four characteristics, although they could show all four.

○ Repetitive motor movements or speech patterns (for example,
   "stimming" behaviors such as pacing, bouncing, or rocking,
   or using the same phrase over and over).

○ Comfort with sameness and dysregulation/distress with unexpected changes to routine.

○ Special interests that are extremely intense and often to the exclusion of other interests.

○ Hyposensitivity or hypersensitivity to sensory stimuli (such as noise, lights, textures, etc.) leading to sensory seeking or sensory avoiding behaviors.

Because twice-exceptional individuals frequently mask or camouflage their differences, gifted/autistic children and teens are frequently identified much later than their same-age peers. The DSM-5 even recognizes this fact and states that while symptoms of autism must be present while a person is young, they "may not become fully manifest until social demands exceed capabilities, or may be masked by learned strategies later in life."[31] In other words, just because a gifted child isn't identified as autistic when they are young doesn't mean they aren't autistic. Many gifted/autistic individuals aren't identified until they are in high school, college, or later.

Gifted, autistic, or both? Differentiating between giftedness and autism can be tricky and the stigma that is associated with a diagnosis of autism adds an additional barrier to appropriate identification. While many characteristics of gifted and autistic people may overlap, searching for the reasons behind the characteristics can shed some light on what is behind the behavior. Table 4 describes some of these overlapping behaviors and their relation to giftedness and autism.

Table 4: Characteristics Associated with Giftedness and Autism

Characteristic/ behavior	Connection to giftedness	Connection to autism
Difficulties with social connection and communication	Gifted children and teens may have difficulty connecting with peers who have interests and ability that are much different than their own. Additionally, the social stigma of being labeled as gifted can cause some social pressures, especially as children reach adolescence.	Autistic individuals may have different preferred styles of social connection and interaction. They may prefer to work or play alone, or they may misread the expectations for social interactions based on neurotypical social norms. Interpreting the underlying meanings of social communication can cause barriers.
Difficulty identifying/sharing emotions	Young gifted children may experience frustration when they don't have the vocabulary to explain their nuanced emotions. Gifted children who experience perfectionism may feel uncomfortable with the vulnerability of verbalizing emotions.	Autistic individuals may have difficulty identifying their emotions. One possible reason for this may be related to sensory differences, such as a hyposensitivity to internal body signals associated with emotions (like not noticing your heart rate speeding up when you are scared).

Characteristic/ behavior	Connection to giftedness	Connection to autism
Difficulty with cognitive flexibility	Gifted kids often have very rigid ideas about what is "fair" or what the "right" way to do something is, generally stemming from advanced logical thinking skills that rationalize their beliefs. They may also be used to being right, so shifting their expectations may feel like admitting they were wrong.	Autistic children and teens rely on consistency so they know what to expect and how to interact in certain situations. Changes that are made without advance notice or that don't make sense can cause emotional dysregulation, especially if the child also struggles with self-advocacy and communication skills.
Intense areas of interest or passion	Gifted kids and teens may have areas of passion that are more intense or developed than their same-age peers. They are generally able to engage in activities that are unrelated to this topic at school or in conversation.	Special interests for autistic people are often the main thing(s) they do or talk about. Using special interests to build relationships and social connection can be very helpful. Autistic kids may have difficulty engaging with or conversing about topics unrelated to their special interests.

You may hear people use terms like "high-functioning" related to autism, and there are several reasons that this can be confusing when talking about autism and twice-exceptionality. First, the term is no longer used diagnostically; "High-Functioning Autism" was originally a term used to describe how well an autistic person was able to navigate the world. It meant they were generally independent in communication and basic life skills. The current DSM designates levels of support (level one for minimal support needs through level three for significant support needs) rather than functioning labels. When talking about twice-exceptionality, though, some people conflate the idea of high-functioning with above average cognitive ability. Gifted/autistic individuals may have a wide range of support needs depending on the environment and situation, which is separate from their general cognitive ability.

It is important to get a correct diagnosis. If gifted/autistic children are considered simply to be quirky, eccentric gifted children, they will go undiagnosed and not receive treatment that could help.[32] An appropriate diagnosis is key to accessing accommodations and supports now and in the future because the more gifted/autistic children know and understand about themselves, the better they will be able to self-advocate.

Practical Solutions

○ When a child has inexplicable or apparently careless errors, they should be carefully evaluated for sensory integration deficits, learning disabilities, or other neurological problems. Parents and professionals should look at the child's reaction to their environment. Some children, for example, experience sensory overload that prevents them from mastering a task. Others may appear inattentive in an educational setting that doesn't meet their needs. Once a formal and accurate diagnosis of a disability in a gifted child is made, parents and teachers can identify and implement appropriate educational interventions to address the problem. A diagnosis can also help a gifted child better understand her strengths and weaknesses, thus enhancing self-understanding and self-esteem. A misdiagnosis or missed diagnosis may result in not only inappropriate interventions, but also a lack of appropriate interventions.

○ The giftedness component should always be incorporated when explaining the diagnosis and in educational planning with twice-exceptional children. Educational options should be tailored to fit the child's abilities, and strengths should be utilized to help compensate for weaknesses. It is important to address the concerns arising from both conditions (giftedness and disability) rather than only one in an either/or fashion. A gifted child may be reassured to understand which parts of their emotions and behaviors are associated with giftedness and which are part of their other exceptionality. With an accurate explanation for the behaviors, a gifted child can then use his intellect to comprehend what his diagnosis means—and also what it does not mean.

○ If you think that your gifted child may be twice-exceptional, consider: (1) getting a comprehensive assessment of the child, (2) creating a thorough learning profile of the child's learning and behavioral strengths and weaknesses, and (3) designing a program of education, therapy, and play to implement at home and school.

○ In your plan, you will want to undertake three fundamental approaches. First, wherever possible, use remediation that will help to "rewire" the brain, teach skill development through instruction, or use a tutor to help develop an academically weak area. Second, use compensation strategies that help a child use strengths to work around areas of weakness. For example, use a child's strength in visualizing to help develop organizational skills. Third, use accommodations where needed. For example, a child who is struggling with poor handwriting may use a keyboard for writing assignments. Accommodations are not ways to get the child out of work, but rather to put the child into situations that will best promote education and skill development and allow her to demonstrate the full extent of her knowledge and skills with minimal impact from her weaknesses.

○ It is important to start the remediation process as early as possible. Because they are in a state of rapid development, children's brains are far more able to be rewired when they are young than when they are older. The adage "It is easier to build children than to mend adults" applies here. If they are misdiagnosed or undiagnosed, twice-exceptional children may slide into an intellectual poverty that could have been avoided, and they also have higher risks for substance abuse and psychological difficulties. Early evaluation and diagnosis of the twice-exceptional child can help address problems that are otherwise overlooked, and this can save the child years of frustration and low self-esteem.

Chapter 3
Complexities of Parenting Gifted Children

Every parent wants to be successful, but what defines success? What are the goals? Parents of gifted children have seven important tasks or goals:

○ Accept and appreciate the child's uniqueness.

○ Help the child like herself and relate well to others.

○ Develop a positive, trusting relationship with the child.

○ Help the child find a sense of belonging within the family.

○ Nurture the development of values.

○ Teach the child self-motivation, self-management, and self-discipline.

○ Allow the child to discover his passions and commit to letting him explore.

This book focuses on approaches and techniques to help you achieve these goals. We recognize that parents have quite different ideas about what is an appropriate parenting style, and usually their style comes from the way they themselves were raised. There is no one best way to rear a child; it depends upon the child. The best way for your family is whatever you and your partner agree upon and implement consistently to accomplish the goals above.

Mistakes are a part of life, and part of parenting. Our parenting will not always be what we want it to be. As the psychologist Haim Ginott declared, no parent wakes up in the morning planning to make life miserable for their child by yelling, nagging, and humiliating whenever possible. Despite our best intentions, we find ourselves sometimes saying things we do not mean or using a tone we do not like. We are wise to learn from these incidents and keep trying to improve.

As with many aspects of life, being a successful parent involves some element of chance or luck. Many parents seemingly do all the "right" things, yet their children still do not turn out as they had hoped. Parenting is a very humbling experience. We must struggle through, doing the best we can. As our children grow, we have to trust that we have laid a solid foundation and instilled proper values in our children, but we cannot know the results of our efforts immediately and may not know for quite some time. We hope that this book will help you plant the seeds of success so that you can watch them flower.

Influences on Modern Parenting

Being a parent of a gifted child is demanding, sometimes even exhausting, and is more complicated now than in previous decades. Parenting has changed in many ways from our childhood and our parents' childhood. In our grandparents' day, it was common for a father to take a young boy to the woodshed and whip him with a leather belt. Child-rearing practices today are more democratic and less punitive. Whereas in earlier times children were to be "seen but not heard," today we know it is healthy to encourage children to talk to us and share their thoughts and feelings. Expectations for our children are different, too. Parenting keeps changing as younger generations strive to keep up with the latest research and expert advice, weighing the new information against traditional values and practices.

In addition, changes in society have weakened the influence of parents and reduced support from extended families. Family members these days may live long distances from one another. Technological, consumer, and peer influences have become increasingly important forces that affect our children. These are just some of the difficulties of modern parenting. In the face of all these changes, parents must find ways to take care of themselves and their relationships as well as the family.

Mobility. The average family in the United States moves much more frequently than in the past, when families lived in the same neighborhood for 20 years or more and relied on neighbors they knew well. There was a sense of safety since everyone knew children by name. Parents knew that if their child misbehaved at a neighbor's house, someone there would correct the child. Now, with each move, there is a loss of community, and many families don't know their neighbors' names. We are anonymous in our communities. Cross-country moves mean children see relatives less often. Extended family members, who can provide a sense of stability, belongingness, and shelter for children, may find it hard to maintain relationships from afar, even with technological advances like video calls.

In the past, at family gatherings, people would talk about shared experiences, including what happened to this or that individual, or how this one or that one achieved success or dealt with tragedy or failure. Children would overhear these stories or ask their parents questions on the way home. These gatherings and conversations conveyed family values, traditions, and a sense of belonging from one generation to the next. Children understood how their own family fit within the larger family context—how they differed and how they were similar.

In the 21st Century, we have a great deal of freedom in lifestyle; we can choose where we live and work and the kind of work we do. We may not even live where we work because remote work is much more available. In many ways, we are more isolated. We have lost the benefits of having family members and neighbors living nearby who maintain an interest in our lives and those of our children and with whom we share holidays and other special occasions. We hesitate to put down roots in our new community, knowing we might move again in a few years.

When there are great physical distances between family members, it is difficult for them to act as a support system if problems arise. When someone is rushed to the hospital following an accident, for example, family members can't simply get in their car to be at the bedside. And when there are relationship problems, family members aren't always there to offer a listening ear. They may call or connect via video, but the physical connection is missing. Where people once turned to family, they now turn to friends or a counselor instead. And often they wait until problems are serious before talking to anyone. While mobility offers freedom, it comes with hidden costs.

Divorce and remarriage. The incidence of divorce and remarriage has increased dramatically in recent years, resulting in many splintered families. Even when amicable, divorce has long-lasting consequences for parents, children, friends, and even grandparents and other extended family members. These consequences m. ay be even more severe for gifted children because of their emotional sensitivity. Issues of custody can create additional difficulties, whether parents live in the same city or in a different city or state. Even the fairest custody arrangements disrupt family life. Although children are resilient, back-and-forth moves between two households are often difficult, with differing expectations, rules, and routines.

Divorce almost always involves emotional distress, disappointment, and disillusionment for the entire family, which undoubtedly affects parenting and family relationships. Disengagement, distrust, and frustration may be frequent. A new level of uncertainty about the family and about life brings stress and anxiety. Remarriage and blending families bring more uncertainty. The adjustment is often difficult.

Faster pace. In the late 1970s, futurists and the U.S. Department of Labor predicted that computers and other technology would eliminate so many jobs that, by the turn of the century, we would all need to work only a four-day week. Businesses would have childcare centers, and we would have more vacation weeks each year. There would be more leisure time, and the futurists encouraged us to start planning and developing interests for that promised leisure. Now that the 21st Century is here, the reality is quite different. Most of us feel more pressured than ever. The COVID-19 pandemic has added varying levels of stress to our lives. Work schedules have been disrupted and many have become increasingly demanding. While many now work remotely, some workers commute to and from work and still bring work home. There is a sense of urgency, even on weekends, to be productive. There is less "down time" for many. Information is everywhere and social media pulls on our time. The faster pace leaves even less time for parents and children to spend with each other.

In his best-selling book *The Seven Habits of Highly Effective People*, Stephen Covey points out that we often find ourselves responding to what feels *urgent* rather than to what is *important*. Helping a child with homework after dinner may be more *important* than the business call that comes in and seems so *urgent*. If we pay attention to what is "important" versus "urgent," we are better able to counteract some of the pressures.

Nothing is unthinkable. With easy access to information online, we get still another unintended consequence. Our children are exposed to actions and events that in previous generations would have been simply unimaginable. Children hear and see peers engaging in unsafe behavior online and watch gruesome and disturbing events unfold in real time. They see death, war, and poverty, for example, and the gifted child's sensitivity, intensity, compassion, and sense of moral justice are often strongly affected by these news reports.

Disturbing role models. Poor role models have always been present but are now more readily seen. Unrealistic portrayals of selfishly rude characters are not only shown as acceptable, but also as humorous, valued, and worthy of copying. Some shows depict bright and talented children as comic figures worthy of scorn and not individuals to be respected or valued. When bright children are mocked in the media, it can be detrimental to all bright children's self-esteem.

Sometimes, parents are shown as incompetent. When parents are ridiculed in the media, successful parenting becomes more difficult. Peers and social media can become stronger influences than parents, adding a layer to parenting not seen in previous generations: parents must more closely monitor their children's online activities.

Consumerism and technology. Our economy and our standard of living is high compared to most countries: food, clothing, and luxuries are plentiful. There is pressure to earn enough to live comfortably in a nice house, own two cars, and buy all the new gadgets. There is always someone enticing you to buy something. The message is that we don't have enough. The pressure to buy a cell phone for your young child, for example, comes from all directions. Unfortunately, some of these technological advances have become barriers to family relationships. Many children these days are far more likely to be engaged with social media than to be engaged in a mutual activity with a parent or other family member. In some families, dinner out means "being alone together" until the food arrives. Playing outside with friends, going to the library to check out books, building something, and cooking with mom or dad are less frequent these days, and there is less time for imaginative play. Technology needs to be managed differently than in the past to be sure it doesn't replace other forms of play or human interaction in ways that negatively affect relationships.

If all of this sounds discouraging, it may be. This is the reality of the society we live in. While we do face barriers, there is much that we as parents can do to counteract these influences when we acknowledge that they exist. We can act within our own families to offset or diminish their influence.

Family Equilibrium

Families can be viewed as a system with relative equilibrium among the individuals and relationships. When challenging events occur, either within the system or outside of it, the equilibrium of the family is temporarily thrown out of balance, and readjustment occurs as the family strives to find a new balance. How long finding anew equilibrium takes will depend on the extent of the disruption. The new pattern may be healthier and more satisfying, or it may be less so. The quality of the new equilibrium will depend on communication and how relationships are managed during the unsettling events.

Stresses and crises—some lesser, some greater—occur in all families over time and change the relationships between family members. A new school, relocation to a new community, divorce, a serious accident or illness, or someone moving out to attend college or get married will create a temporary period of instability that requires readjustment for the family to reach a new equilibrium. When one individual changes, others react and adjust. New roles emerge, particularly for the children. Sometimes sibling rivalry intensifies or self-esteem improves, sometimes family traditions take on new importance, and sometimes there is underachievement, rebellion, withdrawal, or some other unexpected behavior. Assure your children that their fundamental security and belonging within the family are not at risk. A small amount of time spent reassuring children can help them understand that life always involves change, change involves loss, and loss brings new opportunities.

Blended Families and Step-Parenting

One of the most dramatic examples of disequilibrium occurs when remarriages create blended families. Two parents, each with children from a previous relationship and with different ways of doing things, merge to become one new family. If you are in such a situation, you already know the difficulties. Both parents have already spent years with their own children. There are already patterns, traditions, and expectations not only about the children, but also about the role of the other parent. The failure rate of second and third marriages confirms the extent of difficulties involved.

How does a stepparent establish a relationship with a stepchild who is gifted? It depends on the age and personality of the child. It is wise to take an unhurried approach and spend a significant amount of time observing and listening both to the child and to your partner, who has a far longer history with the child. If you are a stepparent who didn't see the gifted child's early development and "quirks," you don't have key pieces of information that can help build a strong relationship. It helps to be aware of the ways gifted children differ from other children. The relationship you establish with a stepchild will likely be different from the relationship you have with your own children, and will require openness and sensitivity. Allow it to grow at its own pace; do not try to force it.

As for the family, it is extremely difficult to instantly blend two separate and functioning parenting styles while simultaneously trying to establish individual relationships and assume new parenting responsibilities. This is even more challenging when one or more of the stepchildren have abilities and talents that are quite different from the other children. It may take years before everyone is comfortable.

A frequent dilemma in blended families arises when a parent becomes the spokesperson for their biological child or feels a need to rescue their child from a stepparent's anger. This not only hinders the ability of the other parent to establish a relationship with that child, but it also ignores and reduces the child's ability to speak for herself. Allowing the child to relate to the new parent on her own terms, in her own time, and in her own words can be difficult but is beneficial to developing positive relationships.

Parents Must Care for Themselves, Too

Pressures of everyday life can leave parents feeling overwhelmed. Children's demands can leave parents little time for their personal life, friends, and hobbies. Lessons and activities put a strain on the family budget. You may feel a sense of responsibility to offer enrichment to these children who show so much potential, but how much can you sacrifice in your own personal life for their sake? In the same way that you set aside special time to spend with each of your children, you must set aside time for yourself. If you do not take time to recharge your own batteries, there will be no energy to give to others.

Parents need relationships with other adults. Taking care of yourself also means taking care of your relationship with your partner and close friends. Some parents, often gifted themselves, are so intensely focused on their own careers that they neglect other relationships. Balancing career demands, adult relationships, and the needs of children can be a daunting task. It's easy for parents to get overly focused on work, or so enamored of their gifted children, that they let other relationships go. Make time to do things without your children, just you and your partner or friend. These intentional special times are necessary for healthy relationships. Activities like date nights, sharing yard work, or simply taking a walk demonstrate a balanced life to your children, and also nurture your relationship. There is no substitute for parents as partners working together to offer children a sense of family solidity and security.

As you reflect on your own needs, also think about what you are modeling for your children. How are you taking care of your own intellectual, emotional, social, and spiritual needs? Children need to see how an adult achieves a balanced life, and home is the best place for them to learn. Children also need to see how adults maintain relationships with others, as well as the skills involved, such as how to be caring, how to argue fairly, and how to resolve conflicts.

Parenting a gifted child can be exhausting for two-parent families, and it is even more so in single-parent families. Along with the absence of the physical, moral, and emotional support from another caring adult, single parents usually have additional financial pressures as well. It can be tremendously exhausting not having another adult in the home to discuss child-rearing and occasionally take over parenting tasks. If you are a single parent, you will likely need extra support to keep from feeling frazzled. A friend, relative, or a grandparent may be able to give you a well-needed break.

Don't pressure yourself to be Super Parent! Allow yourself to be fatigued, worried, and to make mistakes. When your children know they are loved, mistakes can be forgiven. Be assured that it is ok, and sometimes even better, if you don't know all the answers and are not always right, because having a parent who "knows everything" can be a hard act to follow. For example, a young boy proudly described his discovery that Hannibal first took elephants across the Alps, only to have his father tell him that Hannibal's uncle actually took elephants across that same route years earlier. The father was completely unaware of how devastating his encyclopedic knowledge was to other family members. Children in this household learned not to offer facts or opinions for fear of being challenged or put down by their father. Parents who are gifted, intense, and always right can have a powerful—and sometimes harmful—effect on their families.

Gifted Adults

Of course, it is no surprise that many parents of gifted children are intellectually and creatively gifted themselves. As you read this book, you may discover that some of the characteristics of gifted children—such as intensity, sensitivity, or high energy level—are traits that describe you as well, even today as an adult. Giftedness is not something you outgrow when you leave school. Develop an awareness of how your own gifted traits affect your expectations and communication with your family, as well as your relationships with coworkers and supervisors. Just as with gifted children, your passion, idealism, concern for justice, perfectionism, and impatience may be great strengths, but they can also be hindrances. You may even find some personal discontent that stems from issues related to your gifted traits. You may find it helpful to talk with family members about what it means to be a gifted adult, because you are probably not the first gifted person in your family.

CHAPTER 4

Communication: The Key to Relationships

Positive interpersonal relationships are important in determining whether gifted children will be successful, caring, and contributing members of society. Communication is a vital part of any relationship, and parents and other significant adults play key roles in fostering children's communication skills.

From the time children are born, communication occurs through everyday actions and behaviors, and relationships begin. Parents try to understand an infant's needs from cries and other behaviors, and they respond by offering food and comfort. When parents talk, children follow their voice and smile or babble. As parents encourage infants to smile and make sounds back to them, relationships strengthen, and children learn expectations and how to please others. They learn to smile and laugh, say "da-da" and "ma-ma," and later to communicate wants and needs. Time passes, children grow, relationships develop, and communication changes.

As children get older and become more independent, communication can become more difficult, especially if significant adults have not established a strong relationship in the younger years. Communication is even more challenging if there is a major family crisis, such as illness, divorce, or death. Children in such situations may "shut down" communication with their parents, preferring to deal with their thoughts and feelings on their own. Only a strong relationship will reopen healthy communication.

Communication is a fundamental component of any relationship, but particularly with one's child. When there is healthy, open communication, family matters go much more smoothly, and relationships grow stronger. A child develops a sense of who she is within the context of family relationships, and strong communication builds her confidence and self-esteem. With this experience, the child learns how to interact socially and form positive relationships with others, both within and outside of the family.

What Communication Skills Are You Modeling?

Children learn about communication and relationships in three primary ways. First, by how parents interact with them; second, from observing parents as they interact with others; and third, from their own interactions with others. The way parents behave, especially in disagreements or during discipline, can foster or hinder healthy communication by encouraging or discouraging trust and openness. Raising one's voice, yelling, or acting out with physical aggression, for example, can frighten children, who may then not take the risk to share openly. Conversely, using open and assertive communication with "I" statements[1] fosters trust. Here are some suggestions, adapted from psychologist Martin Seligman for modeling positive communication in relationships:

- ○ Model anger control. Slow things down; take time to cool off. Say, "I'm going to go out in the back yard to cool off a bit before we talk about this."

- ○ Don't criticize your partner in front of your child and avoid permanent and pervasive labels (e.g., "Your father always…," "Your mother never…").

- ○ If you do criticize your partner where your child might overhear, use language that identifies specific behaviors rather than global personality.

- ○ Don't use the "silent treatment" and assume others won't notice.

○ Don't ask a child to choose sides between parents.

○ Don't begin arguments with others in front of your child unless you plan to finish the conflict in that same conversation.

○ Resolve conflicts where your child can observe that conflict and its resolution are natural parts of any relationship. Seeing conflicts resolve helps a child learn to look for resolution.

○ Leave your child out of adult issues. Have an agreement with your partner that you will avoid certain topics when children are present.

Communication and Feelings Are Linked

The good news is that barriers to communication can be overcome. First, remember that all communication has an important emotional component. Your tone of voice, inflection, volume, body posture, and gestures all convey your feelings. These feelings influence how your child hears, interprets, and reacts to what you are trying to say. To illustrate, say the first four letters of the alphabet as you normally would. Then pronounce them in an angry, sad, and happy way. Notice how the emotional information being transmitted through your inflection and intonation is significantly different each time, even though the information (4 letters) is the same. As adults setting an example, we must not forget the emotional component of our voice and must pay attention to both the words and feelings we portray.

Next, recognize that communication of feelings also occurs in behavior. When a child slams a door, stomps off, or rolls eyes, we recognize the emotion, but are more likely to criticize the behavior than to respond to the feelings that prompted it in the first place. Recognizing the emotional component that plays a significant role in the behavior will enhance communication with your child. You might say, "I can see that you are really angry, and I'd like you to tell me about your anger rather than slam the door," to help the child talk about what is bothering her—if not at that moment, perhaps in the future.

Emotions can affect a child's achievement, test scores, and even success in life. While it is now widely accepted that emotional and interpersonal skills are important to one's success, some parents and teachers of gifted children may downplay the importance of emotions, viewing them as nuisances that get in the way of what they see as the foremost goal, which is to develop the child's academic achievement. In recent years, the stress of the COVID-19 pandemic has renewed a focus on mental and emotional health.

Ignoring, avoiding, attempting to *control,* or belittling a child's feelings sends the message that feelings don't count or that the child's *emotional development* is not valued. Such negative messages clearly affect communication and relationships. Try to imagine that every time you get upset, someone bigger and taller looks down at you and says in an angry tone, "You have no right to feel that way!" or "You're wrong to be angry about that!" Feelings are personal, and they seem very authentic to the person having them. To judge a child's feeling as "wrong" is as inappropriate as saying that an involuntary muscle reflex is right or wrong. Children need to learn to be aware of their own true feelings, rather than being concerned with what they are *supposed* to feel or what others *expect* them to feel. Of course, children also need to understand how feelings influence their communication with others and learn to manage the behaviors associated with their feelings.

Naming Feelings

Children are not born knowing words to describe their feelings. Part of getting to know and manage oneself is learning to name emotions to communicate better with others. This may sound simple, but young children don't have an extensive vocabulary for feelings and will primarily use basic words like "sad," "mad," "angry," and "happy." As children grow, parents can add to their vocabulary by using other descriptive words like "frustrated," "annoyed," "proud," and "ashamed." Caring adults can also help by actively and accurately reflecting a child's feelings by saying things like, "I notice you are getting frustrated with your project," or "Wow, you seem really excited!" Recognizing and naming feelings are the first steps to managing them. Children can learn to recognize feelings and their impact on communication and relationships through conversations and modeling. There are also books available that help children identify, normalize, and understand strong feelings. As a parent, it helps if you recognize that feelings generally come from underlying issues. The feelings that you see on the surface may reflect deeper concerns. Feelings generally arise because of underlying beliefs and concerns, and it is generally better to focus more on the underlying problems (i.e., the child's beliefs) than whatever topic is currently at issue. For example, anger may be the outward emotion, while the underlying thoughts involve being wronged.

Be careful not to label a child's feelings incorrectly and tell her how she "*really* feels," as though you know what she is feeling better than she does. Saying "You aren't really angry at your brother. You know you love him. You're just tired right now" may confuse a child. First, the parent dismisses the validity of the strong emotion the child is feeling *at that moment*. Second, the parent makes assumptions about both feelings and behaviors, which may not be correct in the child's view. And finally, the parent is suggesting that the feelings are not valid, decreasing not only the child's confidence in her own ability to identify, accept, and manage feelings, but also her willingness to share future emotions with that parent.

Gifted children not only have advanced mental abilities but also unusually strong emotions. While they have the same feelings as others, they may experience them more intensely, making identification and validation even more important for gifted children. It is critical that these intense children learn how to communicate their emotions and manage the behaviors associated with feelings.

Punishing the Child for Being Gifted

Without meaning to, adults sometimes punish a child for having the very characteristics that are inherently a part of being a gifted child. Starting at an early age, gifted children's behaviors and ways of thinking are different from what is considered typical. Parents often describe their gifted children as "difficult," "challenging," or "strong-willed." When asked to explain further, they use words like "stubborn," "argumentative," "bossy," "spacey," "judgmental," "perfectionistic," "hard on herself" or "marches to a different drummer." Sometimes, these comments come from genuine puzzlement as to why such a bright child cannot remember certain simple tasks or responsibilities. Or perhaps the adult is trying to say that they are "no different than anyone else." But of course, the gifted child *is* different in at least one way from the typical child. People around gifted children often respond negatively to the gifted child's differences without considering how their remarks affect the child.

While gifted children's curiosity, intensity, sensitivity, idealism, and advanced skill levels are definite strengths, these same strengths also make them appear different from others and affect communication and relationships. Parents may inadvertently link a critical comment to an inherent trait, saying something like, "If you're so smart, why can't you remember to do your homework?" This tells the child that he might be more acceptable and receive less criticism if he were simply less gifted. A teacher who says sarcastically, "Well, I finally asked you a question you couldn't answer," communicates that the child would be far more acceptable and popular if she knew less and were more mediocre in her intelligence. When parents say, "Why do you always have to be so sensitive?", the child may feel misunderstood, criticized for true feelings, and afraid to show them in the future. Sadly, it appears that the brighter the child—and the further from the norm—the more likely the child is to experience such criticisms.

As caring adults attempt to motivate and socialize gifted children, they all too often communicate in ways they never would with a good friend or a partner. For example, they would not say, "You really didn't plan very well for that dinner party," or "Next time, I'm sure you can do a better job; you just need to pay more attention to the details," or "Don't you have better things to do with your time?" Yet gifted children frequently hear statements like, "I can't believe you waste so much time," and "What were you thinking? I guess you weren't!" One teenager remarked that he would likely be called "dumb" less if he weren't as smart as he is! Negative messages like these demonstrate a lack of understanding of giftedness and have a profoundly stifling effect on communication and relationships with sensitive gifted children, perhaps leading to insecurity and self-doubt. The gifted child may react by choosing to keep feelings and opinions to herself or come to believe that it is unacceptable to think or feel differently; she may even conclude that something is fundamentally wrong with her as a person.

When gifted children get strong reactions from others, they can shut down the honest and open communication that is otherwise natural to them and may try to be more "normal"—more like other children. A child repeatedly exposed to damaging comments may become distrustful of all relationships and develop a style of guardedness where she "puts up a wall" and seldom shares feelings with anyone. Not until a child feels safe will they decide that a high wall of defense is no longer needed.

Because gifted children can be quite challenging and frustrating, most parents, at some time or other, will make a destructive statement. You may get angry and say something you wish you could take back. When that happens, it is important to make amends with an immediate and sincere apology and to explain why you felt so frustrated and angry. It is a fact of life that relationships will have rough times, and it is important to learn ways to make amends. Apologizing to your children is modeling interpersonal resilience and provides an example of how to repair a relationship. It will also convey to the child that you respect and accept his feelings, which may reopen communication.

Media and Technological Barriers to Communication and Relationships

To develop healthy and positive relationships, people need to spend time together, share activities, and communicate ideas and feelings. In today's fast-paced culture, parents and children often find that they respond mostly to what seems urgent, which interferes with communication and relationships. Cell phones and gaming devices may keep people connected in one way, but also pull them in many directions, creating barriers to communication. Children and teens spend hours a day interacting with screens. In 2020, for example, the CDC reported that the average daily screen time rose to 9 hours for children aged 11 to 14. The COVID-19 pandemic led to improvements in connecting with others through screens but did little to decrease our reliance on them.

Although it is exhilarating to have so much high-speed interaction with technological devices, we come to communicate in sound bites rather than participate in lengthy, meaningful conversations, which are necessary to develop rich personal relationships. Parents need to be sensitive to how devices can be barriers to communication within the family, especially at mealtimes. We have all eaten dinner at a restaurant and noticed others interacting more with screens than each other. Family dinners or group meals where everyone contributes something to the conversation are important practice for communication and relationship building.

Media portrayals of communication are not helpful; they offer a twisted view and seldom show healthy relationships. Reality TV is far from reality, and 24-hour news focuses on unusual, sensational, or deviant behaviors like violent demonstrations, shootings, famine, war, and genocide. Any of these can erode a child's trust in others, impeding their ability to develop healthy relationships. These factors contribute to less frequent interactions with other people, and this, in turn, negatively impacts communication and development of relationships.

Other Barriers to Communication

Many parents unintentionally engage in other behaviors that can obstruct communication. Here are some to avoid.

- Being the authority or micromanager; telling the child exactly what to do may inhibit independent thought.

- Using overgeneralizations that harm self-esteem and relationships. Accuracy in both praise and criticism are important.

○ Using sarcasm that criticizes the child. A sensitive child may not recognize the sarcasm and take the words literally. If you do use sarcasm or teasing, be sure your child knows that you don't mean the words literally.

○ Diverting the conversation to protect the child. "Let's forget about it and just play a game," minimizes both the situation and the child's feelings, while sending the message that the child is wrong to feel that way. Take time to understand instead.

○ Saying, "I know exactly how you feel." You can't *really* know what is going on in the mind of the child. Instead, convey that you want to understand, and gain the child's perspective by listening; then share your understanding of his feelings.

○ Interrupting the child when she is talking. Listen with interest; ask questions to clarify when she is finished. We can only fully understand by truly listening. Keep in mind that understanding does not always mean agreement.

○ Asking, "Why did you do that?" Children have difficulty analyzing feelings and understanding their motives, especially when they are hurt or angry.

○ Abruptly denying the child's wish. Rather than hastily saying, "No, we don't have any peanut butter today," offer it in fantasy: "I wish we had some. If you'll remind me next time we go to the store, we'll get some."

○ Denying the child's feelings. After playing with a friend, the child announces, "I don't like Rachel anymore." If you immediately dispute the child by saying something like, "Of course you like her. She's a good friend," you deny the child's feelings, which either stops the conversation or begins an argument. A response that encourages communication, like, "Well, it sounds like you didn't have much fun today," will be more helpful.

You can see from the examples above why communication is so important psychologically for gifted children, and why it is so important that a child's home be a sanctuary where honesty and safety are honored and the norm. There are often not enough places in the child's life that provide a safe haven for open communication.

Communication with your child is literally a lifeline for her. If a child has even one adult with whom she can communicate freely, who accepts and values her, she can withstand a fair amount of frustration with the larger world. You, as parent, are a key person—one who provides a place of emotional safety and acceptance. If you are unable, for whatever reason, to be such a person, perhaps you can find someone else—teacher, neighbor, mentor, or friend—who validates your child as a person and who assures her that what she feels and believes is reasonable and worthwhile.

Practical Solutions

○ *Create an atmosphere that promotes communication.* You cannot force communication, but you can create an atmosphere that encourages communication. Remember that every communication has an emotional component to it that influences the emotional "climate" of the home. Consider asking someone you trust to give you feedback on your tone of voice or body language and the feelings that they convey. Many people are unaware that their voice sounds angry, critical, or judgmental, or that they seem uninterested in others. Parents are often surprised, or even horrified, to learn how their messages may be received by their sensitive gifted child who takes a negative tone to heart and may not hear the positive words. Recognizing and managing the emotional component in your communication helps create a positive atmosphere.

○ *Listen well, if you want to communicate.* Listening well is the single most important element of communication. When you actively listen, you convey to the child that his ideas, feelings, and values are worth listening to. Often, children just want you to listen, and nothing more. They don't necessarily want your comments, opinions, or evaluations—just a chance to share their feelings. Allowing them to share while you actively listen creates a climate where your child can risk sharing more, and perhaps even ask for your input. You might find it helpful to ask, "Do you want comments from me on this, or do you just want me to listen?" The child will know that you have opinions, but it is important for him to also know that you will not share invasively. Doing so builds mutual respect and trust. Keep in mind that listening without giving advice or opinions can be quite difficult for parents because they want so much to "help" by sharing their own ideas and experience. After all, parents have been through some of the same struggles as their children, and they would like to "save" or "rescue" their children from painful situations. Remembering that a child needs experience solving his own problems may help you to hold back your advice and just listen.

If you absolutely *must* give advice, perhaps because the situation is potentially dangerous, remember that a child is much more likely to accept your comments if you first indicate that you understand how she feels. A simple reflective statement like, "I can tell that you are angry and think the situation is unfair," or "I imagine you feel upset over what happened at school," tells the child that you are at least trying to understand her and that you value her feelings.

○ *Accept feelings even when you disagree with them.* When you listen, accept your child's feelings and thoughts. This does *not* mean that you necessarily agree with them; remember, feelings belong only to the person who has them. Each person has a right to his feelings, which are neither "right" nor "wrong." Encourage your child to express how she feels and communicate that her feelings, opinions, and attitudes are important to you. Communicating feelings is a skill your child will need throughout her life, and the best place to learn and practice these skills is in the safety of her own family.

In some families, children learn that feelings are dangerous territory and that talking about them can result in unpleasant yelling and fighting. Children in these families may conclude that it is simply better not to express their feelings—that the resulting emotional chaos is just not worth it—so they learn to keep feelings bottled up inside. When this happens, there is a risk that the accumulated problems will suddenly erupt, creating a crisis. Internalizing feelings can also lead to anxiety and depression, or even physical problems like headaches and stomachaches.

○ *Use reflective listening*. One good way to let your child know that you accept his feelings is to use reflective listening. You often don't have to say much, just paraphrase what the child says to mirror the feelings that seem to underlie his words. For example, when a child comes home from school, obviously upset, you might say, *"It looks like you might be upset about something that happened today."* The child then says, *"Jason called me a name just now walking home from the bus!"*

"Wow. It sounds like that probably made you feel bad."

"Yeah. He said all I do is read books and play with my telescope."

"Sounds like that made you angry."

"Yes! I want to punch him. I might do it, too, tomorrow at recess."

"You're thinking of fighting him."

"Well, what else can I do? I hate him for saying that in front of my friends."

"Sounds like you're thinking of some kind of revenge."

"I suppose I would just get in trouble at school."

"Seems like you're wondering if there are other options."

"Yeah. I guess I should just ignore him and forget it, but it sure isn't fair."

"It doesn't seem fair, does it?"

"No. He really doesn't know me."

"He doesn't know what you're really like."

"Yeah. I like baseball and stuff just like he does."

"He doesn't know you like the same stuff he does."

"Yeah. Well, maybe he'll find out some day."

Notice in this example how the parent really doesn't add much new information other than labeling some feelings. The parent restates the comment or asks it in question form. The power of reflective listening is that it helps you accept the child's feelings without making any judgment that they are good, bad, right, or wrong. Reflective listening helps the child clarify his feelings, as well as think through how he might decide to handle those feelings so that he can solve problems on his own.

In the same scenario, if the parent had said something like, "Why don't you try ignoring Jason tomorrow?", the child could conclude that you are jumping in with a solution, as if his problem is an easy thing to solve, or that he should listen to you instead of the other way around. When you use reflective listening, you listen to the child's point of view and help him solve the problem himself. Reflective listening is difficult to do at first and takes practice, but it is a valuable tool to enhance future communication.

○ *Seek to understand your child's silence.* Silence can communicate considerable feeling, as many frustrated parents have experienced, and it is important to understand why a child is suddenly silent. Is it because she is angry and withdrawing as a way of punishing you? Is it an attempt to gain control by refusing to participate? Is it a way of protecting herself because she is afraid you will not understand if she tells you? Or is it simply her way of relishing a poignant experience? It is easier to help when you can figure out the motivation behind a child's silence. Sometimes it is completely appropriate to simply let long silences occur, because that communicates to the child that you accept her as she is and respect her wish for privacy.

○ *Set aside special time.* Special time is one of the most important techniques parents can use to encourage communication, regardless of the child's age. Spending time with your child is the single most important technique you can use to enhance your relationship. Each parent individually gives each child a few minutes of complete and uninterrupted attention every day, if possible. This special time does not have to last very long—three to fifteen minutes—but it does need to happen several times a week. Five special times of five minutes each will be far more powerful than one special time of an hour. The consistency and the frequency are more important than the length of the time. If you have several children and are concerned that they may interrupt one another's special time, use a timer. If siblings interrupt, add another minute for the child you are with.

During special time, give your full attention, unless there is an actual emergency in the household. If your phone rings, ignore it or say, "This is my special time with my daughter right now; I'll call you back." When you refuse a phone call to spend time with a child, your child will know that your relationship is a high priority for you.

You can use special time to do virtually anything the child wants, but don't let them choose a competitive activity. With competition, there are winners, losers, and usually hurt feelings. During special time, you want to send the message that the child is *always* important, not just when he is winning or achieving. You are modeling future relationships the child will have, helping them understand that relationships take time and attention; neglect does not sustain them.

With older children, you may consider creative adaptations of their special time. Parents can take turns driving a child to school, or perhaps eat breakfast at a restaurant before school. This time could be taking a bike ride or a walk. Perhaps you would like to take one child at a time on a special outing—to a movie, the library, a museum, or fishing, camping, hiking, shopping, or even on simple errands. The important thing is that you are giving your child a segment of time when she has your full, undivided attention. Just being with your child sends the message he is important to you.

When your child is old enough to travel, you might take her along on a business trip, visiting city sights in your "off time" or adding time to the trip for that purpose. These times will create memories that last throughout your child's life.

With young children, special time can occur at bedtime or shortly after a parent gets home from work. Some children like to have special time in a certain place, like sitting on their bed with their stuffed animals, or in a certain corner of the family room. In some cases, the place itself becomes associated with feelings of support and caring. *What* you do or *where* you do it is less important than *that* you are doing it.

Older children may say, "I'm not interested in special time right now." If that happens, the parent can say, "Is there a better time for you later today? If not, I'll be available for the next five (or seven) minutes in case you change your mind."

○ *Create family "Super Saturdays."* One day each week, or one day a month—perhaps a Saturday—each family member is allowed to plan the events for the day, or part of the day, on a rotating basis. Parents, of course, set the parameters for the day, which could involve monetary limits and time frames. All family members must participate and agree to try to enjoy the events scheduled by the family member in charge. This gives a gifted child some control over the environment and a voice in the family's events. Super Saturdays can help develop relationships and mutual respect.

Children are usually very excited about this kind of opportunity. This strategy can provide an outlet for perfectionist tendencies since planning can get very detailed. Some gifted children put together itineraries, complete with specific directions and times for various activities throughout the day, while others may be less structured. Super Saturdays provide quality family time, opportunities for communication, and respect for each other's ideas and interests.

○ *Assess emotional temperatures.*[2] Many gifted children are reluctant to talk about feelings, particularly if they are not in the habit of doing so. If this is the case, you can try a shorthand way of communicating about their happiness level in which the child doesn't have to reveal much—a sort of "emotional temperature reading." For example, "On a scale of 1 to 10, with 10 being absolute joy and happiness, what is your emotional temperature today?" The child can respond with a single digit, without elaborating, to describe how she feels. If the number is low and the parent does not pry further, the child almost always asks, "Don't you want to know why?", opening the door to more communication.

○ *Share feelings.* Communication is always a two-way street. As a role model to your child, you should make a point to appropriately express and talk about *your* feelings in various situations—whether you are satisfied or frustrated, proud or dismayed. You may sometimes want to share your emotional temperature. Practice expressing your emotions in healthy ways, and then identify them so your children can objectively view another's emotions. You can say, for example, "I'm really angry right now about a problem at work." When you talk with your children about your own feelings, you send the message that they are yours, they are sometimes complex, and they are an important part of your life.

○ *Monitor your own intense feelings.* With their sensitive antennae, gifted children will know you are having feelings, whether you state them or not. Trying to hide or deny your feelings only creates distrust, lack of confidence in the relationship, and emotional estrangement. If you determine that your feelings are too personal or too powerful to share, you can simply say, "Right now, I have very strong feelings about this, and I'm going to need some time to let them settle before I can talk with you." Such a statement lets children know that adults can manage their feelings.

○ *Use "I-Statements"* Saying, "I feel disappointed when you do not listen to an adult who is talking to you," will be far more effective than saying, "You were inconsiderate and rude to your uncle just then." The latter statement accuses the child and puts him on the defensive. The earlier statement starting with "I feel"—the "I-statement"—stresses how the behavior affected you, the one who observed it. Without blaming the child, it opens the door for the child to respond and more easily save face with an I-statement such as "I'm sorry." Saving face is important for gifted children, who tend to be hard on themselves, and I-statements can help a child recognize the impact of his behavior on others.

In a similar fashion, you can use I-statements to recognize a child's positive accomplishments by expressing how *you* feel and how *you* interpret the child's feelings, rather than by evaluating her. For example, you might say, "I feel happy and proud when I see you mastering a difficult project, and I imagine that you must feel good about your work, too," rather than saying, "You are good at so many things!" The latter statement puts out an expectation, and a gifted child may feel some pressure to continue to be good at many things. The danger in this is that the child will think that she is valued only when she achieves, rather than just for being herself.

○ *Separate the behavior from the child.* Remember during communication to praise or reprimand the behavior rather than the child. If you disapprove of a child's behavior, simply say, "That behavior is not allowed here." This is important because it separates the behaviors from the child, and both positive and negative comments directed at a specific behavior are usually more accurate and effective than those directed at the person. Changing comments to focus on the behavior rather than on the child will take practice, but the result will be better communication. Some parents have found success with a simple, calm "Try again" response to inappropriate comments or behaviors.

○ *Remember your own past.* Sometimes you can help create a positive communication climate by talking about situations you experienced as a child. Simply share some of the emotions associated with your past experiences by saying things like, "I remember being furious with a school bully," or "I had a problem like that with a girl once." Gifted children can be particularly responsive when adults admit to having delicate feelings such as hurt or fear or embarrassment.

○ *Teach interpersonal skills.* Your child may be unaware of the impact of his communication style on others. For example, if he comes across as bossy or judgmental with other children, he might benefit from some fictional role-play situations exploring how different voices look or feel to others. Gifted children sometimes need to be specifically taught to make eye contact and speak in a friendly manner. Role-playing these skills can help a child better understand his role in social interactions with his friends.

○ *Avoid untrue or contradictory messages.* A parent's words can sometimes indicate one feeling or idea, but their voice tone and body language say something different. When one mother said, in a rather monotone voice, "Your piano playing is really improving," her gifted son, resenting the lack of sincerity, answered, "Why don't you tell that to your face?" The same message with a kind tone would have felt supportive. If said with a smile, "I'd like to know what you did at your friend's today," shows interest and invites sharing, while a dark or sarcastic tone implies concern. Be careful about sending a message you don't really mean to send.

○ *Communicate with touch.* Another important yet often-overlooked technique to promote communication is the simple act of touching. Our society has less understanding of the value of human touch, even within families, yet there is good evidence that touching and hugging are important for feeling healthy and connected to others. Putting your hand gently on your child's arm or around her shoulder may help her focus and ensure that she really hears what you are saying. Touch conveys connectedness and caring while fostering a climate of better communication. Some families are more demonstrative with physical affection than others, and families that are more reserved may need to make a conscious effort to add touch to their interactions.

Teenagers may react as though hugging is only for little kids, and they may resist hugs. If that happens, a parent can say, "Okay, I know *you* don't need a hug, but *I* need one." Even a reluctant hug from a teenager conveys a very important message—that there is a family love connection. Hugging and cuddling that starts when the child is very young is easy to keep up as the child grows. Your child may no longer be sitting on your lap, but you can still have an occasional warm, physical connection.

○ *Avoid gossip.* Adults are usually careful to avoid gossiping about other adults, but far less careful to avoid gossiping about children. In fact, even the most caring adults often do it right in front of them! Psychologist Sylvia Rimm describes this as "referential speaking," in which parents and teachers talk about (or refer to) a child's behaviors within easy earshot of the child, as though the child is not listening or cannot hear. The talk may be about good things the child has done and thus is positive for the child to overhear. "She worked hard and got an A on her biology test this week. Isn't that great?"

But more often, the talk is negative. "Tyler was supposed to be studying for his algebra test last night, but I found him playing a video game in his room, so he's grounded for two days." These words might be said to a friend on the phone or between parents in the child's earshot. Regardless, talking negatively about the child within the child's hearing is not appropriate. With their sensitivity and tendency toward perfectionism, gifted children can be hurt deeply if they overhear you talking with others about their shortcomings or problems. The hurt from these overheard comments may sting for a long time and can undermine the child's trust in you as a loving parent. If you do talk about your children to others, separate the behavior from the child and do it when the children are not nearby to overhear.

○ *Reward honesty.* Gifted children generally want to do the right thing, but like other children, they sometimes forget the rules, particularly if they are in a hurry to do something exciting. You may notice a few cookies missing from the cookie jar, and the child admits that yes, she took one or two. In this situation, you could say, with a sense of humor, "Well, I definitely appreciate that you like my cookies so much that you took a few on the sly, but even more, I appreciate that you are honest about telling me. I hope you'll always be honest like this with me." This non-threatening approach avoids an angry confrontation over a minor incident and fosters future communication.

Usually, when you already know that a child has done something against the rules, you are better off simply letting him know that you know, rather than asking him to confess. Avoid creating a situation that might encourage him to lie or deny it. Otherwise, the child is in a no-win position in which he will be punished if he is caught lying, but he will also be punished if he is honest with you. If you know what he did, skip the trial and, if a consequence is necessary, move straight to the penalty phase.

For example, your child runs outside, leaving the screen door wide open behind her, even though you've repeatedly asked her to close it. Now there are flies in your kitchen, and it's obvious she did it. Rather than asking with impatience if she left the door open and giving her an opportunity to lie, or delivering an angry lecture that begins with, "Can't you ever remember to shut the screen door behind you when you go outside?", you can simply say, "I notice you left the screen door open. What do you think we should we do to help you remember to close it?" Rather than inadvertently conveying that the child is hopeless and may never improve, the kinder reaction to the mistake assumes that the child *wants* to do the right thing, but she forgot and now is willing to help make things right. Once you establish a pattern of honesty, don't use stories like these to punish, tease, or embarrass a child later, as it will only discourage honesty and communication in the future. Perhaps one day, the child will feel comfortable sharing and be able to laugh about it.

○ *Establish a complaint department.* Successful businesses often have complaint departments, and many successful families have them as well. Your child needs opportunities to say how she feels, which includes complaints. Otherwise, she is likely to feel that her views are unimportant, and she may accumulate grievances until she is carrying a heavy load. Then one day, an explosion of angry feelings is likely to occur. To encourage your child to express concern, have a place to air them. Whether it is a box or a place on the family whiteboard does not matter, as long as it is convenient and available to all. Discuss complaints and validate feelings at the next family meeting to work toward resolution.

○ *Reassure your child that feelings need not be logical or orderly.* Feelings are often *not* logical. That is the nature of feelings. One gifted teenager wrote, "The worst part of being gifted is the loneliness.... I struggle with difficult issues like religion, morality, philosophy, and politics, and there simply isn't anyone I can talk to. I have to deal with things all by myself."[3] Some gifted children share feelings easily—almost too readily—while others, particularly those who prefer a world of logic and order, are uncomfortable talking about them. These children may attempt to steer conversations toward facts or other intellectual subjects that seem more concrete and comfortable to them. They need reassurance or they may avoid emotions and opinions that seem illogical, imprecise, risky, or even scary in their intensity.

○ *Respect your child's feelings, and don't intrude.* Some feelings and situations are special and private. Privacy is a necessary condition for being an independent person separate from others. Respect your child by allowing him to have aspects of his life that are truly private, not to be shared with you or others without permission. This can be scary for parents of teenagers, who want to know for safety's sake what their children are doing and thinking. It can be a delicate balancing act to decide what things you need to know, and what can be simply allowed to exist without your knowledge or approval.

○ *Handle sensitive topics delicately.* Because gifted children's feelings are so intense, they may feel vulnerable when they share feelings openly. Parents should be particularly gentle when discussing them. Although sharing one's deepest fears and hopes can establish intimacy and closeness, it also increases the likelihood of being hurt. Some gifted children learn not to share after once being hurt and may decide to go it alone rather than risk the distress of being criticized, misunderstood, belittled, or even ridiculed. They may appear on the outside not to have feelings, but internally, they may feel very deeply. Help your gifted child find the courage to be vulnerable and explore sensitive emotions with trusted others.

If a child would feel embarrassed talking directly to the parent about a sensitive topic, consider using written communication or discussing while driving to avoid eye contact. For the former, the child can write a question or concern in a notebook and leave it for a parent. The parent answers in writing and leaves the notebook for the child, creating a written dialogue.

○ *Appreciate temperament differences.* Children differ in temperament, including how they express feelings. Some children are typical; some are masters of drama; some are logical but seem to have little concern for the feelings of others. Different children require different communication approaches. Unless they appreciate children's differences, parents may try to make children into something that they are not. The result can be that the parent feels frustrated, and the child feels misunderstood. As one parent said, "Communication became much easier once I realized that I couldn't change an oak tree into a dogwood tree."

○ *Avoid too many "observations."* Sometimes parents may feel that they are "just making an observation" about how things are or what they see. For example, a parent might say, "I see your room is pretty cluttered today," or "It looks like you decided not to finish your homework," It is important, though, to consider these observations and *how* you give suggestions that stem from them. Do your comments imply a criticism that the child is not doing something right? Or not doing a good enough job? A casual observation will not have a major impact on a relationship, but too many imply that the parents are keenly watching—and evaluating—what the child is doing.

○ *Avoid making promises; they can be difficult to keep.* Sometimes your child may ask you to keep a secret or make a promise before you know the details. Since you don't know what the child might tell you, you cannot agree to such a sweeping promise. In these situations, it is important that you are honest with your child about what you can and cannot promise. You can respond by saying something like, "I can't promise unconditionally, but I will do everything I can to respect your privacy." In some situations, a parent must not keep a secret if the situation involves someone in serious trouble or danger, such as when a child tells you a friend is contemplating suicide or is engaged in a dangerous activity such as illegal drug use. In potential life and death situations, appropriate action, such as notifying parents or authorities, must be taken. Help your child understand that your priorities involve keeping her (and perhaps others) safe, and you cannot promise anything that might jeopardize that. Your relationship is certainly important, but it cannot be held hostage by a promise you cannot keep.

○ *Use written notes tucked here and there.* Handwritten notes can enhance communication and provide a powerful message to the recipient. A quick note saying "I love you" or "Good luck on the test" slipped into a lunchbox or backpack can provide a mid-day lift. Notes can praise behavior as well. "Great work on the science project!"

○ *Avoid over-sharing.* Gifted children, with their advanced vocabulary and comprehension, can seem so much older and more mature than they really are, and some parents unwittingly fall into a pattern of sharing more adult feelings than are appropriate. Parents who do this can become enmeshed in an unhealthy way, using their child as a substitute for more appropriate adult relationships. A parent who is upset over a partner's alcoholism or a pending divorce should not share all details of current and past disappointments with a child. Children do not have the life experience or emotional capacity to handle such complex issues; they need to have a life independent of adult worries. A parent who looks to a child for emotional support in troublesome situations puts the child in the very inappropriate role of taking care of the parent. Putting this burden on the child, even if the child is as old as 12, 15, or even 20 and seems mature enough to handle it, is unfair to them. While it is tempting to share with bright children who often seem like adults, parents in difficult circumstances should get help and support from friends, relatives, or a professional, not from their children.

Similarly, a parent should not make comments that will prejudice the child against the other parent. Doing so robs the child of the chance to make her own judgments and choices, and it can have lasting effects on her relationship with both parents. Of course, parents can certainly acknowledge their feelings in unpleasant situations. But they can do so without casting aspersions, saying, "I'm very sad about the divorce, but I'm definitely looking forward to living without the fighting that's been going on."

○ *Solve Communication Problems.* With their intelligence and strong-willed nature, gifted children will inevitably get into arguments with you—sometimes heated ones that lead to an impasse or a painful power struggle. When possible, do not allow these difficulties to linger. In these instances, it is helpful to take a step back and evaluate not only the situation, but also the emotions involved. Why did you respond that way? How could this situation have turned out differently? Why are your feelings and theirs so strong on this issue? Once the feelings are recognized, accepted, and better managed, the underlying issue can be addressed. This does not mean things will be easily resolved; whenever there are strong emotions, there is a reason. Both parties have definite ideas that conflict, and resolution usually takes time and effort.

The techniques described in this chapter can enhance communication and lead toward possible resolution of relationship problems. Communication problems don't appear overnight; nor will they be resolved overnight. Good communication, like problem-solving, requires effort and willingness over time. As a parent, you can initiate practices that will improve communication and encourage positive, rewarding interactions.

CHAPTER 5
Motivation and Underachievement

Gifted children are usually enthusiastic about learning, passionately engrossed in many ideas and activities, and intensely curious about the world around them. So how does it happen that some of them drift into patterns of underachievement? How does their innate motivation diminish? How can parents nurture motivation so that these children will develop their interests and abilities? How can caring adults prevent underachievement?

How Can Motivation Become a Problem?
Young gifted children generally show excitement about the world around them. One mother described her seven-year-old daughter's motivation this way:

> I'll never forget her first day of kindergarten…she was so excited she was almost vibrating. She couldn't wait to get in the schoolhouse door. I was eager to have her go to school because, frankly, she was wearing me out. [She] was a whirlwind of energy who never stopped talking or questioning.[1]

When such a curious, enthusiastic preschooler grows into a bright but unmotivated teen, parents are understandably puzzled. How does this change occur? It could be that, in those curious preschool years, far too many gifted children hear messages like "Slow down," or "Wait," or "We're not studying that today," or "We're going to learn about that that next week (or next semester or next year)." When gifted children enter school, many of them are placed in classes where they have already achieved the grade level standards before the teaching has even begun.[2] Though sometimes boredom can simply be an idle complaint or an excuse for not participating in class, more often than not, these children, from first grade to high school, really dislike many school activities because they are not challenging. The seeds of underachievement in middle or high school are often planted in elementary school with coursework that is inappropriate or too easy.

With each passing year, these children become more concerned about fitting in with their peers and less concerned about their level of performance. After all, they know how bright they are; they're top students in their class. They've been told that their performance at this level is fine—their desire to learn more is unnecessary, their questions can wait, and they should enjoy "being a kid" and not care about "adult" issues. The older they get, however, the more parents and teachers begin to tell them that they are not living up to their potential and are just following their peers. These confusing messages play a big role in the issue of motivation.

Are these the only reasons that so many gifted children develop a wide gap between potential and performance? What causes so many to lose their spark? Can a parent do anything to renew it? Can their energy be channeled after it is restored? There are many paths to underachievement and loss of motivation. Fortunately, there are also many ways to stimulate an unmotivated child.

Why Wouldn't a Gifted Child Be Motivated?

To understand this question, it may help to think about situations when your own motivations lag. You are not always as motivated one day as you are the next. Even within a single day, your motivation levels fluctuate dramatically. No one gives 100% all the time, and your performance might fall below your potential in exercising at the gym or cleaning the garage. Are you underachieving? Well, it depends on whose perspective is used to answer that question.

There are many factors that influence motivation. It is usually not enough to simply know why a person is not reaching his potential.

Most people understand why they should exercise or clean the garage, but knowing why doesn't change their behavior, because there are other things that are motivating them in other directions. Remember, if a child could change his motivation that easily, he probably would have done it some time ago (and your garage would be tidy by the same principle). Instead, there is probably a good reason, from the child's perspective, not to change. When you see a lack of motivation in a gifted child, approach the situation by first considering some of the many factors that influence motivation.[3]

Health. Physical reasons can play a role in underachievement—vision or hearing problems, a lingering infection, lack of sufficient sleep (particularly in teenagers), poor nutrition, or possible substance abuse. All of these should be examined and ruled out. Some children, for example, seem simply to run out of calories during the period before lunch and again in mid-afternoon. During those times of hunger, the child is "off-task," has difficulty concentrating, and starts to underachieve. Once parents eliminate physical causes, they can then turn to other possible reasons for the underachievement.

Disability. Some children have a learning disability or a wide span in abilities due to asynchronous development. A learning disability (like dyslexia, dysgraphia, or dyscalculia) is easy to overlook, because giftedness often masks the disability, and the child's frustrations lead to motivation problems. Gifted children can also be diagnosed with other neurodevelopmental diagnoses, like ADHD or autism, that can affect motivation.

Family. What are the expectations for achievement within the family? Are children expected to achieve equally well in all areas? Do parents expect too much? Too little? Does one parent send messages about achievement that conflict with those of another parent? Some parents are more concerned with a child being happy and content than with academic achievement. Other parents are very concerned that their children become high achievers. Some examples of influences within the family include an unstable family situation, a pending divorce, frequent quarrels within the family, a recent move that results in the child losing friends, death of a relative or a pet, major disruptions with siblings or peers, or (with adolescents) being jilted by a close friend. Any of these events can cause worries that intrude during the school day and disrupt the concentration of even the brightest student.

Relationships. Interpersonal relationships are extremely important factors in motivation. One of the most common reasons for lack of achievement in school is that the gifted child wants to fit in with peers. Many gifted children are torn between their need for achievement and their need for connection with peers. Some are teased because of their unusual abilities and are called names like "nerd," "brainiac," or "geek." It can be uncomfortable to always score the highest, and gifted girls may purposely mask their ability in order to be accepted by peers who reject them for having advanced vocabulary and knowledge.[4] Gifted boys may attempt to live up to the "Boy Code," which approves of athleticism but not intellectualism.[5] African American boys may find themselves accused of "acting white" if they are high achievers.[6] The pressures to conform are immense for the gifted child, and this often contributes to motivational issues.

School. For many gifted children, the ordinary school setting quickly becomes uninteresting and unexciting. The enthusiasm, curiosity, and excitement quickly disappear. Gifted students frequently report frustration because they must wait for peers to finish their work before the class can move on to the next concept.[7] They may quickly feel out of step with peers. When early success comes quickly without much effort, gifted students may not develop the motivation and work habits necessary for success when effort is required. While no school or teacher intends to discourage gifted learners, they have a difficult job trying to address the educational needs of each child, especially when those needs fall outside the norm.

Educational modifications can nurture and restore the motivation, zeal, and enthusiasm of a gifted child. Acceleration and differentiation, described in chapter 11, are examples of such modifications. It is important, though, not to simplistically think that all underachievement and motivation problems can be solved if only the correct educational options exist. While the educational system has a role, strong family relationships can balance or even overcome a difficult school situation. Many parents can keep their children motivated despite less-than-optimal educational settings or other obstacles that ordinarily might reduce motivation.

Other factors. Discovering additional obstacles that might block motivation is essential to positive intervention. Children's behaviors are not just random events. All behaviors, even maladaptive ones, are motivated to meet some need. What need is the unwanted behavior serving? Are there other ways to meet that need? You can help your child by identifying and removing whatever obstacles are hindering motivation. Encourage your child, help him feel connected and understood, and explore reasons why he might want to learn.

Collaborating to Build Motivation

Most children are not unmotivated. More likely, they are not motivated in areas where others think they should be. In daily life, motivational issues usually appear only in certain areas. For example, a child wants to learn about all kinds of things in her areas of interest, but she doesn't want to learn grammar, spelling, or good handwriting. She doesn't want to show how she derived the math answer; she just wants to write the answer that she figured out in her head. His bedroom resembles a garbage dump, but he doesn't want to pick up after himself. As you work to support your child and collaborate with them to find ideas for motivation, the following prompts can help you find a starting point.

What accomplishments does the child see as important? Remember that underachievement is in the eye of the beholder. Often, gifted children's areas of motivation simply aren't the ones that *we* think are important. Those areas just do not seem relevant to them—at least not at the time—or other things seem more important. From the child's point of view, a grade of C may be considered adequate; after all, it's a passing grade. Or a child who is doing marginal academic work may be a very high achiever in other areas, such as sports, band, cheerleading, or social events. Your goals and her goals may simply differ. At the time, there are other things that are more important to her than the things you want her to do. Her current needs dictate her agenda, which doesn't match yours.

Sometimes, parents and educators, in their attempts to motivate the child, use tokens, stickers, or money as rewards or punishments for behavior modification programs. This can temporarily alter behavior. However, these systems may not work well in the long-term because children view them as attempts to manipulate and control them. Many strong-willed children would rather give up privileges—even endure drastic consequences for their behavior—rather than give in to what they see as a "power play" by adults. In addition, these rewards may actually decrease motivation because the child starts doing things for the reward and not for the love of the activity.[8] Although material things provide temporary motivation, a sense of belonging and independence will lead to sustainable motivation.

Are you understanding or demanding? It doesn't usually work to simply demand that a child motivate himself with statements like, "Because I said so!" or "If you just put your mind to it, you could bring your grades up. You're certainly bright enough!" or "I want you to start taking schoolwork more seriously, or else!" Extended lectures and punishment are not effective in improving motivation, and they certainly take a toll on relationships. Many workplaces have a tongue-in-cheek sign that says, "The beatings will continue until morale improves." Employees enjoy the humor because they recognize that corporal punishment is not effective.

Trying to motivate the child who is underachieving and has "turned off" can be challenging and time-consuming, but there are several methods and procedures that you may find useful. Keep in mind that it can take significant time, sometimes weeks or months, to motivate a child who is mired in a long-standing pattern of underachievement. Since the problem did not come up in a day or a week, it won't go away in a day or a week. It will take a good deal of patience, and progress will be slow and occur in small steps. Also, keep in mind that underachievement is usually sporadic, occurring in some classes but not in others, or in some years but not others. The pattern of underachievement and subsequent *learned helplessness* can be difficult to break. Connecting through empathy and attempting to problem solve together will help to work toward the long-term solution of independence.

What are the child's interests? It is generally more effective to start with the child's areas of interest and gradually work toward a transfer of motivation through encouragement and success. Too often, parents insist that the child change by immediately doing what the parents want. They may say, for instance, "If you get your grades up and keep them up this semester, then we will talk about whether you can have the new bike (or other desired item)." For most children, this is difficult. If the desired behavior were really that easy for them, they would have done it long ago.

What is your child interested in now? Does she have any particular passion? If you can find and identify enthusiasm that already exists within the child, you can find ways to build on that motivation, redirect it, or refocus it. Perhaps you can find ways to transfer that motivation to new areas that—up to now—the child has had little interest in. For example, a child who has little concern for spelling, grammar, or handwriting may have an enduring passion for South American insects. You might encourage him to write a letter to an author in *Nature* magazine to ask some questions that were not answered in an article. You might gently point out that, in order not to be dismissed as only a child, it will be important that the letter be neat, with good grammar and correct spelling. You or someone else could perhaps check it over before it is sent. Now the previously unimportant tasks of spelling and grammar become relevant to the child's interest and therefore important in his eyes. The motivation has transferred, and the child learns something in the process.

It is vitally important to maintain a child's eager attitude, regardless of the interest area. For example, reading, no matter what the topic, proves itself later in higher achievement. If the child wants to read only sports magazines or graphic novels, let him. At least he is reading! He will gradually move on to other reading material and interests, perhaps with a gentle nudge toward sports novels or the chapter book version of his favorite graphic novel as the next step. It is particularly important to help a gifted child develop and maintain an "island of excellence"—a place where he is continually growing and stretching with enthusiasm. He might be enthusiastic at a museum, learning about cars, studying astronomy, or reading gruesome mystery novels. Even if the special interest is outside the school experience, there will eventually be some transfer.

How can the child have ownership of the process? It is important to nurture assertiveness, independence, and self-reliance in gifted children. Gifted children can learn quite early in life how to speak up for themselves and negotiate so that they feel some involvement and "ownership" in what they are doing each day. Perhaps the gifted child can negotiate with her teacher a "learning contract" that will allow her to "test out" of work that she has already mastered, giving her time to pursue something of interest. This negotiation can not only empower the child, but also provide the teacher with an opportunity to transfer the child's motivation.

Letting a child feel more involved in setting priorities increases involvement, investment, and a sense of personal responsibility, which can heighten motivation generally. Children who develop a sense of emotional independence from teachers and peers are better able to manage themselves, and they typically show more curiosity, assertiveness, and achievement. Children who are not allowed to voice opinions or complaints at home or at school may come to believe that there is no caring person with whom they can communicate about reactions and concerns. They may become overly reliant on others and feel discouraged with few ways to change the situation. They learn to be helpless. Encourage active, appropriate involvement to avoid this "learned helplessness."

Practical Solutions

○ *Build a strong relationship with your child.* Personal relationships are influential motivators, but the results aren't necessarily immediate. Occasionally, a significant amount of time passes between when parents encourage their children and when they see the results. Parents and teachers may work diligently to promote a good relationship with a child, but the child's motivational spark still does not ignite. Don't give up. Continue to work on your relationship and communication with the child. Communicate acceptance and convey your confidence in her and in her ability to change. Over the long term, it is these relationships that mold a positive future outcome. Parents who love learning and who share and encourage others in their own passions foster lifelong learning and help children develop confidence and self-esteem.

○ *Focus on effort, not just outcome.* Sometimes, gifted children exert little effort, even though their performances or outcomes can be tremendous. For example, a gifted child may get straight A's or carry a 99% average in all classes with only minimal effort because the tasks are not appropriately challenging. If you focus only on the outcome, you are rewarding minimal effort, and the child does not learn the connection between effort and outcome. It is better to reinforce good effort, even when an outcome is only partially accomplished. Of course, finding effort to reinforce can be tricky for the child who effortlessly maintains good grades, and parents may have to look outside of academic activities.

○ *Recognize accomplishments.* Most parents recognize that it is important to notice accomplishments, yet sometimes they draw more attention to a child's failures. For example, avoid the "7 A's and 1 B" discussion. When a child brings home a report card with all A's except for one B, a parent may immediately ask, "Why did you get the B?" It is far better to say, at least initially, "You must be pleased with all those A's!"

Referring only to the B can send a message to the child that, once again, she has not done enough, thereby inadvertently fostering negative and perfectionist thinking.

○ *Avoid power struggles.* Power struggles can destroy a climate that nurtures motivation. These are not minor annoyances, but rather protracted power struggles, such as with an adolescent who, though very bright, simply refuses to do homework or participate in classroom quizzes, and as a result has been getting failing grades for several months. If you are in a non-productive power struggle with your child, do your best to withdraw, because that may be the only way to move past the struggle. Indicate that you are concerned that your relationship is being jeopardized and that you have confidence that together you can find a better solution.

○ *Maintain high expectations.* In an effort to promote success, many who try to intervene for the unmotivated or under-achieving gifted child will lower their expectations. Instead, raise expectations with challenging activities that are related to the child's interests. Successful coaches have found that it works best if they expect slightly more than the athletes think they can do, but these coaches also provide substantial encouragement as well. Challenging activities can be more engaging than rote memorization. Incorporating challenge, while providing the necessary support that leads to success, can help build both confidence and constructive work habits.

○ *Break down big goals into manageable and achievable steps.* To maintain motivation, gifted children must learn to set realistic and attainable long-term goals. Breaking these big goals down into basic and realistic tasks is needed to give children a sense of control, foster continued motivation, and prevent discouragement. Adults can guide the process by helping identify intermediate steps and sub-goals as well as target dates for reaching them. This clearly sets points of progress in concrete terms, and the child can give himself frequent rewards for achieving the partial successes of the sub-goals, providing both reinforcement and "rest stops" along the way. A sense of achievement comes from accomplishing intermediate steps, and the long-term goal now appears more attainable to the child. The focus is on progress, which can help the gifted child the first time he encounters a task that is challenging and demands sustained effort. Many gifted children wish, for example, to play an instrument or to build a complex model. Mastering a simple tune or constructing a component of the model would be short-range goals.

○ *Avoid "goal vaulting."* Gifted children must learn the skills associated with setting and achieving goals, even more so than the typical child, because the gifted child tends to "goal vault." That is, they will set a goal; then, when they are close to achieving it, they suddenly set a new and higher goal. They "vault" past the original goal on the way to that second goal. When they are close to that second goal, they set another still higher goal. When they do not achieve their ultimate goal, many gifted children don't recognize their progress as success and feel like they have failed. The process of goal setting and breaking tasks down helps clarify subgoals to avoid "goal vaulting."

○ *Build on small successes.* To foster motivation toward a challenging task, begin by reinforcing even the smallest movement toward a goal or simply the effort toward the goal. Success on increasingly difficult tasks breeds more success and confidence, and you can build on that by stacking successes. While the initial motivation may come from external rewards, satisfaction and intrinsic motivation will increase with continued success.

○ *Communicate expectations in advance.* In movie theaters, often amidst the lengthy previews, there is a message that thanks patrons for silencing their cell phone. This technique can be used at home to communicate expectations before having to correct inappropriate behavior by praising the behavior you expect. For example, your son may be just coming in the door from school and taking off his jacket to drop it on the floor (as he usually does). At this "teachable moment," you can say, "Thank you for putting your coat in your room. I very much appreciate your being so helpful!" Your son may not have had that thought in mind, but your clear communication reminds him of expectations, increases the likelihood that the behavior will occur, provides reinforcement, and avoids criticizing him for past behavior.

○ *Use declarative language to share observations of your child's behavior.* Rather than relying on praise or critiques of your child's behavior, you can use declarative language to provide a neutral observation of the behavior. Declarative language provides the opportunity to invite feedback from your child because the observation is framed in a neutral way. For example, you might say, "I noticed that you got started on your homework when you got home from school," or, "It seemed like getting ready for school this morning was slower than usual." These types of observations feel safe. Parents who use declarative language remove themselves from giving or taking away approval and offer an opportunity to talk about the observed behavior if the child wants to do so.

○ *Participate in joint activities.* Sometimes, parents do their work in one part of the house or at a specific time of day and expect children to do theirs somewhere else or at a different time. In these homes, children seldom have opportunities to see how their parents deal with issues of motivation and achievement. By doing joint projects where you and your child work together, your child can see your motivation and work habits. It can be helping in the yard or garden, assisting with a home maintenance chore, or participating in sports or a hobby. Or perhaps they can see your passion for something work-related. Projects provide opportunities for them to see your pleasure and excitement in doing things well. These shared activities communicate your values, work attitudes, and other principles like patience or tolerance for frustration that are important to you. Shared activities enhance relationships, and good relationships likewise make activities more enjoyable. Many activities you now enjoy as adults first became enjoyable because you did them as children with your parents or other people close to you.

○ *Avoid "Yes, but…" statements.* Often, parents praise a gifted child's efforts in a "Yes, but…" fashion. "You did well, but it would have been better if you had done it this other way." These types of statements are particularly harmful to a child's self-esteem because the "but" negates the positive that comes before it, and often it is the "but" that is remembered by the child. The message is, "You aren't quite adequate as you are, but perhaps with a little more success, you will be acceptable." Try using "Yes and…" instead to accentuate the positive *and* help the child see other options.

○ *Avoid ridicule and sarcasm.* Gifted children, with their sensitivity, are often deeply hurt by ridicule and sarcasm. Even if they use it themselves, they do not always recognize it when they are on the receiving end. Some gifted children misunderstand and take sarcastic comments literally. Ridicule, sarcasm, and humiliation do not motivate sensitive gifted children.

○ *Be sensitive, but also specific.* Be sensitive to your own feelings and to the child's and try to avoid making statements that broadly label or evaluate him. Pronouncements such as, "You really need to try harder and not be so lazy," or even "You have so much potential," are not helpful. Try to be specific when giving constructive criticism, but generalize about positive behaviors. Be sensitive to how the child might feel about your evaluation. One useful approach is to express how *you* feel and how *you* infer the child might be feeling by using "I-statements" talked about in the previous chapter on communication.

○ *Teach negotiation skills.* Negotiation is a skill gifted children will use throughout their lives, but few families consciously teach these skills at home. While some gifted children do appear to be talented in the art of negotiation, particularly in the heat of a power struggle, some refinement of the skill is necessary for situations outside of the home. Other gifted children become such skilled negotiators that they want to negotiate at every opportunity. Teaching negotiation skills and the appropriate time and place for negotiation will help gifted children navigate their world. The ability to negotiate can help with self-advocacy in school, which may prove useful in motivating a gifted learner.

○ *Seek mentoring opportunities.* Formal or informal mentoring opportunities help motivate a child by allowing an opportunity to see a professional at work in an area of her interest. "Shadowing", or watching a parent, college professor, veterinarian, or chemist at a local company, can provide a new perspective and add a "real life" slant to the importance of education. As students progress in their education, more formal internship opportunities with professionals can also help middle or high school students get into more competitive programs. Even if the child decides the career isn't one they want to pursue, it can still be a valuable learning experience and an opportunity for parents to praise effort and risk-taking.

Find the Balance

Parents want their children to become highly motivated, but still feel content as people and be intimately connected with others. No one wants children's achievements to be a refuge from unpleasant surroundings or a way to retreat from uncomfortable interpersonal relationships. Parents must recognize and praise the child's special qualities, while being careful not to dote too much on trophies. Expose children to a variety of experiences to broaden their view of what is possible, and help them develop their own interests in ways that fit with their talents. Nudge, encourage, and challenge your bright children to reach their potential, but also avoid drifting into power struggles in which the child underachieves and refuses to perform simply because parents or teachers emphasize it.

As parents, we must balance our roles of nurturing emotional development and fostering achievement because there is a connection between the two. It can be difficult for a child if the emotional side and the achievement side don't develop in tandem. For each family, that balance is different. How much do you push? When is it time to nurture? How will you know when you are pushing too much? With strong relationships, these questions will be easier to answer. Remember, gifted children are almost always motivated toward *something*. Through personal relationships, goal setting, building on success, and other techniques, you can build on their existing enthusiasm to shape, transfer, and channel their motivation. Their high degree of motivation and achievement in one area will usually spread to other areas.

CHAPTER 6
Establishing Discipline and Teaching Self-Regulation

Parents want children to become self-disciplined in the same way that they want them to be self-motivated. Discipline is an important part of parenting. Through experiencing limits set by parents, children learn to take responsibility for and regulate their behavior. As with everything related to parenting, discipline involves both modeling and teaching the behaviors you want children to practice.

Most parents fret over discipline issues, wondering how many rules bright children need and how best to help them learn self-discipline. Some parents tell us they feel that they need to set down many rules because their intense children are undisciplined. Other parents believe that bright children need few, if any, rules. Two parents in the same family might disagree on how to discipline their child. Other parents believe they will be good parents if they try to be their child's best friend or buddy and use little discipline, which, though tempting, detracts from the fact that a key part of parenting involves teaching discipline.

How can you, the parent and most important teacher, help your exuberant, intense child learn to regulate their actions and emotions? No single approach works with all children, but there are some basic principles that provide a foundation for shaping and modifying behavior, teaching self-discipline and the kind of self-assurance you want your child to have as an adult.

Discipline and Punishment

For many parents, discipline means time-out, grounding, or some other punishment. This is unfortunate because discipline, unlike punishment, encourages self-knowledge and behavior management. For gifted children, punishment can be emotionally threatening, offers no guidance, and should be used sparingly, as a small amount goes a long way. We use the word "discipline" to describe ways to help a child learn to manage her own behaviors—to achieve self-regulation and responsibility while learning to manage her own life.

Discipline is learned both from consequences (imposed or natural) and from others around us who demonstrate self-discipline. Effective parenting involves discipline that shows children not only what they have done wrong, but also what is important to do next time. When you say, "Storybooks are not for coloring with crayons; the paper tablet is where you can use your crayons," you are giving your child clear direction for how to act differently next time. Too often, parents focus on what children do wrong without telling them how to improve their behavior, which is the more important part of learning self-discipline.

Punishment only shows a child what not to do, and repeated use of harsh words, a harsh tone, and harsh punishment not only decrease communication but can damage relationships. This advice against punishment may be quite different from what you grew up with, as parents often believed in swats or even hitting with a stick or a belt. Child discipline was based on a philosophy of "spare the rod; spoil the child." It was expected that parents would physically punish children. Families were autocratic rather than democratic systems. Schools regularly used corporal punishment—even a wooden paddle—for infractions. We now know that corporal punishment leads to increased rates of anxiety and depression. While punishment may get short-term compliance, it does not teach necessary skills for self-regulation.[1]

Fostering Self-Direction

The goal of discipline is self-direction—developing a strong inner sense of what is right or wrong and what is appropriate. For gifted children, self-direction is vital. Because they are different in many ways from others, they will need to rely throughout their lives on their own judgment more than that of others. Their unique thought processes often lead to unusual conclusions, and their evaluation of a situation may be quite different from that of others. Learning self-direction and self-discipline is essential if gifted children are to become autonomous, lifelong learners.[2]

Whereas punishment comes from the outside, usually from someone older and bigger, discipline comes from the inside. Discipline focuses on teaching a child to depend upon her own ability to think and act appropriately, rather than out of fear of punishment. Parents teach their children to understand their actions and the natural or imposed consequences of those actions. This understanding of discipline focuses on positive ways to teach self-monitoring, to develop self-direction, and to learn to act responsibly in predictable, mutually satisfying ways that eventually lead to self-regulation.

This shift in thinking highlights the differences between punishment and discipline. It is easy to see that punishment does not foster independent thinking and can lead children to depend on others to indicate how they should behave. In addition, punishment often provokes a strong reaction of fear or anger from gifted children because they are independent, strong-willed, and quick to react to something they think is wrong.

Because gifted children are both bright and strong-willed, they have an advanced ability and inclination to think, reason, and question— anytime and anywhere. They are not likely to accept orders or arbitrary parental directives without an argument. If they do, it is likely out of fear, which can later breed resentment. In guiding gifted children, it is helpful to understand that they may at times talk back or become angry, rebellious, or defiant when we use a phrase like, "Because I said so!" These children want to know an actual reason that makes sense to them.

Discussions with a gifted child can be difficult at times. For example, one child challenged his parents by pulling out a copy of the *Declaration of Independence* and saying, "See, it says here that all men are created equal—it is an inalienable right! You can't tell me what to do; we are equal." His mother responded, "This says *men*; you are *seven*—you are not a man!" The child promptly went to the internet to find out *when* he was going to be a man. He came back with some interesting information, which led to more questions. (Life with a gifted child is never dull!) Fortunately, this parent didn't stifle the child's curiosity and need to question with a "Because I said so" response. Even though incessant questions can be tiring, avoiding strict or non-negotiable parenting styles with gifted children will produce more positive relationships and better outcomes in the future.

Consistency Is Important

The most important guideline is to set (and enforce) rules and limits as consistently as possible, and it is also important that parents agree on those limits. When parents differ in standards, limits, and expectations, their guidelines for children are unclear, and the result is often underachievement, power struggles, or the manipulation of one or both parents.[3] While gifted children often need fewer limits than other children, limits are nonetheless necessary. Setting only limits that you can and intend to enforce will increase trust and the likelihood of success.

Whether a child is young or a teenager, guidelines, rules, and limits help to be in control and make sense of the world. There are rules in society—red means stop, yellow means caution, green means go. People who don't obey these rules may get a ticket. No running is allowed at the pool, or there are consequences. If you forget a second time, the consequences are more severe. Rules and laws in society and at home ensure that people live together safely and cooperatively. Helping your child understand reasons for rules and consequences allows the opportunity to make better-informed choices about behavior.

Although they may not admit it, children are more comfortable and secure when limits are clear. Even if your child strongly protests rules, they offer unfailing stability. He knows you set limits because you care, that they will guide and protect him, and that you will always enforce them. As a result, he knows you are trustworthy because when you say something, you mean it.

If your child doesn't learn trust in the home, she may not trust others. Clearly stated and mutually understood limits, rules, and expectations for conduct give your child a sense of security, stability, and predictability that are important for children from infancy through the teenage years. On occasion, children will test limits, try out new behaviors, and watch for your reaction to see if the limits are still there. Some of these limits, such as being on time or respecting others' privacy, involve family values, and help a child to understand themselves in the context of family and the outside world.

Develop Rules as a Family

Working with your gifted child to collaboratively establish family rules can provide a sense of belonging for young people in your family. A family meeting to discuss rules for chores and family interactions can be a wonderful learning experience. We are not suggesting that children should be allowed to *set* the rules, or that parents allow themselves to be manipulated. But when children take part in the discussion and feel that their opinions and ideas have been *considered*, they are much more likely to accept and obey the rules. You might also ask your gifted child to use their advanced logic skills to help search for any of the loopholes in the proposed rules.

Just as gifted children are more willing to comply with rules when they see the need for them, they are less likely to go along with rules they see as arbitrary or merely displays of adult power. Listen to your child's reasons before making decisions; sometimes they are valid. Gifted children vary greatly in their abilities, judgment, and behaviors, meaning rules will vary, depending upon your child's age, experience, and maturity.

It is easy to fall into the trap of expecting too much from gifted children because they talk and act so much older than they are, due to their asynchronous development. Although their high verbal ability makes them sometimes appear and sound adult-like, their sense of experience, emotions, and maturity are usually still closer to that of a child their own age. It is unreasonable to punish a six-year-old for being a six-year-old, even if they often act more like a 10-year-old. To find appropriate balance, remind yourself that knowledge and intellect are not the same as wisdom and experience. Consult books about normal stages of development and observe other children of the same age to understand the differences in your gifted child.

Establishing Consequences

What will you do when the rules are broken? We recommend that you enforce limits by allowing natural and logical consequences to occur, rather than enforcing a consequence or punishment that *you* create for the child. Natural and logical consequences are almost always more effective than ones that are imposed.

Natural consequences. Natural consequences are really the best way for children to learn, as learning occurs naturally without someone "teaching." Nonetheless, using natural consequences consistently is easier said than done. Here's an example: if 10-year-old Andrew forgets to bring in his skateboard from the driveway, the natural consequence is that he cannot find it the next day, or it gets rained on, or perhaps even stolen, all of which are far more effective in the long run than if you bring the skateboard inside for him and later give a lecture or impose a consequence.

Allowing natural consequences to occur is one of the hardest aspects of parenting. First, it requires refraining from a lecture, which is difficult; next, it involves standing back to allow your child to fail or feel hurt or loss (as in losing the skateboard). Suppose you notice that your child is forgetting her math homework. You don't remind her because it needs to be her responsibility. You let the homework sit on the kitchen table, knowing there will be a natural consequence—she will lose points or get in trouble with her teacher. The value in this lesson is clear, but for parents, it is extremely difficult to avoid "rescuing" the child. "False rescue" will not allow natural consequences to occur. Clearly, there are times when our children are truly in danger and we must rescue them, but false rescue deprives the child of learning from natural consequences. (Note: Natural consequences for homework issues don't work particularly well for children with ADHD. These children will need checklists and reminders monitored by parents until self-management and self-monitoring become more of a habit.)

Natural consequences allow your child to discover consequences on his own and ultimately learn self-management, while helping you avoid being caught in conflicts that are not *yours*. Allowing natural consequences to occur helps avoid power struggles, and preserves the relationship because you can't be blamed for the outcome. You didn't impose the consequence. Instead, you can be supportive and say, "I'm sorry that happened. Let's see if we can think of a way to keep it from happening again." You can be genuinely sympathetic and perhaps even relate a story about how you learned from similar situations when you were young. Using natural consequences allows you to be a supporter, encourager, and commentator in a positive fashion, instead of the angry parent disappointed with failed expectations.

Logical consequences. If you must enforce disciplinary consequences for your child's misbehavior, make the consequences logical ones, rather than ones that are unrelated to the behavior and that come from your anger. For example, if a child leaves her science project strewn all over the kitchen, there is no need to lecture, saying, "You are so inconsiderate; how do you expect me to cook dinner!" The logical consequence is to say, "I can't cook dinner with things all over the kitchen counters. There simply isn't enough space for me to do it." To say that you cannot cook in that situation says that the family will have to do without the meal, at least for now, and this will (hopefully) prompt the child to rectify the situation. Such logical consequences tend to be much more effective than punishment, like banning the child from watching a favorite show, which is unrelated to the problematic behavior.

Show your child how a logical consequence will affect him, as well as how it affects others. If the child breaks a toy that belongs to someone else, then the child must buy a new one. Your teen is caught lying about completing their homework, so you decide that they are no longer allowed to do their homework in their bedroom and must do it at the kitchen table. The consequence logically follows from the behavior.

Imposed consequences. Parents sometimes need to enforce limits by imposing their own disciplinary consequences. Natural consequences may be dangerous or otherwise inappropriate, or perhaps there is no obvious natural or logical consequence. Clearly, using natural consequences to teach a child not to run into the street is absurdly dangerous. Imposed consequences come when the limit is simply one that you, as the parent, have set and must enforce. You set the rules, define the boundaries, and enforce the consequences.

The most important element of imposed consequences is consistency. If you are unable or unwilling to enforce the limit, it is better to not set it rather than to set it without following through. Not following through teaches a child that you may not be serious, or that you may not follow through the next time. Avoid being tentative, changing consequences, or giving mixed messages when you impose conse-quences. You might feel bad about setting limits, and then enforce them tentatively or even apologetically. Giving such mixed messages through changing consequences creates doubt, and increases both the possibility of non-compliance with future limits and power struggles about them.

By experiencing and understanding consequences, and through participating in defining boundaries, gifted children can learn early to set their own limits. This is the beginning of self-discipline, which is the ultimate goal. As soon as a child is able to communicate, work to develop rules or limits jointly with him. This does not mean that gifted children get to set the rules, but it helps greatly if they are a part of the process. As he develops and matures, he will be better able to evaluate his own actions—not rely upon adults to do it for him.

Power Struggles over Discipline

Self-discipline is necessary to withstand peer pressure and to achieve, both in and out of school, but children are not born with it. They learn this vital skill only after years of practice and encouragement from significant adults who model it. Sometimes, gifted children discover their independence at appropriate times and places. At other times, their strong will generates an angry stand-off. Despite all good intentions of helping children learn self-discipline, parents sometimes find they are drifting into serious and unpleasant power struggles.

If it feels as if your nine-year-old is holding her ground and refuting your every point, you may be in for larger power struggles in the teen years ahead. With this type of child, discipline often involves extensive, protracted, and painful discourse. As the parent, you want to avoid getting caught up in a power struggle that has the potential to damage your relationship. Although right now your child's skilled attempts at asserting herself, manipulating others, or defying authority may be causing hurt and strife within the family. But later in life, this same persistence and reasoning skill may be an important asset for her. Try to view these behaviors not as a threat to your authority, but as a potential strength for your child. Keep your sense of humor as you deal with her refutations. Help your child learn to use her reasoning skills productively and proactively. In 10 or 20 years, this same person may be a leader—a skilled business negotiator, lawyer, or CEO.

When you find yourself in a non-productive power struggle, try the following approach.[4] If your teen wants to stay out later than usual, tell her that you will carefully consider her request and that she should prepare her case and present it to you, say, after dinner. You then listen to all of her reasons for the request and agree to render a final decision at a later specified time (for instance, after talking it over with the other parent at 7:00 P.M., or at dinner the next evening). This honors the child's request, shows respect for her, and forces her to plan ahead and think through the reasonableness of her request. It also helps parents avoid responding with a knee-jerk "No!"

Once the child has presented her case, she has no further opportunity to plead and no opportunity to appeal when the verdict comes; the decision is final. In this process, the child will learn that her views are important, and she will also learn the importance of preparation and patience. When a positive decision is rendered, there will be no need for further exchange other than the parent setting the final parameters. When a negative decision is rendered, reasons can be included. Your daughter may suddenly realize she has forgotten a point or two and try to add arguments. However, the consequence is that, because there is no appeal on the decision, she will have to prepare a better case next time. If the child begins to engage again, the parent simply does not respond.

Praise and Encouragement Guidelines

The long-term goal is for your children to learn self-discipline, self-regulation, and self-direction. This does not imply that you should never impose your will. External limits and consequences may help your child understand the significance of breaking an important rule or limit. But in the long run, praise will be far more influential in helping your child learn self-management and self-direction, because your praise conveys to him that you believe he is competent and that these are behaviors you would like to see repeated. The child who believes that he is competent is better able to take responsibility for his behavior.

Praise is a particularly powerful reward and is used far too seldom in relationships with children. Because we want our child to do her best, we don't always notice or compliment her for what she does well. Instead, we focus on what she still needs to improve. Children need us to notice their efforts and positive behaviors. Do we admire the way he attempted a task? Do we tell a child how pleased we are with her happy disposition? Do we say we appreciate the child helping us cook, or set the table, or get the house ready for company? Or are these things we simply expect and take for granted?

Although some parents balk at reinforcing "expected" behavior, saying "Good job" or "Outstanding! Thanks!" helps reinforce a desired behavior and shows respect. Your child should be praised for expected behavior precisely because it *is* expected behavior, and behavior you would like to see repeated. It helps if parents recall how good it feels when a partner or friend shows appreciation for us and our behaviors, even if they are "expected" behaviors like cooking dinner or picking up a child after swim practice. For our child's self-concept and our relationship with him, it is important that we still provide plenty of positive messages.

Praise should be accurate, valid, and specific. When using praise, be sure that you are not overstating it or being inaccurate. Your gifted child will easily see through comments like, "You are the best baseball player ever!" or "That's the best picture I have ever seen!" If you provide inaccurate or extreme praise, you will lose credibility with your child or risk producing a false sense of confidence. "I like the way you got in front of that ground ball" or "I love the different blues you chose for this picture," are examples of specific praise.

Praise the behavior, not the child. Similarly, praise and statements of appreciation are more effective when they are connected to a specific behavior. Praising a child's general brightness or ability is not very effective in enhancing self-esteem, while praising a child's efforts in a *specific* task is more helpful.[5] Instead of saying, "You're very talented at the piano," or "You're so quick in math!" you might say, "I admire how you keep practicing that same part until you get it the way you want it," or "I'm proud that you try different ways of solving math problems until you find the way that works best."

Catch the child doing something right—frequently. Frequency of reinforcement is one of the most overlooked dynamics in helping people learn to change behaviors, especially in the beginning. When a child is trying to learn a different way of behaving, it is not enough to just *occasionally* admire, encourage, or compliment him. The rewards must be frequent enough to sustain the new behavior until other factors, including new behavior itself, provide the reinforcement. In the beginning, the frequency and regularity of rewards is far more crucial than the size of the reward. Initial frequent reinforcement is needed, but rewards should gradually become less frequent and even sporadic as the behavior becomes more regular. Intermittent reinforcement (think of a slot machine—rarely a jackpot but just enough to keep you playing) has more lasting effects and helps wean the child from becoming dependent upon rewards.

Use the sandwich technique. When discipline and limits are sandwiched between two complimentary comments, the constructive criticism is usually more palatable. For example, you might say, "I admire how you are learning to be more patient with others; however, when you interrupt adult conversation, I am disappointed, and I would appreciate it if you would try again not to interrupt. I know how much you enjoy talking with older kids and adults." Be careful when using the sandwich technique because it can easily turn into a *"Yes, but…"* statement if you forget the encouraging ending or spend too much time on the criticism.

Discipline around Screens and Social Media

Although most parents express concern about the time children spend on screens, research is still emerging about best practices for children and adolescents. Small links to aggression, mood, and sleep disturbances are documented, and we also notice that screen time can restrict physical activity, create distractions from other activities, and expose children to age-inappropriate material. In contrast, screen time can enhance social connections for gifted children who lack those connections in real life. Finding balance is necessary.

Parents should take care to communicate, teach, and model good habits regarding technology. Remember that categories of screen time differ, including educational, social, gaming, and passive consuming. Education time is necessary and appropriate. Social gaming time should be monitored and managed, while individual gaming and passive screen time should be limited. The emergence of e-sports (video gaming as a competitive team sport) has been a blessing for some teens, but an added frustration for their parents. Practicing for e-sports requires additional time in the same ways that practicing swimming or gymnastics does.

As with all other family rules, parents should be explicit and communicate clear, specific limits. Supervise interactions when necessary and limit social media, especially with young children. There are many options for parental control that can minimize the direct power struggles over screens. Limit screen time as much as possible in the child's bedroom. Technology and screen time should end 30-60 minutes before bed; allow only calm content in night-shift mode between one and two hours before bed because active and aggressive content can interrupt sleep. Especially with young children, technology is best stored away at night to avoid distractions. Having a device overnight is a privilege that must be earned when responsibility is shown. Remember that it is easier to provide more time and privileges related to technology, and much harder to decrease time or privileges already provided.

Practical Solutions

○ *Acknowledge emotions first; then address discipline.* When behavior problems occur, respond initially not to the *incident*, but to the *emotions* that prompted it. If you show the child that you understand his feelings—though perhaps not his behaviors—you can reduce the likelihood that your discipline will be rejected. Acceptance of a child's feelings helps him understand his own reality, whether or not anyone else feels the same way. It is extremely difficult to think clearly and logically when experiencing strong emotions. If you handle feelings first, your child is more likely to learn from the situation and consider behaving differently in the future.

Handling feelings before discipline helps preserve relationships. If gifted children are predisposed to power struggles, why should we insist that the child do it only our way? If we are rigid, with no consideration for a child's feelings or other methods to resolve a situation, then we are creating a win-lose situation. We may use our parental power and authority to obtain temporary adherence to our rules, but not lasting self-discipline. Unless a child understands the reason for the discipline, she is likely to be angry, perhaps wanting revenge, and she will probably do things her way as soon as she is able.

It may help to think about how *you* feel about a particularly rigid boss. You may have put on a façade of conformity, but inside you felt growing discomfort, disrespect, and distance. Now think of another supervisor who listened to you, sought your suggestions, and directed and corrected you more gently. Which one helped you learn and perform better?

○ *Assess the child's needs.* Disobedient behaviors often indicate that the child needs or wants something. It could be something as simple as reassurance, comfort, or attention. Children sometimes misbehave just to get emotional reassurance. They want to know that you really care about them, and they want their feelings recognized. When you determine the goal of the behavior, you can respond more appropriately.

Regardless of motivation, unwanted behavior must still be addressed. Understanding the child's needs will help you behave with respect during the discipline process. Your expression of empathy can help the child understand why you are disciplining her. Even though she may not like the consequence, at least she will know that you care about her—that you are not just trying to control her. With any age child, it is important to communicate that you care about her and her feelings, that you believe in her ability to achieve self-discipline, and that you are not adversaries.

○ *Choose your battles.* Maintain positive relationships by minimizing conflict over small matters. Too much talking and too much emotion can get parents in trouble. Not every problem is worth an angry confrontation, and sometimes the price of getting compliance is too expensive. Avoid rigid, excessive, or arbitrary limits. While we might be able to force our children to do exactly as we wish every time, the resulting resentment would be so great that we would most likely do serious damage to the relationship. We need to ask ourselves whether obedience in every instance is really that important, or whether we perhaps should focus on more important issues. For example, if a limit of 10:30 P.M. is set and the child arrives home from a party at 10:45 P.M., the extra 15 minutes may not be worth arguing about, especially if being late is not a pattern. Ask for an explanation and consider accepting the reason if it is valid.

What about arguments and refutation? Since gifted children are highly verbal, they will often argue and try logically to defend their behaviors, reasoning, or viewpoint. Parents should expect this and should be ready to actively disengage from such arguments by saying, "I am not going to argue about that." Too many limits or those that seem "plucked from air" will likely bring questions that can turn into unnecessary power struggles.

○ *Use giftedness to explain behavior, but not to excuse it.* The intensity or sensitivity of a gifted child will create situations where giftedness drives a child's behavior. Sometimes, that behavior will be inappropriate. While giftedness can explain why the behavior occurred, it does not excuse it. If a consequence is necessary, provide one, rather than saying something like, "Oh, she is our creative one!" while minimizing the inappropriate drawing on the wall.

○ *Offer choices but avoid the illusion of choice.* By pointing out options and by giving your child choices, you will be encouraging her to take responsibility for herself and her actions. Just be sure that they *are* real choices. For example, don't ask for a behavior when there is no option. Instead of asking if she would like to clean up her room ("No, not really, but thanks for asking."), provide a meaningful choice. "Would you like to do it yourself, or would you like me to help?" False choices or the illusion of choice demean rather than encourage. Viable choices foster mutual respect and encourage self-sufficiency and self-discipline.

○ *Examine your expectations.* Sometimes we need to consider the possibility that our expectations are not appropriate for today's world. Do we really need to *insist* on a particular behavior? Is it imperative that the child make her bed every day or finish every single bite of food on her plate? Brushing teeth regularly is certainly important for dental health, but making one's bed every day without exception is not necessary. Perhaps just a quick fluff of the comforter will do. Seeking too much control can lead to unnecessary power struggles. Examine the reasons behind your insistence. Are you replaying messages you heard in your own childhood? Are you afraid that if you give in, your child will have too much power? Do you listen to your child's arguments and respect them? Does your child feel you are being unreasonable? Have you allowed for some freedom within the limits? Reviewing your position honestly can be helpful in examining your expectations for your child.

○ *Make expectations clear.* Does your child understand the behavior you want from him? One way to check is to ask him to reiterate the rule you have just explained to see if he understands. If he does not, you can clarify. If you give a clear, understandable direction that the child is able to accomplish and the child does not comply, then you know that it is more likely due to compliance issues than lack of understanding. Making expectations clear decreases the chance of misunderstanding or noncompliance.

○ *Support the other parent.* If one parent sets a limit, the other parent should not change or undercut it except in extraordinary circumstances, and even then, not in front of the child. For example, suppose you believe that your partner publicly humiliated your child at dinner last week in a restaurant. Don't go behind the other parent's back to say anything like, "I'm sure your mother didn't mean what she said. I'll speak to her about it." Instead, empathize with the child's feelings of frustration, and encourage him to think about what he might have done differently to bring about a different and better outcome. Later and privately, you can talk with your partner about the child's reaction and different ways to handle the situation in the future.

○ *Touch your children to get their attention and to show affection.* Although all children are different, sometimes touching a child lightly on her hand, arm, or shoulder can help her focus on what you are saying. A light touch lets the child know that you care about her and are setting a limit because you *do* care. Parents usually know when a child would like to have an adult arm around their shoulder, a warm pat on the back, or a hug. Younger children in particular respond well to hugs. Teenagers, however, may come to avoid hugging and touching, finding it appropriate for younger children, but not for them. They might prefer a handshake or fist bump instead.

Be aware that touch doesn't work with all children, and it won't work if a child is angry with you. Some children are sensitive about being touched by anyone and will flinch as if to say, "I don't want you to touch me right now!" It is important to respect the child and not invade his personal space. For children who are sensitive about touch, you can increase the chance that it will be received positively by making sure they expect and understand such contact.

○ *Convey trust that your children will act wisely.* Gifted children need to feel that their parents trust them to do the right thing. By setting limits and gradually giving them the chance to experience freedom within those limits, you are preparing them for making good decisions about setting their own limits. If you expect them to follow your guidelines for behavior and they do so successfully as young children, they will continue to be trustworthy as teenagers. As you talk with them about their activities and friends, you can let them know that you trust them to know what to do in various situations. In return, they will show you they are worthy of your trust.

○ *Gradually loosen rules and increase freedoms.* Stricter limits are needed when the child is young, and the number of rules can be reduced as the child matures. As time goes on, parents can comfortably pull back the safety net and encourage children to begin setting more limits for themselves. Parental limits are always there, but the developing child has more freedom as he demonstrates responsibility. Don't unwittingly relinquish control early and turn it over to the child; it is easier to loosen than tighten up. When parents suddenly begin to apply limits to a child who has not had many rules or limits before, there is a strong likelihood that the child will either rebel or simply refuse to comply.

○ *Avoid Feeding the Monster of Negativity.* Think about the emotion involved when you tell your children "Thank you!" or "Good job!" Now think about how much louder and sharper your voice is when you rebuke or redirect your children with shouted messages like, "Leave your brother alone!" or "Hurry and get dressed!" Often, there is far more emotional emphasis given to negative statements than to positive ones. Avoid blasting out "no's", and be sure to voice, not merely whisper, compliments and appreciations.

○ *Be patient; don't give up!* Recognizing the effectiveness (or lack of effectiveness) of your disciplinary strategies is the first step to improving them. Many parents describe with great distress how they have tried several different approaches to disciplining their children, but they have all failed. They tried one approach for a few weeks, dropped it, then later tried a different method for several weeks, and then still another. It didn't occur to them that their children had learned to just "wait it out" for a few weeks before they could go back to their usual ways. Learning and practicing new strategies takes patience and persistence. Don't give up until you have tried a new approach for a month or more. If you respect and maintain the new approach, your child's behaviors *will* change.

CHAPTER 7
Perfectionism, Stress, and Trauma

While giftedness can be a protective factor for many mental health concerns[1], some characteristics of giftedness, combined with environments that don't support the needs of gifted children and teens, can exacerbate stress and anxiety[2]. Gifted children with advanced verbal abilities may be exposed to and cognitively understand topics that are distressing, but they lack the life experience to put them into context and the agency to do anything about them, resulting in feelings of helplessness. Gifted children who are unchallenged in the classroom may internalize messages about how learning is extremely easy for them, perhaps leading to anxiety, perfectionism, limited perseverance, and low resilience when faced with more difficult tasks.

It is easy to overlook the fact that gifted children, who have many strengths and abilities, can experience high levels of stress that require professional help. Parents and teachers may not see warning signs because gifted children are skilled at masking, intellectualizing, or minimizing their distress, especially when they believe they should be able to manage their social and emotional problems as quickly and easily as they handle most academic challenges. They may be reluctant to ask for assistance, fearing they will lose their status as "bright and capable". If unmanaged and unsupported, everyday stress can manifest in physiological symptoms, like headaches or stomachaches, or it can lead to depression or thoughts of suicide, crossing the threshold into clinical anxiety.

Like all children, gifted children must learn to manage stress and anxiety. Everyone needs resilience and a system for organizing oneself and coping with problems when they occur. Life contains adversities, events that require us to change in some way. When we make a mistake in performing a task, we need to change our way of doing things. We are disappointed if something goes wrong in a relationship. Resilient people feel stress, and they learn ways to prevent worries and doubts from overwhelming them. The gifted child's mind can be her worst enemy in creating stress, but it can also be her greatest ally in managing it.

Overall, gifted children generally have higher self-esteem,[3] which suggests that they feel good about themselves and their situation. Some studies show that gifted children who are in suitable and appropriate programs in public schools generally have lower levels of anxiety than do students with lower IQs.[4] Research suggests that the degree to which a school's program is a good educational fit for a child's giftedness (for example, verbal, mathematical, visual-spatial) also helps control a child's stress level.[5] While there are factors like an improved educational fit or finding appropriate peers that minimize a gifted child's stress, there are other factors that create stress as well. Table 5 shows some stressors experience by gifted children and teens.

Table 5: Factors Influencing Stress in Gifted Children or Teens

Factors Influencing Stress in Gifted Children or Teens	
Intrapersonal (Caused by internal factors)	Interpersonal (Caused by external factors)
• High levels of intensity	• Upward comparison from peers
• Unusually high standards and expectations	• Negative reactions from others about ability
• Asynchronous (uneven) development	• Lack of intellectual challenge
• Fear of failure (long-term or on the first attempt)	• Poor educational fit

Factors Influencing Stress in Gifted Children or Teens	
Intrapersonal *(Caused by internal factors)*	*Interpersonal* *(Caused by external factors)*
• Fear of success	• Excessive expectations from others
• Feeling pressure due to potential in many areas (known as multipotentiality)	• Lack of common interests with same-age peers

Asynchronous Development

Asynchronous development can cause stress in gifted children, particularly when judgment and emotional maturity lag behind intellect. The cognitive ability of gifted children is usually well above their chronological age, but judgment is often much closer to it. Even though an eight-year-old gifted child may be able to understand mathematical concepts like a 12-, 13-, or even a 16-year-old, the younger child's judgment about how to act will likely be closer to their actual age. Intelligence and knowledge are not the same as emotional maturity, understanding, or wisdom. A gifted six-year-old may be able to discuss computer applications or do complex puzzles with the skill of a 12-year-old, but she may still need to be tucked into bed at night with a favorite toy or blanket.

Asynchrony of emotional and intellectual maturity. To have the intellect of an older child or an adult, but still have age-appropriate emotional development, creates stress. While he can understand the physical forces that create natural disasters like hurricanes, he does not have the emotional capacity to handle the tragic and far-reaching results of such events. As Leta Hollingworth (an early leader in the education of gifted children) noted, "To have the intelligence of an adult and the emotions of a child combined in a childish body is to encounter certain difficulties."[6]

Adults who are unaware of a child's asynchrony can fall into the trap of expecting the child to act her 'older' mental age rather than her younger chronological one. As with children who appear older because they are taller than their peers, gifted children who speak like adults may also be perceived as older than their years. Adults may be puzzled when the child seems emotionally immature, since they are noticeably more mature in other areas. Adults can easily make the mistake of assuming that a child who is comfortable with sophisticated words and concepts should also be able to handle complex emotional and interpersonal situations and discussions even though the child's emotional development is not similarly advanced. Because the child is emotionally like other children the same age, stress increases for the child when adults express criticism or disappointment about emotional behaviors that do not meet the emotional maturity level inappropriately expected by the adult. If a child is showing asynchronous behavior characteristic of a younger child (for example, with social skills or attentional regulation), it is important to consider whether they may also be twice-exceptional (see Chapter 2).

Asynchrony of abilities. Asynchrony involves more than judgment and emotional development lagging behind intellect. Gifted children show asynchrony in other areas, too. For example, it is common for a younger gifted child working on completing an art project to be frustrated that her fingers will not do what her mind wants them to do. She can visualize with advanced understanding how a finished product should look, but her fine-motor skills are not yet sufficiently developed to create it. A gifted child with above average math skills but more age-appropriate processing speed may be frustrated when they struggle with timed math tests at school.

Gifted children with extreme asynchrony related to academic skills may be exhibiting characteristics of learning disabilities, such as dyslexia, dysgraphia, or dyscalculia. Such asynchrony can lead to low self-esteem and depression.[7] The discrepancy between their overall ability and difficulty experienced when attempting certain academic tasks can be frustrating and overwhelming. The child may regard tasks that come easily to him as trivial, and ones that are difficult as evidence of his lack of intelligence. His self-worth, in his eyes, is focused more on tasks that are difficult for him than on ones that are easy, and he judges himself by what he *cannot* do instead of by what he *can* do. Without support for the areas of difficulty, children with this learning profile may develop learned helplessness.

Interpersonal asynchrony. Still another type of asynchrony exists when one doesn't seem to fit with the world around her. Gifted children recognize that they are different at a young age, and often feel "out of step" with family and friends. Even when parents try to provide an atmosphere of acceptance and support, gifted children may still feel that they don't fit in. They can feel at odds with peers, traditions, and society in general, or feel out of place in school. The highly gifted, creative, and independent-minded are particularly likely to experience this social discord in environments (especially classrooms) that aren't created with their needs in mind.[8]

Perfectionism

While perfectionism is not exclusive to gifted children, there are factors that are unique to how or why some develop perfectionistic tendencies. One of the major factors that influences the development of perfectionism is the lack of challenge in academic environments. Gifted children learn early on that they can breeze through school while giving only a small amount of effort and internalize this lesson as evidence of their intelligence. When they eventually face an academic task that is difficult, it undermines their sense of identity. Gifted children who are praised for their intelligence may internalize the message that if they are smart, things *should* be easy.

Gifted children often envision ideal behaviors, performances, and settings—for themselves, for society, and even for the world. They see the potential, but they also clearly see how they are missing the mark or how society falls short. Their high ideals often cause them to feel pressured to make a significant difference in the world. Because they have great potential, others may expect more of them. The resulting stress can be burdensome when the child's perfectionism makes them expect the world to be perfect. These children often have difficulty tolerating the imperfections and frustrations of daily living.

Healthy and unhealthy perfectionism. Perfectionism in the pursuit of excellence can be a valuable driving force. Setting high personal standards and finding places where perfectionism is valued is necessary for success.[9] In neurosurgery, precision and exactness are essential—a healthy place for perfectionism. But perfectionism that involves a "driven" pursuit of unrealistically high goals, with intense stress and suffering if goals are not met, is not healthy. Some perfectionists feel it is catastrophic if they do not meet their own high standards. They feel they are valued only for what they produce, as opposed to being valued for their whole, fallible self.

Differentiation between healthy and unhealthy perfectionism is a useful distinction. Healthy perfectionism can be viewed as the pursuit of excellence, meaning doing the best you can with the time and tools you have, and then moving on. Unhealthy perfectionism leaves one continually dissatisfied, as the work is never "good enough." Psychologist Maureen Neihart said, perfectionism is like cholesterol; there's a good kind and a bad kind.[10] Children (and parents) benefit from understanding both kinds.

Types of perfectionistic students. Parents may look around their child's room, or at their messy backpack, and think there is no way their child is a perfectionist. But perfectionism has several manifestations that look different than expected, especially as it relates to academic performance. Jill Adelson and Hope Wilson outline several styles of perfectionism that can be observed in gifted children[11]:

- ○ **The Academic Achiever**—The student who must achieve 100% on every task and is extremely hard on themselves when they don't succeed.

- ○ **Aggravated Accuracy Assessor**—The student who restarts assignments or tasks repeatedly because it isn't "just right."

- ○ **Risk Evader**—The student who will attempt a task if they feel they can do it perfectly but will avoid it entirely if they can't.

○ **Controlling Image Manager**—The student who either doesn't try at all or puts in only a small amount of effort to be able to claim they could have done it perfectly if they had wanted to try harder.

○ **The Procrastinating Perfectionist**—The student who can't begin a task because they keep thinking about how they want it to turn out; fear that it won't measure up to their mental image blocks them from starting.

Styles of Perfectionism

Some parents are concerned that they have created perfectionism by expecting too much. Most often they have not, though they may unintentionally foster it. Understanding the pressures that trigger perfectionism helps parents support someone struggling with perfectionistic tendencies. The Multidimensional Perfectionism Scale, developed by Paul Hewitt and Gordon Flett, describes three styles of perfectionism: self-oriented, socially-prescribed, and others-oriented.[12]

Self-oriented perfectionism. Self-oriented perfectionism comes from a source within a person. The drive to pursue excellence (healthy perfectionism) or insist on unrealistically high standards (unhealthy perfectionism) is based on internal drive. In general, if a student can develop an awareness of their own strengths and weaknesses, self-oriented perfectionism is often the least damaging. A gifted student who recognizes that their self-imposed standard to take all possible Advanced Placement courses in high school (and get A's in all of them) is unrealistic and opts to drop two while focusing their efforts on the courses that they enjoy is exhibiting healthy perfectionism. The student who refuses to drop any because they "should" be able to manage the workload is risking becoming overwhelmed and burnt-out, both results of unhealthy perfectionism.

Socially-prescribed perfectionism. The student who shows perfectionistic traits because they feel pressure from family, teachers, or peers is experiencing socially-prescribed perfectionism. The family is often the first area where these traits may be unintentionally fostered. It is easy for a family to drift into a pattern in which performance and achievement are emphasized and rewarded more than other aspects of the child's life. Even parents who want the best for their children can unintentionally nurture perfectionism. They check homework to make sure the child answered all questions correctly, and they insist on corrections if there are mistakes. They are vigilant. They call attention to the one B on the report card rather than the six A's, unintentionally fostering perfectionistic behavior. The parents' goals are admirable; it makes sense to set and maintain high achievement standards if we want children to attend competitive universities or reach a desired profession. But when the pursuit of achievement interferes with daily life and causes a great deal of stress, it is time to reduce the pressure.

Others-oriented perfectionism. Perfectionism that is outward-facing, or others-oriented, is often not recognized as perfectionism. The student who corrects the teacher for minor errors or is highly critical of other students and is unable to collaborate amicably in groups, may be showing signs of others-oriented perfectionism. Unrealistic expectations for others can impede the development of healthy social relationships. Sometimes, this type of perfectionism stems from a gifted child's attempt to be helpful, though they misinterpret others' feelings about being corrected. In other situations, it may be an attempt to impress others with their knowledge or reconfirm their belief that they are smart.

Managing Perfectionism

One component of perfectionism for bright learners is the difficulty they can experience tolerating ambiguity. A child who feels most comfortable when there is a clear right or wrong answer may become paralyzed at the prospect of a task that has multiple correct responses or—even worse—no right answer at all. Perfectionism can drive gifted students to become risk-averse to ambiguous tasks. A complex math problem is viewed as manageable, while an open-ended response about their interpretation of an essay is a harder task to manage. Recognizing that the ambiguity is daunting, and not the task itself, helps gifted children. Finding a "good enough" response and building resilience to tolerate the discomfort of this type of risk-taking is key to managing perfectionistic paralysis.

While it is not likely that a person with perfectionism can completely stop being perfectionistic, it is possible to learn to manage perfectionism so that it becomes a healthy and realistic pursuit of excellence combined with a gentle acceptance of self. A child can ask three questions about their performance to help manage perfectionism: (1) Is it good enough? (2) In the long run, will it really matter? and (3) What is the worst thing that could happen?

Another idea to help balance perfectionism is the *5-5-5 Question*, which asks how long the impact of an imperfect result will last. Will this matter in 5 days? 5 months? 5 years? (The intervals used vary depending on the situation and age of the child; the intervals might be minutes, hours, and days.) Zooming out from the situation can help put it into perspective in the larger scheme of things.

Children who are extremely resistant to or anxious about imperfections might be encouraged to be *intentionally* imperfect to build tolerance of the discomfort, fostering resilience. One of the best ways to overcome the fear of not getting 100% on a test is to intentionally choose the wrong answer on a few problems. Panic about turning in something that is only partially complete can be mitigated by intentionally experiencing the feelings of turning in something that isn't perfectly completed. Gifted students (or their parents!) may balk at this idea, but the point is that by experiencing such mistakes in a controlled environment and realizing that there is no long-term impact, they lose the power they hold over the perfectionistic child.

Trauma and Gifted Children

Gifted children may experience the same types of trauma that their peers do. There is "big-T" Trauma, such as severe neglect, surviving natural disasters, and witnessing or experiencing violence or physical abuse. There is "little-t" trauma, which can be more subtle, but still impactful. Little-t trauma might include being chronically bullied, vicariously experiencing a traumatic event, or being an unidentified or unsupported twice-exceptional learner.

Trauma that is unsupported can cause a child to have difficulty regulating their emotions. Individuals who've experienced a traumatic event can be in a constant state of heightened emotion that impacts every part of life, including relationships, academic or work performance, and general life satisfaction. Different people can experience the same event and have quite different reactions to it. For little-t trauma, it is not an event *per se* that creates stress or trauma, but how one perceives the event. One person might get through the situation with little long-term impact, while another might be significantly traumatized. Personality, coping skills, and external supports can mitigate the negative experience of traumatic events.

After a traumatic event, individuals who are struggling with the aftermath can experience hyperarousal, including an inability to focus, increased physical signs of stress (like rapid heart rate), being easily scared or startled, increased test anxiety, or aggressive behaviors. Hypoarousal can also indicate a trauma response, when children withdraw or shut down, avoid tasks, or appear apathetic.

There is minimal research about the impact of trauma on gifted children or adults. However, if we view trauma through the lens of giftedness, we can develop an understanding of how gifted children might be influenced by traumatic events. There are several risk factors to consider concerning how gifted children might be impacted by trauma:

○ *Advanced verbal ability.* A child with verbal comprehension above that of their peers can understand and internalize the messages they receive, whether from adults arguing in their presence or exposure to tragic events on the news. But because of their age and the limited resources available to them, they might have a traumatic response. Developing a sense of agency to reduce feelings of helplessness, combined with opportunities to feel supported, are key to minimizing the negative impact of trauma. For example, helping a child find ways to raise money to support starving children in a war-torn country will provide a sense of control as they cope with understanding world events.

○ *Atypical peer relationships.* A gifted child who struggles to find friends because peers with similar interests and abilities aren't available may become vulnerable to trauma because they don't have a support network. Additionally, these children might be at increased risk of being targeted by bullies because they are more isolated than other students.

○ *Chronic stress and unhealthy perfectionism.* Gifted children who are in highly competitive academic environments and push themselves to take every honors or advanced placement course can experience a traumatic response to the perceived intensity of expectations. Internalizing perceived failures rather than processing them with a strong support system can lead to future trauma responses in similar situations.

○ *Inappropriate academic fit.* A student placed in a classroom that is under-stimulating or with a teacher who doesn't understand, value, or support gifted learners is at risk for trauma because their needs are being neglected. Twice-exceptional children are at higher risk because it is not uncommon for one or more of their unique learning needs to be unrecognized or unaccommodated.

Gifted students can pull from their strengths to overcome traumatic experiences. Abstract reasoning skills and advanced imagination can help children talk about and process their emotions about trauma in a safe way. With the support of the adults in their lives, they can use their ability to generate ideas to take helpful action in traumatic situations, leading to a sense of agency and power over such events. Giving a sense of control and removing the fear of being helpless are key factors for reducing the impact of trauma. Though a gifted child cannot undo trauma they have experienced, they can work to gain control over certain aspects of their life to minimize the effects of trauma.

Stress and Self-Talk

Our inner voice—"self-talk"—is what decides whether something feels like a catastrophe or an opportunity to learn and grow.[13] This idea has existed for centuries. Shakespeare's Hamlet said, "There is nothing either good or bad, but thinking makes it so." (Act II, Scene ii). Mark Twain once observed, "I…have known a great many troubles, but most of them never happened." Self-talk is the little voice in our head. It's what we say to ourselves about a situation, our behavior, or an interaction. We use self-talk in many ways. Sometimes we use it to remind ourselves of tasks, to stay organized, to keep focused on a project, or to avoid making an inappropriate comment. We also use it to evaluate ourselves, often negatively. We're more likely to say to ourselves, "I did a dumb thing just then," or "I'll never succeed at this," than, "Good job!" or "Way to go!"

Self-talk is such a regular habit that most people are unaware that they use it continually. Since many gifted children develop language early, some use self-talk by the age of two or three. Younger children often self-talk aloud, for example, "Don't forget to brush your teeth." As they get older and more aware of their surroundings, self-talk becomes more private. Self-talk helps children achieve self-control as they repeat the same directives, warnings, and corrections that parents say to them, such as, "I should be careful not to let the cat out," or "I shouldn't be too rough with my baby sister."

A person's self-talk can be a sign of resilience or insecurity. Resilient self-talk focuses on solutions and putting things into perspective. Insecure self-talk is self-critical and focused on negative outcomes. Gifted high achievers, as well as gifted underachievers, suffer from feelings of inadequacy and engage in negative self-talk.[14]

Self-talk plays a major role in a child's day-to-day life and is closely connected to self-concept and self-esteem. Because self-talk influences mood and behavior, children must learn to manage it so that it helps rather than hinders them. Capitalizing on the critical thinking and verbal skills of gifted children is useful in this regard. Many gifted children can grasp the idea behind self-talk earlier than their peers and understand how our thoughts influence our behavior and emotions.

Cognitive-behavioral therapy techniques were among the first to integrate the importance of recognizing and implementing self-talk to help build resilience. Building awareness of thought patterns that undermine resilience is key to reframing those thoughts in more productive, healthy ways. Self-talk mistakes made when trying to manage stress and anxiety include:

○ *The mental filter:* Instead of focusing on the many things that have gone well, the mental filter focuses only on the one (often small) negative thing that has occurred. Using the analogy of a single drop of black ink (representing the negative event or thought) coloring an entire pitcher of water (representing all neutral or positive things that have occurred) is a helpful comparison to explain the concept of the mental filter. The mental filter causes someone to go from thinking the day was good to being ruined because one small thing didn't work out.

○ *Discounting the positive:* In some ways, this is the mirror image of the mental filter. Instead of ignoring the positive, this self-talk mistake actively minimizes the importance of successes or other positive outcomes. Gifted children who learn very easily are prone to discount the positive, thinking that positive events aren't valuable or important. "I didn't really try very hard on that test, so the A doesn't really count" is an example of discounting the positive.

○ *Binocular vision:* Hyper-focusing on a single, small event or situation and exaggerating the impact of the event is called binocular vision. It also causes one to be so focused on a problem that they lose sight of the big picture. A gifted student who gets a C on a quiz might feel like a failure, even though all other grades for the semester have been A's.

○ *Illogical beliefs:* The greatest stress arises when we incorporate illogical, unreasonable beliefs into our self-talk, leading to inappropriate "should" statements. Most often, the "should" comes from values others have instilled in us, or from our own intense idealism. Wherever possible, replace "should" with the phrase, "It would be nice if...," which sounds less crucial and compulsory. So instead of, "I *should* be more organized," the self-talk becomes, "It would be nice if I were more organized." Such phrases lessen the urgency of expectations and help us be more realistic about behavior. Table 6 provides examples of some common illogical and unreasonable beliefs.

Table 6: Illogical and Unreasonable Beliefs[15]

- Everyone must like me, and I should like everyone.

- If someone treats me badly, I should hate him and never speak to him again.

- I must be perfect in every way.

- If I do something I shouldn't, it means I am a bad person.

- I can't handle it when things aren't going the way I want them to.

- Life is unfair, and I can't change anything to make it better.

- I should be able to immediately find a perfect solution to every problem.

- If I'm unhappy, it is because of what other people have said or done and I can't do anything about it.

- When something bad happens and my mind gets stuck on it, there's no way I can move on.

- There's something wrong with me if the things that make other people happy don't make me happy, too.

- I can't escape the negative things that have happened in the past.

Encouraging Healthy Self-Talk

How can parents help children avoid self-talk errors? Changing self-talk and evaluating accuracy is not something parents can teach in one instance. These skills develop over time. First, help children understand the impact of self-talk and thinking on both behavior and emotions. Then, talk with them about the examples of self-talk mistakes described above. Understanding self-talk is the basis for monitoring it and its consequences.

Children who are aware of their self-talk will be less likely to base future self-talk on hidden "shoulds," because they can evaluate whether they are setting unreasonable expectations for themselves and others. If no one teaches them about common thinking errors, they will remain unaware of the impact of negative self-talk on their moods and behavior. They may continue to engage in these self-talk blunders until they become deeply embedded in their way of thinking, profoundly affecting mood and outlook on life. Unnecessary stress, poor self-acceptance, and emotions like disappointment, frustration, anger, and rage toward the world can result. Parents can remind children that it is not events that cause their stress, but what they say to themselves about those events.

Because gifted children's self-talk is so quick and well-practiced, pointing out the pitfalls seldom does enough to help them manage it. In fact, pointing out these errors may create more stress if the gifted child does not have sufficient tools to manage the self-talk. He may think, "Oh, there I go thinking 'wrong' again! Stupid me." Children will need practice and coaching to learn skills to avoid negative self-talk. The language we use with our children becomes fundamental to their inner monologue. By building awareness of self-talk and coaching our children toward healthy ways to reframe their thoughts and manage uncomfortable emotions, we help them become resilient and flexible in the face of adversity. Table 7 shows other strategies to manage negative self-talk.

Table 7: Strategies for Overcoming Negative Self-Talk

Strategy	*Discuss self-talk.*	
	Rationale	**How-to**
	Parents rarely discuss self-talk explicitly. Encouraging children to build awareness of their self-talk is a good foundation for both understanding their emotions and developing strategies to self-regulate distressing emotions. Explicit conversations about self-talk builds rapport and provides insight into the child's thought process.	Explore their thoughts. Ask your child specific, neutral questions about both mundane and emotionally distressing events. For example, "Tell me about what thoughts were going through your head when you saw that on television," or "When that happened, what thoughts were you having?" Try drawing a cartoon with thought bubbles to help build awareness of their self-talk if they have a hard time identifying it.
Strategy	*Develop and name an imaginary character in the child's mind, to separate negative self-talk from their sense of self.*	
	Rationale	**How-to**
	Externalizing the negative self-talk by creating an imaginary character who is responsible for the internal dialogue helps kids feel less threatened by their negative thinking. Referring to the "Worry Bully" or "Negative Nelly" reminds children that they aren't being blamed for negative thoughts, and provides an opportunity to "talk back" to the negative thoughts.	Empower the child. When talking to your child, say, "Wow, it sounds like the Worry Bully is really beating up on you today. I hear him sending all kinds of negative messages through your self-talk. What can we do to take the power away from Worry Bully?" Work to reframe the negative thinking so it is neutral.

Strategy	Practice predicting outcomes.	
	Rationale	**How-to**
	For children who automatically expect a negative outcome of events or situations, learning the skill of making realistic predictions is valuable.	Explore alternatives. Have children think through and predict three possible outcomes to a future event or situation: (1) the absolute worst outcome, (2) the absolute best outcome, and (3) the most likely consequence of the situation. Afterward, ask them to evaluate their predictions and discuss why they may have been leaning toward a more negative outcome. Brainstorm ways to avoid this in the future.

Strategy	Is it my problem, or does it belong someone else?	
	Rationale	**How-to**
	Sensitive children may internalize critical comments from others, especially when they come from peers or teachers. Expectations of others can produce stress, especially if they are dramatically different from the child's own expectations. Teaching your child that someone being critical of their behavior doesn't mean they have to change is a healthy way to learn self-protective boundaries.	Find the root. Coach your child to ask: "Is this my problem or someone else's?" Help her to decide whether to give in to the expectations or beliefs of the other person. Analyze the logic of critical statements and decide how or whether to respond. Knowing that she has a choice about whether to accept or respond to criticism can give a gifted child a feeling of strength.

Strategy	*Expect progress, not perfection.*	
	Rationale	**How-to**
	Many of the benchmarks of success are product- or outcome-oriented. Did you get an A on the test or win the chess tournament? But focusing on the process, and the progress made while moving toward the goal, is a better measure of success.	Identify progress. Encourage your child to reflect on various outcomes, both positive and negative. What were the growth points throughout the process, even if the desired outcome wasn't achieved? Modeling this through conversation builds this skill into your child's internal self-talk.
Strategy	*Stop playing the blame game.*	
	Rationale	**How-to**
	While it may be true that someone else's actions have influenced the outcome of a situation, saying someone else is to blame for a bad situation does not lessen stress. Blaming others increases feelings of helplessness and frustration; it also leaves us in a passive mode rather than an active, assertive one. Gifted children must learn ways to avoid feeling helplessly trapped by their situation and take an active role in reducing their stress by viewing challenging situations as learning experiences.	Take responsibility. Help the child focus less on who is to blame, and more on the challenging emotions associated with the situation. Discuss what actions they may take to mitigate the situation in the future. Instead of "It is my teacher's fault that I got a bad grade on this test because they didn't even go over some of the material that was on the test," help your child reframe this: "I felt really frustrated and annoyed that there were items I wasn't expecting on the test. Now I know that the teacher test on items from the book, even if she didn't go over them in class. I'll make sure to study more completely next time."

Strategy	Look for evidence to disprove negative thinking.	
	Rationale	**How-to**
	When our feelings are hurt, we believe negative self-talk, have difficulty assessing a situation, and fail to look for evidence that would contradict our thoughts. If we say to ourselves, "I am stupid," we may ignore information that disputes it, increasing our frustration, stress, and negative mood.	If we do not look for evidence, we will never find it. Look for data to disprove negative thoughts by asking, "What is the evidence that things are bad?" Identify other aspects previously not considered, which will help manage negative self-talk and its resulting stress effectively.

The Mind-Body Connection to Stress

The connection between physical wellbeing, stress, and how we handle uncomfortable emotions is sometimes overlooked. Building greater awareness of the physical signs of stress helps us proactively take steps to regulate emotions before they become overwhelming or explosive.

If you are noticing that your child's mood changes quickly throughout the day, ask yourself if your child has any physical stressors that may be increasing their distress. For example, "hangry" is the perfect colloquial term for the increase in irritability and decrease in frustration tolerance caused by hunger. Many children struggle with identifying specific physical sensations associated with hunger, and are unlikely to realize that hunger influences their mood. Building your own awareness and helping them identify the association between physical discomfort and mood can provide some quick and easy solutions for emotional dysregulation. Discomfort with clothing, room temperature, or physical illness are other possible explanations. The acronym HALT—Hungry, Angry, Lonely, Tired—is another tool to help identify and address causes of dysregulation.

Stress not only causes physical discomfort, it also triggers specific physiological reactions in the body. When children notice these signs of stress before becoming dysregulated, they may be able to proactively regulate their emotions. A child who notices that their cheeks get hot when they are embarrassed would be able to leave a situation before their embarrassment turns to frustration and anger. Help your child learn to recognize the signals their body sends when they are stressed; help them create a diagram of a body indicating their specific signs of discomfort (like upset stomach, flushed cheeks, clenched fists, or increased heart rate).

Using Mindfulness to Reduce Stress

The term "mindfulness" has been broadly used for a wide range of strategies and techniques to improve mood and reduce stress. For our purposes, the term specifically refers to the intentional connection between our present experience, our focus, and our attention, whether that is internal (within our bodies) or external (in our environment). Research on mindfulness strategies shows that using them can help protect gifted students from depression, anxiety, and unhealthy perfectionism.[16]

Some gifted children may be skeptical of using mindfulness techniques to reduce stress. It can seem silly to them, or they may feel like they've tried it and it didn't work. However, research on biofeedback techniques and polyvagal theory provide evidence that we can not only influence our bodily reactions to stressors, but we can reduce the intensity of uncomfortable emotions and return to a calm state of mind more quickly by using mindfulness.[17] These techniques relax both our minds and bodies, helping manage the discomfort of stressful situations more easily.

When a person experiences stress, breathing and heart rate become rapid, the stomach tightens, and the neck and muscles throughout the body become tense and "on high alert." People experiencing a great deal of stress can seldom think calmly and clearly. Reducing physical tension helps. Deep breathing, muscle relaxation techniques, and visualization exercises take time to learn but can be powerful tools of self-control. The child can use these strategies to "reset the system" after a stress reaction, or simply to reduce daily stress.

Slow, controlled breathing is a technique that can control stage fright and even panic attacks. When people are anxious, they breathe in a shallow, rapid fashion that does not allow sufficient clearing of the carbon dioxide from the lungs, resulting in even more anxiety. Focused deep breathing changes this pattern and gives the child something other than the stress to concentrate on.

It is important to teach these techniques when things are calm, rather than during a crisis; the middle of a storm is not the time to teach navigation. As with any new skill, a child needs practice to be able to rely on these mindfulness techniques during times of stress.

Bibliotherapy and Cinema-Therapy

Another way to teach children about managing emotions and difficult situations is by reading books, or watching other people, either real or fictional, manage the same challenges. Most gifted children love to read and can easily identify with characters in books. When children see characters coping with the same stresses, they can learn coping strategies and feel less alone. When presented in a non-threatening way, books can help children gain perspective on various issues without direct confrontation. Books, either fiction or nonfiction, can help gifted children explore intensity, sensitivity, perfectionism, aloneness, differentness, and relationships. Biographies can also be powerful learning tools for gifted adolescents and young adults. There are also many books written especially for gifted children that provide coping strategies for common issues.

Movies are another engaging and safe escape into a world of characters and their life challenges. Some movies portray gifted characters dealing with stress; others present fictional scenarios that relate to struggles in a gifted child's life. Guided discussion about these movie characters can help children develop insight, see alternative perspectives, and increase the likelihood of positive change.

Bibliotherapy and cinema-therapy each have drawbacks. Not all content in books or movies is appropriate for all children, and accuracy in depictions may be questionable. Parents must choose carefully and avoid the trap of being too direct. Books and movies can provide a gentle approach for children to develop social and emotional skills; the gifted child's mind will make the connections between the characters and themselves, without parents connecting the dots for them. Bibliotherapy and cinema-therapy are not meant to replace actual therapy or counseling, but they can help a child gain insight and can gradually begin to change a child's understanding and behavior.

Practical Solutions

○ *Don't ignore or deny problems.* Discussing problems validates the importance of both acknowledging and addressing them. Situations that cause stress need to be identified to be solved. Ignoring or denying a problem signals that the situation is not valid or important. Even if we are unable to solve a problem, reviewing the situation and its accompanying thoughts and feelings will be beneficial. An unresolved challenging situation does not facilitate healthy problem solving, and may discourage a child from sharing difficulties in the future. Talking allows problems to be addressed more effectively. Take time to listen to your child and to discuss their stresses and worries. Validate their emotions by naming them: "I can tell you feel really *frustrated* by that situation." Do not dismiss their concerns with comments like, "Well, that really isn't a big deal," or "There's no need to worry about that."

○ *Provide age-appropriate information about adult problems.* Gifted children who perceive adult problems may magnify them in their minds, extrapolating a severity beyond what is likely. A child's image of a problem can be far worse than the real thing. A gifted child with little or no information may speculate wildly, filling in gaps with creative ideas. You must balance giving enough information and context to reassure them without burdening them with information that is too mature. These conversations build trust and open communication. Recognize the child's worries and let them know the situation is being taken care of by adults. "Dad and I are watching our finances. You are fine; we are not suddenly going to be without money. We are just putting extra focus on careful planning this month."

○ *Listen, but give little direct advice.* Providing direct advice can invalidate a child's experiences. Comments like, "You're just being too hard on yourself," or "Why not just turn in your project as it is and forget about it," can add more stress. They imply that the child, who already feels as if there is something wrong with her, *is* wrong. Instead of providing unsolicited advice, encourage your child to think "out loud" about the situation, describing the solutions she has attempted and her reactions. Follow this with an invitation to problem solve ("What ideas do you have to solve this problem?") to let them feel their autonomy and a sense of control over an uncomfortable situation.

○ *Avoid parental over-involvement.* A parent who is overly involved in a child's daily life encourages a dependent relationship, which does not allow self-management tasks to be mastered. Also termed "helicopter parenting" or "snowplow" parenting, solving kids' problems for them undermines their independence, removes growth opportunities, and can lead to learned helplessness. Teach children to take responsibility for their own actions, assume a fair share of tasks and chores, and manage normal stress as part of their path to self-management.

○ *Relieve tension with humor.* Someone once said that a person without a sense of humor is like a car without shock absorbers—jolted by every pothole in the road. If children hear family members laugh at their own imperfect actions, they begin to see humor in situations and become more likely to take mistakes in stride. Laughing at one's own foibles helps neutralize perfectionism and promotes acceptance of mistakes. Encourage light-hearted humor, but discourage sarcastic humor because it can be misunderstood and hurtful.

Explore real vs. false alarms. Sometimes, we experience stress or anxiety when there is no real threat. If there is no real danger or concern, teach the child to "reset" and move on. For example, when mom doesn't arrive home exactly at the time expected, a child may experience anxiety, thinking about terrible things that might have occurred. Recognizing the false alarm, exploring other realistic explanations, and resetting through mindfulness strategies can help.

○ *Learn to say "no."* Gifted children tend to over-commit themselves, then feel stress and guilt if they are unable to manage all that they have taken on. Successfully managing stress means setting priorities and deciding which activities are the most meaningful and worthwhile—then saying "no" to over-involvement.

○ *Use journaling.* Journaling allows a child to write down thoughts and feelings and develop life perspective. By writing regularly about significant events, feelings, strategies, hopes, and aspirations, gifted children can learn to identify their goals, crystallize decisions, and find meaning in their own unique lives.

○ *Encourage pride in attempts.* Too often, bright children succeed without effort and begin to believe it will always be so, failing to connect effort and outcome. Encouraging them to persist when things become difficult will develop the work habits and confidence necessary for success. Mastering any skill takes practice, and mistakes are important and helpful, because they help children learn better ways to do things the next time. Many famous people have failed before succeeding, and some of the most important discoveries in science, medicine, and other fields came from unintended mistakes. Find ways to highlight persistence in a non-threatening way.

○ *Convert problems into opportunities.* In the same way that mistakes can result in new discoveries, problematic situations can provide new opportunities. Help your child get beyond the negative self-talk of disappointment and frustration to realize the new opportunity. Not making the sports team means more time for other activities; missing your plane means extra time to relax or meet someone new. Help the child realize that one always has choices, even in maddening or disappointing situations.

CHAPTER 8
Idealism, Unhappiness, and Depression

The idealistic gifted child often seeks change, seeing how things can be different. Challenging the status quo, however, may come at a cost—distress, frustration, or even isolation. How do idealism and these other factors affect the gifted child's emotional well-being? Are gifted children more likely to be unhappy? Are they more likely than other children to get depressed? To attempt suicide? What could make a talented child so unhappy and so desperate as to not want to live? Fortunately, most gifted children are resilient and able to handle disappointments and cope with stress. There are unique stressors that gifted children and teens experience that can impact their mental health, but there are also assets within their giftedness that can promote their resilience.

The idea that any child or teen can experience depression is surprising to some adults, but there are definite steps parents can take to reduce the likelihood of children becoming depressed, or at least to lessen its intensity. Depression may even be turned into a positive, so that it becomes fuel for a person's motivation to undertake meaningful work, enhances humility, or provides clarity to see faulty situations as they really are. For example, documented stories of Abraham Lincoln and Lou Holtz describe how they used their depression as an agent of growth to develop strength of purpose and conviction. The ability to do this will depend on the child's ability to learn resilience, manage perfectionism, and acquire stress management skills. Unhappiness and depression are difficult topics, but they are important to understand to guide gifted children.

How Widespread Is Depression for Children and Adolescents in the General Population?

In 2020, 17% percent of adolescents ages 12-17 reported having experienced a major depressive episode within the last year. This was an increase from 2017, when 13% of adolescents reported a depressive episode, and 2007 when it was 8%. The pandemic disrupted lives and triggered mental health concerns for many students, but even prior to this event, reports of depression in adolescents were rising. When the 2020 statistics are analyzed by gender, they show that depression impacts girls more than boys, with 25% of females and 9% of males between the ages of 12-17 experiencing a depressive episode. Younger children also experience depression; however, it can be difficult to determine, as statistics showing the rates of early childhood depression are often lumped in with those of adolescents. When the age range is expanded to include children from ages 3-17, the rate of diagnosis of depression between 2016-2019 was 4.4%.[1]

These age group statistics are derived from the general population; finding reliable data concerning gifted children and teens is difficult, primarily because the CDC, which tracks information about mental health, depression, and suicide, does not include information about individual cognitive ability. Additionally, a lack of consensus about the definition of giftedness further complicates a clear understanding about mental health and giftedness.[2]

Risk Factors for Depression in Gifted Children and Adolescents

Current research shows that overall rates of depression in gifted versus nongifted people are not significantly different. However, there is evidence of unique factors in gifted children and adolescents that influence the presence of depression or suicidal ideation. The three main categories of risk factors for depression include: biological (such as family history of depression or identifying as LGBTQ), psychological (such as low self-esteem, poor emotional regulation, negative thinking, and anxiety), and environmental (such as academic difficulties, loss of a loved one, bullying, abuse, discrimination, or other trauma).[3] Parents can be on the lookout for various risk factors that might influence a child's mental health.

Mismatch in Environment

The Person-Environment Fit Theory in psychology examines how the learning or work environment a person is in influences their well-being. A strong match between the student and the environment predicts both academic success and affective benefits (like feelings of confidence, self-efficacy, and hopefulness).[4]

Gifted students often are often placed in an academic environment that is under-stimulating. They may have already mastered much of the content that is presented, leading to difficulty staying engaged with material. Teachers who are unable or unwilling to provide educationally appropriate material to bright students undermine their drive to learn. Additionally, this mismatch can lead to feelings of social isolation.[5] A student who is twice exceptional is also at risk for this type of environmental mismatch because meeting both strengths and weaknesses is doubly challenging for educators. In these cases, it is not giftedness *per se* that is causing the problem, but the mismatch or inability of the teacher or system to meet the gifted child's needs.

Meeting the educational, social, and emotional needs of gifted children offers them protection from depression. Providing a stimulating and challenging learning environment among peers allows them to grow and is one of the most effective ways to increase academic fit, reduce isolation, and decrease the likelihood of depression.

Socially Prescribed Perfectionism

Children and teens who experience socially-prescribed perfectionism may be at higher risk for poor emotional resilience or depression.[6] (The different types of perfectionism are discussed in depth in Chapter 7.) The belief that one can never live up to the expectations of their parents, teachers, or society can feed hopelessness and helplessness, which are strongly associated with clinical depression.

The high-stakes coursework and competitive environments that many gifted children and teens experience can be a double-edged sword. On the one hand, they need these courses to challenge them and allow their skills and abilities to grow. On the other hand, the stress, pressure, and comparisons to other high-ability students can foster socially prescribed perfectionism. Cultivating resilience, encouraging students to ask for help when needed (rather than powering through and feeling like they must figure it out on their own), and fostering relationships with adults who do not solely focus on academic performance can help balance any tendencies toward socially-prescribed perfectionism.

Social Isolation

While social isolation and loneliness are a risk factors for depression in all people, regardless of intellectual ability,[7] gifted children may experience barriers to developing social relationships due to their asynchrony or atypical interests (see chapter 9). Fulfilling relationships are protective when it comes to mental health. Creating and maintaining the type and quantity of friendships someone wants will foster wellbeing.

Elementary children often want to be friends with the smartest students in the classroom, which helps gifted children develop the relationships they desire at younger ages. As children get older, the appeal of being friends with the "smart kids" can wear off, and gifted adolescents may find themselves struggling to find the friends they want.[8] Gifted children may put up a façade that masks their depression and reveals only the superficial parts of themselves that they think others will accept, such as their physical attractiveness, sports talent, or ability to tell jokes. But relationships built on superficiality are seldom rewarding or long-lasting. Some gifted youth become overly dependent on—almost addicted to—recognition outside of themselves, such as honors and awards. When they lose that recognition—and they all do at some point—they begin to doubt themselves.

Finding like-minded peers in the school setting can be difficult for students who are constrained by arbitrary age limits. The understanding and awareness of what a friendship can and should be may differ for a gifted child compared to their same-age peers, leading to additional difficulties in developing strong friendships. Additionally, the stigma surrounding being in an exclusive program "for the smart kids" can give the perception of inequality, inhibiting the development of strong friendships.

Overcommitment and Burnout

Gifted children are often talented in multiple areas. This is sometimes referred to as *multipotentiality*. Some with multipotentiality can be successful in many areas. Imagine a gifted student who holds first chair for violin in the school's orchestra, participates on the school's debate team, plays on the tennis team, and competes outside of school in local and regional chess tournaments. Additionally, they are taking a heavy load of Advanced Placement courses and get excellent grades. How long do you think it would take for this bright student to get overwhelmed and burnout due to the many commitments?

This pattern of overcommitment and burnout is often seen in gifted individuals. The enjoyment of doing something (and doing it well) is hard to pass up. Additionally, adults in their lives may encourage them to try new things and pursue such endeavors. However, without a strong awareness of how one is managing stress and the ability to self-advocate by declining opportunities when needed (or quitting them when they get to be too much), burnout is inevitable.

Emotional exhaustion, feelings of cynicism, and reduced personal accomplishment are tell-tale signs of burnout.[9] The characteristics of burnout strongly align with the signs of depression; burnout can easily become clinical depression when not addressed. Helping gifted children and teens prioritize their goals and necessary time commitments can help them preserve their energy to prevent burnout and depression.

Idealism and Disappointment

Gifted children are often disappointed in themselves when they believe they have failed to live up to their own (self-imposed and unrealistically high) standards of achievement, morals, or values. This can lead to depression. As one gifted teenager said, "When I get anything less than perfect, it's like the world ended. No one else is that way. They can do anything and be happy."[10] Another gifted adolescent described it like this: "I worry too much. I worry about 'losing my talents.' I worry about becoming average. I worry about my lost childhood and the opportunities I've missed. I worry I will burn out or overspecialize. I worry about how successful I will be in my career and whether my colleagues will accept me (and whether they do now)."[11]

Gifted children have high ideals for themselves, for their peers, and for the world. Their zeal and intensity drive them to reach these ideals. When they can't measure up, or the people around them don't see things the way they think things ought to be, or the world continually lets them down, they may feel helpless in pursuit of those ideals. Such idealism, combined with uneven or asynchronous development, can result in unfulfilled expectations, which can lead to cynicism and depression.

Existential Concerns

While many begin to experience existential awareness around adolescence, a gifted child's ability to think deeply and critically from a young age can lead them to question existential aspects of their life and ponder these topics at an earlier age.[12] Existential awareness can cause discomfort and anxiety. Once existential issues are brought into conscious thought, they must be continually addressed; you cannot return to a time when they did not exist. Without support, these existential dilemmas can lead to more serious depression.

Existential issues include big humanitarian problems like war, poverty, starvation, climate change, dishonesty, and cruelty. Even at a young age, gifted children can worry passionately about such issues. Why do these problems exist? Surely there must be a way to solve them. Basic issues of human existence—freedom, isolation, death, and meaninglessness—

can be difficult for gifted children to understand and lead to worrying. They don't have the life experience or emotional regulation skills to put these fears into context. Many parents have found that their children find support, feel empowered to make the world a better place, and can combat the source of these fears, if they are involved in volunteer work with organizations that strive to improve conditions in society. The idealistic gifted child may find such involvement connects them to other idealists and adds meaning to life by helping others. Giving time to a cause increases the child's personal sense of control and gives her a positive direction with specific work to do. The volunteer work might be serving in a food pantry or reading to elderly patients in a nursing home. The type of service is less important than the fact that the child is with others who care and are similarly involved.

Compared to the general population, gifted adults are more impacted by existential concerns, which persist throughout life.[13] It is certainly difficult for adults to deal with questions about the purpose of their life, inevitable death, and free will. Gifted children without like-minded peers to connect with about these issues can benefit from discussing them with trusted adults; knowing that they aren't alone with these questions is one of the few ways to handle existential anxiety and depression.

Idealism and Challenging Traditions

Situations that prompt children to challenge customs and tradition will arise from their idealism, particularly when the traditions seem unreasonable or when customs conflict with their own moral standards. For example, a child may conclude that, "We let material things control our lives far too much, and we should live more simply." Or "We should stop eating meat because it requires that we kill other living creatures; besides, feedlots are inhumane and harmful to the environment."

Even at young ages, idealistic gifted children are often willing to forsake the comfortable predictability of the status quo to search for improved ways of living and being. They see possibilities for change.

They may want to help the homeless or want their family to become vegetarians or purchase a lower emissions car. They may design a project to raise money for a special cause.

When strong emotions attached to traditions are coupled with the gifted child's intensity, the challenges can escalate into potentially disruptive situations, threatening rifts in the family or with peers. This is especially likely when a family or group has little tolerance for the traditions of others. During the civil rights era of the Deep South, many parents found themselves very uncomfortable when their idealistic children sought to change segregationist customs.

We certainly want our gifted children to be creative problem solvers, because new solutions are needed for many problems facing not only this country, but also the world. But persistent questioning and tradition-breaking by some gifted children can cause discomfort for family members, teachers, and others who find their behaviors embarrassing, uncomfortable, or even threatening to their own beliefs or ways of life. Insisting on challenging rules, or questioning simply for the sake of questioning, or just being different, is both a noble search for truth and a painful way to exist for gifted children and those around them. Parents may find it difficult when their teenagers challenge traditions or express uncomfortable anti-establishment views. Gifted children approaching adolescence are even more likely to be irritated by the inconsistencies and hypocrisy they see around them.

Gifted children, with their exceptional analytical ability, can be right in saying that a certain tradition *should* be challenged or defied. Of course it seems more acceptable if it's not a tradition that we ourselves happen to cherish. For example, in the 1970s, many young mothers went back to work even though their parents thought that they should stay home with their children—the tradition until then. The fights for equal pay for men and women, raising the minimum wage, and legalization of gay marriage, as examples, break with traditional expectations and customs, which often makes people uncomfortable. Why is she upsetting the status quo? Where will it lead? We've always done it that way! But when idealistic gifted children can see how things might be, they want to put their ideals into action. Isn't that what we want them to do? Sometimes, though, it happens sooner or more dramatically than we would like!

Challenging societal tradition can be beneficial, even though these changes temporarily distress other people, particularly those who don't immediately see the benefit. It took a Civil War to stop slavery. It took years to legalize women's right to vote. It took more time after that for African Americans to vote and attend public schools. Although we've made progress in racial and gender equality, there is still room for improvement. Someone had to see that things could be different and take action to make it so, causing discomfort in others along the way.

The world is surely better because creative, caring, and courageous people have challenged traditions. Rosa Parks challenged racism on buses in the South and so contributed to racial equality. Martin Luther King Jr. challenged traditional beliefs and assumptions about African Americans and brought positive change through the civil rights movement. In England, Joseph Lister challenged the notion that diseases were not spread in hospitals and developed sterile procedures. The Wright Brothers challenged the traditional belief that humans could not fly in machines heavier than air. Amelia Earhart challenged the belief that women could not fly. Gay men in San Francisco challenged the notion that homosexuality was wrong, bringing sexual equality into social awareness.

Most advances in our society came about because someone challenged a belief and was determined to prove it wrong. One gifted middle school girl staged a boycott over the inequality of funding and opportunities between boys' and girls' after-school sports at her school. She organized a walk-out by convincing other students to gather and sit in silent protest until the principal came out to speak to their concerns. She got results: the students went to the school board with a proposal to put more money toward girls' sports, and the school board voted to do so. Undoubtedly, many were uncomfortable with the challenge of authority, even though the cause was just. We must help our children understand the costs involved with such challenging, but discomfort should not dissuade people from pursuing their convictions. Progress in knowledge and in society simply would not happen if traditions weren't challenged.

As we have shown, tradition-breaking behaviors can result in a positive change. Unfortunately, they can sometimes come at a great cost for the gifted individual. When they meet resistance, they may doubt themselves or lose faith. The road can be long. They may lose friends or other close relationships as they try to remain true to themselves and their desire for change. When these struggles persist, the idealism can breed unhappiness and cynicism. Depression may emerge if the child cannot find appropriate outlets and support.

Symptoms of Depression

Many people are surprised to learn that young children can be depressed. We have an image of childhood as a happy time, where sadness is short-lived and children are cheerful and resilient. In teens, depression is often shrugged off by adults as developmentally normal—just a stage. Identifying true depression in children and teenagers can be difficult, because early symptoms are hard to detect and are often attributed to other causes such as the "bad influence" of peers, lack of sleep, or poor eating habits.

Depression is more than ordinary unhappiness, sadness, or even the temporary grief that we all experience from losses. The Diagnostic and Statistical Manual (DSM-5-TR) defines clinical depression as a mood state that lasts at least two weeks. During those two weeks, some of the signs that might occur include: [14]

O Feelings of sadness, emptiness, or hopelessness almost every day. Tearfulness can be an outward sign that parents might notice; alternatively, in children or teens, parents might notice a change in mood that looks like irritability.

O A reduction in the level of interest or enjoyment in most activities.

○ A change (either increase or decrease) in appetite that might result in weight loss or gain.

○ Changes in sleep patterns, resulting in an inability to sleep or an increased need for sleep.

○ An increase or decrease that is noticeable by others in psychomotor movements. For example, a significant increase in fidgeting or other movements or the appearance of moving more slowly than usual.

○ Feeling tired or exhausted almost every day.

○ Thinking or believing that oneself is worthless or feeling extremely guilty without a reason.

○ A decrease in the ability to think or concentrate; difficulty making simple decisions.

○ Thinking a lot about death, dying, or suicide.

Some of the symptoms of depression are similar in children and adults, but others are different. Depressed adults characteristically have intense feelings of low self-esteem, sadness, weepiness, hopelessness, self-blame, helplessness, and general despondency. They may spend more time sleeping or may feel immobilized by their sadness. By contrast, children and adolescents who are depressed are likely to show a mood that is more irritable than sad. They may act out their depression in angry ways such as temper outbursts or poor school performance.

Whatever the surface behaviors, most depressed individuals feel hurt and angry inside, as well as feeling helpless to do anything about it. Though unhappy with their current life situation, they feel powerless to make the necessary changes, even if they know what changes are needed. Their self-talk emphasizes hopelessness, and they seem unable to muster enough energy to even attempt helpful problem solving. People who are this severely depressed describe their feelings as vague, elusive, diffuse, and timeless.

Depression can be difficult to conquer, and it is far better to take steps to prevent depression from occurring. If you notice even a few signs, there are ways to talk to your child, or you can find a mental health professional who will help sort through your child's challenging emotions. Being proactive when you notice some of these signs is the best way to help your child learn to identify and overcome these experiences.

Self-Injury and Suicide

One of the most difficult things to talk about related to depression is the possibility of self-injury or suicide. But it is always better to address these concerns openly and without judgement. Talking about these topics openly is important to avoid having them become taboo; if children and teens get the message that there is something to be ashamed of if they have thoughts along these lines, they may not ask for the help they need.

Approximately 17% of adolescents between ages 10 and 17 engage in non-suicidal self-injury at some point; females are more likely to do so than males.[15] While we do not have specific data about prevalence in gifted children, we know from clinical experience that it happens, and can estimate that it happens at least as frequently as in the general population. When people think about non-suicidal self-injury (NSSI), they often associate it with cutting. There are other behaviors that may be associated with NSSI, too, such as scratching, burning, preventing wounds from healing, or hitting. NSSI is generally not associated with a desire to die. Some of the reasons children and teens self-injure include wanting to punish themselves, to feel "something" (rather than emotional numbness), to distract from emotional pain, or to have an outward manifestation of the internal pain they are feeling. Adults should be cautious about dismissing any sign of self-injury as "attention-seeking." A mental health professional can help determine the reasons behind self-injury and strategies to help stop the action.

Suicidal ideation is always a concern when talking about depression. Suicide is the second leading cause of death for adolescents and young adults between the ages of 15 and 24; about 11% of all teens and young adults in this age group state they've thought seriously about suicide, and 1-2% of them have actually attempted it.[16] Although suicidal thoughts do not always result in suicidal behavior, they should *always* be taken seriously, particularly during adolescence; this is especially true for a gifted child trying to find his identity. or experiencing conflict between the need for achievement and the need for peer affiliation.

Educator James Delisle says, "Today's gifted adolescents are enmeshed…in a world that often seems uncaring and uncompromising. But with the support of significant adults and peers, these troubled adolescents may come to see options less severe and less definitive than suicide."[17] An honest, open, respectful, and caring relationship with your child will go a long way toward warding off serious, extended depressions. Your awareness of these important issues, and compassionate efforts to address them when they arise will enhance your relationship.

Practical Solutions

Fortunately, families can do many things to enhance resiliency and lessen the likelihood of serious depression. Here are eight guiding principles for parents and teachers.[18]

- ○ *Notice how long the child has been depressed.* Most often, periods of depression last only a few hours, or a few days at most. If the depression lasts longer than a few days and seems to recur, parents should seek professional advice. Do not dismiss depression as "a stage."

- ○ *Listen to the child.* Parents and teachers who do not listen to the child give the message that she is not worth listening to. A child who is depressed does not need another blow to her self-worth. She is already being very hard on herself. It may be difficult to get your depressed child to open up to you. You will probably need to express extra support, showing that you want to help her make life as enjoyable as it can be.

○ *Accept the concerns.* Try to see how the depression appears from the child's point of view. Sometimes it is the loss of a tangible thing (a beloved pet or a familiar school because the family moved) that prompts grief and depression. Other times it is something intangible, such as loss of a friendship, loss of trust in another, loss of self-esteem, or loss of a certain protective naiveté. Loss always highlights the impermanence of life as we know it and promotes crisis and stress. Many have lost much due to the COVID-19 pandemic. While some of these losses may seem trivial to others, it feels very real to the individual experiencing it.

Be careful not to ignore or minimize the intensity of the child's feelings. Avoid saying things like, "You have nothing to be worried (or depressed) about," or "You shouldn't feel that way." To do so suggests a lack of respect not only for his feelings, but also for him as a person. Such statements can prompt more guilt and confusion about his intense, negative feelings. Remember, these feelings are real and very painful to him.

If you protest to the child that she is wonderful, she may respond with reasons why she is not. If you point out that she has many friends, numerous achievements, and other positive attributes, she might think your comments irrelevant. Reasoning with a depressed gifted child is usually not effective. Instead, reflect and accept the child's feelings. Support your child, but also leave the door open to alternative ways he might see himself or the situation. You can recognize and accept his feelings and also point out that your view of him is different. Remember to listen and respect feelings. Do not deny or minimize the problems and provide gentle but not superficial reassurance.

○ *Give emotional support.* A child needs to feel that someone really appreciates the depth of her concerns. Your support, through careful listening and being there, conveys to the child that she is important to you, despite how she feels about herself right now.

Part of a parent's emotional support involves a gentle but firm insistence that the child engage in some outdoor activities, preferably physical ones such as hiking or biking. People who are depressed often become sedentary and stay indoors, which only worsens the depression. Activities help because, when the child is with others, not only does he have a greater likelihood of receiving emotional support, but also of turning his interests to others and away from himself. Exercise also releases endorphins, which stimulate a more positive attitude.

○ *Evaluate the level of depression and degree of risk.* Signs that indicate when a child's depression is serious or severe include sudden changes in sleeping or eating habits, inability to concentrate, talk of dying or preoccupation with death, giving away valued possessions, withdrawal from family and friends, and a recent loss of social supports. Any of these should be considered a sign of depression. Involvement with drugs or alcohol is another risk factor for depression and suicide. An absence of focus on any future goals or accomplishments suggests serious risk, too, whereas talk of future goals lessens the concern.

○ *Ask about suicide.* This can be a difficult step for a parent or teacher, but it is necessary. Ask the question, "Are you thinking of suicide?" Asking does not put the idea into a young person's mind. If you are concerned enough to ask, it is likely that the thought has at least crossed her mind. Most often, a child takes the question as a sign that you care. If she denies thinking about suicide but acts as if she is not being completely honest, you can also ask, "*Would* you tell me if you *were* thinking about it?" It is important to try to find out if the child is thinking about acting on suicidal thoughts by directly asking the next question: "Have you decided how you would do it?" People who have a specific plan and the means to take the action are at far greater risk of suicide than those who have only a vague notion and have not yet chosen a time, place, or means.

○ *Consult with others.* If you are worried about suicide or about the severity of your child's depression, seek professional help. In the U.S., calling or texting 988 connects you with the Suicide and Crisis Lifeline. You can also find help by contacting, a counselor, your family physician, a psychologist, or a psychiatrist, or you can even take your child to a hospital emergency room. Ask the child for an agreement not to harm herself until she has had at least one appointment with a professional who can help her develop a specific safety plan.

○ *Take action.* Depression should not be ignored—any threat of suicide is a cry for help. Some parents may wonder if talk of suicide is an attempt by the child to manipulate or punish them. Perhaps it is, but it still needs to be taken seriously. Talk to a professional to get an informed opinion. Even if it seems like manipulation or "just a suicidal gesture" rather than a potentially lethal act, you need to convey how much you care by taking action.

CHAPTER 9
Acquaintances, Friends, and Peers

Every child—gifted or not—wants to feel connected with others. Our interactions with friends and family connect us to humanity. We learn how others think or do things, we compare perceptions, and we develop a sense of whether we are valued. Parents of younger gifted children might say, "My child would rather read books than spend time with other children," or "She doesn't seem to have many friends in her grade." They sometimes seem surprised or frustrated that their child would rather spend time talking to adults than playing with children their age.

Parents and teachers may think, "She *must* learn to get along with other children. She *needs* to be well-liked by others if she is to be successful in this world." Yet on the other hand, as children get older, peer pressure is not always a good thing. In middle school, the concerns change from "I wish she would be *more* like others her age" to "I wish she would be *less* like others her age!" Parents of teenagers complain about their children being too eager to follow along and fit in, while not thinking for themselves. "She used to be such a good student, but now all she cares about is acting and looking like others!"

Peer relationships are issues for almost every gifted child because of their asynchrony. Their interests and behaviors are often unusual and different from others their age, resulting in fewer same-age peers in their school or neighborhood. Gifted children with unusually high intellectual abilities, intensities, and sensitivities can have even more difficulties finding friends among children their age. They may prefer playmates who are two or three years older, or even prefer interacting with adults.

Some gifted children are popular with their peers. Many extraverts are inherently social and have few issues with friendships because their nature leads them to interpersonal contacts. This type of gifted child usually has fewer problems connecting with others, but—unless they are the leader—they may be at risk for being overly concerned with peer influences. As they strive to fit in with their peer group, they may deny or downplay their gifts or give up their unusual interests. Ideally, a child will find peers who will not force her to choose between the need for affiliation and the need for achievement. The ideal peer will appreciate both aspects of the gifted child's being.

Very bright but more introverted gifted children may feel different and alone and have few peers. These children need to find peers who can balance the need for interaction with the need for time alone. In both cases, one of the best things parents can do to promote healthy social and emotional development for gifted children is to improve their access and exposure to true peers.

Who Is a True Peer for a Gifted Child?

Is it another child of the same age? Are there other first graders who know the names of all the different birds, reptiles, Pokémon®, or planets? Peers generally are those who share an interest and have a similar knowledge or skill level. While gifted children may need different peers to meet the various athletic, intellectual, and emotional needs, their basic need may be just a friend who helps them laugh at life. Because their ability and developmental level can vary widely due to their asynchrony, gifted children, perhaps more than any other group, will need a variety of peer groups. With that in mind, perhaps the younger gifted child's peers for photography will be older, but his peers for soccer will be closer to his age. He may not find any peers for his interest in geography unless he lives near a museum or other historical sites, where he can talk to the curator. They may have one group of friends their own age with whom they play in their neighborhood, but they may prefer to be with older children or adults for sophisticated computer games or chess. A true peer for a gifted child, then, is not necessarily the same age. Adults generally have a variety of friends of different ages with whom they share different interests. The people they go to concerts with are not always the same people they hike with, and these people are different still from friends at work. Just as adults have different peer groups, so do gifted children.

Are other gifted children the best peers? Sometimes yes, particularly if the other gifted children are about the same age and intellectual level and share similar interests. When a gifted child is fortunate enough to have a best friend, that child is often another gifted child. When a gifted child finds a friend who shares her ability and interests, the situation is exciting, although the level of energy is usually exhausting for adults who happen to be around. The enthusiasm is palpable, and the intensity of two or three gifted children grouped together is magnified; they seem to eat, sleep, drink, breathe, and live each other's enthusiasm. From the gifted child's point of view, it is very exciting to find a peer who can jump from topic to topic as rapidly as she and who has new information, interests, or skills to share. Helping a gifted child understand who can be a peer will normalize the seemingly atypical relationships they have.

Peer Relations within the Family. Family plays a large role in a child's peer relationships. When a gifted child finds herself feeling different from peers in school, it is particularly important that family accept her with all her gifted traits and encourage her to develop and use her abilities. Parents and grandparents can provide a lifeline for an isolated gifted child by simply affirming that it is acceptable to have different friends for different activities. They can foster insight and adjustment by talking about their own peer pressures, at work and in the neighborhood, and how they decide to handle them. Significant adults outside of the immediate family, including aunts, uncles, and cousins, may enjoy playing board or card games with a child, being silly, or just the simple pleasure of sharing laughter. Even neighbors can be good peers. For example, a 13-year-old considered his 60-something neighbor to be his peer in chess, and he became a mentor when the teen showed an interest in the retired man's former career.

Older Peers and Other Special Relationships. Encourage your child to foster a diverse network of relationships that will help him appreciate the value of friendships and acquaintances. When a gifted child's vocabulary and other abilities are so advanced that he quickly leaves age peers behind and social problems result, it makes sense that he might gravitate toward older children or adults whose vocabularies and interests more closely align. It is not unusual for gifted children to have friends who are much older at places like museums, veterinarian clinics, or libraries. Take, for example, the gifted child who built her own computer, knew all the employees at the local computer store, and considered some to be peers. Although mixed-age relationships offer certain advantages, some can be problematic. Parents and educators need to monitor interactions with older children to assure a balance between age peers and intellectual peers that best serves that gifted child. While online communities provide opportunities for connections based on interest rather than age, parents should be aware that they can be difficult to monitor and may expose the child to unwanted or inappropriate subject matter.

The gifted child who is academically accelerated (e.g., subject-accelerated or grade-skipped) is more likely to fit with older children intellectually, but might encounter social difficulties, including fewer possible same-age friendships. Some may see the child as trying to appear too grown up, or accuse the parents of "hurrying" the child. Additionally, older playmates outside of class may expose the child to topics that are simply too mature.

Regardless of age, many gifted children usually find at least one or two persons with whom they develop a special, close, and often lasting friendship. Usually, these relationships are with someone who shares the child's interests, and the friendships are very intense and seem to consume all waking hours. These are truly strong bonds, and the relationships grow over time. Some special friendships develop with those who provide a feeling of acceptance, and that friendship, whether with a peer or a mentor, becomes a haven. Sometimes a gifted child's friendship needs are satisfied by this one special, intense relationship. When a gifted child finds this kind of friend, perhaps at a special event for gifted children, the friendship continues through social media or online gaming until they can see each other again in real life.

Special friendships are important, and most people can recall two or three friends with whom they shared much intimacy. They provided validation and a safe place to explore ideas and perceptions. Parents might worry that their sensitive child is getting too close to the other child, and such intense friendships can lead to problems, particularly when they end. The intensity is so great that sadness, tears, hurt, and anger may result. Although the pain is sharp, the end of a friendship also provides an opportunity for conversations to help a child learn about the complexities of relationships and make the best of a difficult situation.

Peer Relations in College and After. For many gifted children, college is a place where they finally find others like themselves. Peer relations can still be an issue in college, though, for students who are very achievement oriented. Some shy away from organized leisure activities, which limits social connections, while others become overly involved at the expense of academics. Finding a balance is necessary. Although many gifted students find friends during their college years, issues of intensity, sensitivity, idealism, and impatience still haunt some of them. They may wonder about equal investment in relationships or feel like the odd one out. Even after graduation, some experience problems finding people to have satisfying discussions with or to share their passionate idealism. These young adults can be keenly impatient with limitations—at work, in society, with relationships. They want to do it all or fix it all, and right now. They remain discontented with the average standards of quality which they see all around them or dissatisfied with others who don't share their search for personal meaning. Relationships with others, whether at the workplace or at home, can suffer as a result. The characteristics of gifted children, though perhaps more refined, continue into adulthood.

How Many Friends Does Your Child Need? Many adults say that they have only a few close friends, some of whom they see regularly and others they see sporadically. Their other relationships are best described as acquaintances or work associates, not friends. This reality offers perspective on how many friends your gifted child really needs. It is also valuable when gifted children understand that relationships are on a continuum of closeness, understanding, and friendship. A peer is not the same as an acquaintance.

Parents should also be aware that what adults would regard as acceptable peer relationships may be quite different from what gifted children consider to be satisfactory. Some gifted children, particularly ones who are exceptionally gifted or introverted, are comfortable with very few friends and do not feel a strong need to fit in. Others want a wide range of friends and may want to be popular, even at the sacrifice of some of their own abilities and interests. They may try to fit into several groups simultaneously, and their behaviors may differ drastically depending on whether they are with intellectual peers or social peers. Parents may be surprised at the age span of their gifted child's friends.

Some gifted children have few or no friends. There are many possible reasons for this. Some simply have little interest in spending time with others, preferring to be alone. Others have few friends because they have missed learning basic skills for making friends and turn children off with their awkwardness. Some may not have been exposed to supervised group situations, such as Girl Scouts or T-ball, where these skills can be learned. Others spend so much time with computer and video games that they limit opportunities for interaction to school recess. And some simply try too hard, as when they tell a joke or story that the other children don't see as either interesting or funny.

When considering what types of friendships and how many is the "right" number, understand that your needs and desires can influence your beliefs about what children want and need. If you enjoy having a wide social circle, but your child tells you they are satisfied with spending time alone or with their online friends, recognize that your discomfort may stem from your personality and relationship needs, not theirs. On the other hand, some parents may suspect that their child really does wish for more friends but is hiding their loneliness due to pride or social anxiety. Seek assistance, if necessary, when you find yourself in this situation to make sure that you aren't projecting your own needs onto your child.

When Do Peer Problems Begin?

Navigating the complexity of peer relationships, regardless of age, can present problems for the gifted child. Peer problems for some gifted children appear early. A preschooler may not relate well to her classmates. A school age youngster may irritate others with advanced vocabulary or puns. A gifted child with a strong personality may emerge as a leader, or he may find it difficult to tolerate other children.

Preschool peer problems. Peer problems can arise for bright preschool children, and for their parents as well. The four-year-old child who reads recipes from cereal boxes and knows how to add and subtract may wonder why the other four-year-old children don't know how to read. Gifted children can often be impatient with other children because they see themselves as normal. It should not be surprising, then, that age-mates are not necessarily good peers for gifted children. Even at young ages, a child may comfort alone or with older children. Some preschool children seem bossy, inventing complex games with precise rules, only to find that other children think the game is too complex, or that the child is too bossy trying to enforce the rules.

Parents may also begin to experience isolation while their gifted child is in preschool. They may find that they cannot talk with other parents about the things their child is doing. The other parents may see them as bragging or exaggerating. Well-intentioned but misinformed others may accuse a parent of pushing the child to *grow up too fast*. "You should let him just be a child!" Sometimes the negative myths about gifted children permeate these early interactions, which quickly become uncomfortable because others fail to understand the important implications of giftedness.

Peer concerns in school. When entering a traditional kindergarten or first grade, advanced learners experience even more intense peer pressures. Most schools have a clear set of expectations as to what a child should be able to do upon entering. The gifted child is suddenly grouped with many other children whose abilities, interests, or behaviors are different. When the general curriculum moves in a carefully prescribed fashion at a set pace, gifted children may become frustrated.

Even though children have varying rates of learning and retention, we often expect intellectually advanced children to find friends and peers among those of the same age in their classroom. If an environment emphasizes conformity and 'fitting in' over individuality, and has clear expectations for performance that are well below a child's true abilities, two things can happen. Either the child learns to 'fit in' and conform to meet the lower expectations in a socially acceptable way, or the child stands out. Either situation has the potential for peer difficulties. In the first, the child is not being true to himself and learns to put on a façade to be accepted. In the latter, the child highlights visible differences early and may begin 'turning off' potential peers.

Peer pressures from home. Gifted children sometimes feel pressure from parents about how they should interact socially, and with whom. Most parents of younger gifted children emphasize the importance of belonging to a peer group, while parents of teenage gifted children worry that their child is being too influenced by peers and are concerned with how much she is conforming. It is a delicate balance for parents to monitor their child's friends but not interfere too much. It can be particularly challenging for an extraverted parent who has many friends to understand their introverted gifted child who is comfortable with just one friend.

Peer pressures for parents. Parents themselves experience peer pressure. Parents who want to modify circumstances for their gifted child, such as skipping a grade or receiving single-subject acceleration, may find other parents or educators pressuring them to just sit back and let their child fit in. Parents frequently receive strong but often incorrect advice about raising gifted children and must carefully avoid misinformation. It can be reassuring for parents to read biographies of eminent adults who grew up in homes where parents had strong opinions and resisted peer pressures.

How Important Are Social Skills?

Most parents and teachers want children to be sociable. Many say they want a child to be "well-rounded," meaning they want them to be well-liked, get along with others, participate in sports or other extra activities, and generally fit in with others in our world. Our society puts high value on social skills, emotional intelligence, and the ability to recognize and influence the behaviors and emotions of others. In most settings, one is expected to relate well to others regardless of feelings about them. Parents spend a great deal of effort teaching children the manners that will make them acceptable in polite society. They understand the hurt of being considered unpopular and so prefer their children to be somewhat conventional. They want their children to feel accepted, and they worry that their children will suffer ill effects from not fitting in well.

At what point, though, should a child disregard compliance and conformity? Is being traditional more important than achievement, creativity, discovery, or establishing a sense of personal autonomy and independent self-worth? How much does a gifted child need to engage in an ordinary social life? Not all great achievers were immediately socially adept. Eleanor Roosevelt had no peer group until she went to boarding school and found other girls like herself. Maya Angelou, who suffered personal trauma, withdrew into herself for years before becoming a personable and admired poet and public speaker. Temple Grandin, who was diagnosed with Asperger's Disorder (a diagnosis now subsumed under the Autism label), was uncomfortable with people her entire life, but obtained a doctoral degree, authored several books, and became a passionate advocate for more humane treatment of animals. Many successful gifted adults mention that they did not have a peer group until late in life, such as in college or even graduate school.

Perhaps the best solution is that all children need to at least learn "business friendly" skills—that is, behaviors that will allow them to do business with other people in a friendly manner. This does not require them to be best friends or adopt the other person's beliefs, values, or behaviors. Initially, most people are "business friendly" with new acquaintances. Then they decide whether they'd like to get to know the other person better. Parents can demonstrate "business friendly" behaviors for their children in public arenas like the library, subway, grocery store, and other places of business. They can talk with children about how it is important to be respectful to others, even if one doesn't agree with the other person's statements or opinions.

Developing Friendships

Gifted children can struggle with fundamental issues of friendships. They may wonder if they really are part of a group, or even if they want to be part of a group. Peer relationships can be a challenging balancing act as they progress through different stages. Some gifted children are leaders of groups and quite popular with their peers. Others have a hard time fitting in or simply decide that it is not important to them at this point in their lives. They often find a way to be comfortable with their situation, whether with one or two close friends or a larger social network.

In developing friendships, we tend to care about and feel affection for those who share a common concern or focus, who value our role in the relationship, and whom we can count on to contribute similarly to the relationship. Gifted children sometimes benefit from understanding some of these basic concepts about how people relate to each other. You can help your child understand that relationships must develop, often slowly, progressing from acquaintance to peer to good friend. For young children, a playmate is often another child who lives nearby or a child she knows from daycare or preschool. For school age children, friends are people they can talk to or people who give them help and encouragement. As the child matures, she becomes more aware of the importance of common interests, making compromises, and reciprocity. Mature friendships are ones that have an enduring, intimate dynamic based on reciprocity and common values.

Children must figure out how active and assertive they want to be in developing and maintaining successful friendships, and it is helpful if parents explain to their children the differences between aggressive, passive, and assertive. Children who are passive allow others to make decisions for them, keep quiet about their own thoughts and feelings, often lack confidence, and are afraid that something bad might happen if they are assertive or aggressive. Aggressive children routinely make decisions for others and state their feelings openly and often tactlessly. They, too, often lack confidence and try to avoid being vulnerable, but attempt to compensate for this by being demanding, dominant, belittling, intimidating, and even bullying toward others. Assertive children make their own decisions and convey their thoughts and feelings easily to others in a tactful manner. They believe in themselves and their capabilities. They seek—and reach—their goals in a direct, respectful manner, which will help as they search for appropriate peers.

It is hard for parents to see a child suffer for lack of friends. When your children are struggling, consider discussing and role-playing typical friendship situations. Because gifted children usually have excellent imaginations, you can help your child think through what behaviors might bring what responses from others. For example, you might say, "What do you think would happen if you…?" "And then what might happen?" "What do you suppose that person would do (think, feel, etc.) then?" "How could you respond to that?" "What else might you try?" Acting out these behaviors with the child can help her see what others might feel or think. If you use role play, consider switching roles from time to time. One time you can play the child, and then next time you play the person your child is trying to talk to. If you have a good relationship with your child, you may even try making your point by being melodramatic so that the child can laugh while learning. Role playing like this can help children create a solution, which is often more useful than giving one.

You can also model behaviors to show a child what he looks like when he is not listening or paying attention to the cues of other children. A parent can demonstrate various types of body language that invite social interaction or display real-life friendship-making behaviors. This can help a child see what kind of facial expression they have when not interested in talking with someone and how they look when they are happy or open. Table 8 shows other ideas for parents to help their child increase social connections and improve relationships.

Table 8: Increasing Social Connections and Relationships

○ Make time for friends and take initiative to open doors for possible friendships.

○ Learn to be a good host.

○ Give compliments to others to show appreciation for their good qualities.

○ Learn ways to deal with teasing, bullies, and rumors.

○ Join an enjoyable group activity, even if it's in an area of weakness, to create friendship opportunities.

○ Practice friendship skills in low stress situations, perhaps with a peer during a shared activity.

○ Be a good listener to show interest and caring for others.

○ Be sincere about abilities but avoid excessive bragging.

○ Learn to be a good sport in winning and losing.

○ Be accepting of those who think and act differently than you.

If these at-home strategies aren't enough to help your child, parents can also enlist the help of a teacher, coach, or other supportive adult by saying, "Liam could use some tips on making friends, so if you see him struggling, will you please help him out?" Most adults are happy to assist, especially when they know that a child will accept help. Some school counselors conduct small group sessions for children who need help with things like making friends. Additionally, there are several helpful books written to address social skills concerns for autistic children. Some of these contain cartoon-strip scenarios of children acting and saying things that discourage friendship, and on the opposing page, children acting and saying things that encourage social interactions. These resources can be valuable in helping gifted children see new ways of interacting.

Introversion and Alone Time

Introverts are not likely to approach new children; they are more likely to wait for others to initiate friendship. They need time to observe a situation before joining in and don't feel the need for as many friends as extraverts do. Sometimes these children just haven't learned *how* to make friends. Some are so preoccupied with their own thoughts and interests that they inadvertently ignore others. It is important for parents and teachers to both realize that the child's inner world may be more important to her than social behavior with peers and help her understand that others might be put off by her actions. Encourage change by raising her awareness that weak socialization skills may be self-defeating.

Introverts tend not to like surprises; they appreciate warning about what will happen next. A well-meaning mother planned a surprise birthday party for her daughter. When the guests arrived, the "birthday girl" hid behind the couch and refused to interact with the other children. Parents who are sensitive to the basic introvert or extravert aspects of their child are better able to plan or intervene appropriately.

Parents sometimes worry about their child being content to play by himself. They say, "He would rather stay home and create than play with other children. At school, he would rather read a book than play outside with the group." Gifted children can find peers in the characters in books during alone time. Most of us can remember the immense satisfaction we got as children (and still get today) from burying ourselves in a good book and identifying with the characters and themes.

Alone time is important to many gifted children, particularly introverts. It may even be a necessary part of developing one's abilities. Barbara Kerr's research found that gifted girls who later became eminent as adults shared a common trait—they all seemed to need large amounts of alone time to read or think or follow other pursuits Some gifted children, although quite capable of interactive play, choose to spend substantial amounts of time alone in solitary play, manipulating objects, creating things, or just reading quietly.

Alone time is not necessarily detrimental. For example, the childhoods of actors and musicians, as well as athletes who later become Olympic medalists, are usually far from typical. They spend many hours alone, developing their talents, and are often homeschooled or study with special tutors. They have limited social lives during peak training times or performance events. Many of these children turn out to be reasonably adept as adults, regardless of whether they continue to perform in their talent area. Developing intellectual talent may require similar dedication.

How much alone time is too much? Few gifted children want to be socially isolated. One guideline is to determine whether the child is spending time alone out of choice, or whether it is due to a lack of social skills, an inability to form relationships, or something like anxiety or depression. If a child is regularly able to interact happily with playmates who share interests and abilities, then there is little to worry about—being alone is likely just a preference and not a problem. Many parents can relate to having been at a social event and wishing they were home instead. Even so, if you find legitimate reasons to be concerned about your child's limited social interactions, consider professional consultation and advice.

Peer Comparisons and the Gifted Label

Schools are not only places for learning, but also places for socialization. Children get feedback about themselves, they practice social and behavioral skills, and they learn how they appear to others. They find themselves compared to others outside of their family, sometimes for the first time in their lives. Physical size and skills, social skills, mental skills, and even style of dress are bases for comparisons made by classmates as well as teachers. Soon, gifted children begin comparing themselves with others as they develop their self-concept. If they compare favorably, they feel accepted. If not, they will seek the approval of others, perhaps by hiding talent.

The "gifted" label creates expectations and comparisons. Teachers may see or hear that a child is gifted and immediately think she will perform academically with ease. They assume competence in many, if not all, aspects of school, and the gifted child may also expect easy success. There may be concern that a gifted child will see herself as *better than* others because of her talents and ability. Peer comparisons may lead children who are not labelled 'gifted' to assume that they are somehow less valued. These children may taunt the gifted child with name-calling or some other kind of bullying.

Comparisons lead to self-evaluation, and sensitive gifted children often recognize the differences and seek ways to fit in. In these situations, gifted children experience comparisons with and by other children who may be very different. One anonymous teenager confided, "I have no friends at my school, only acquaintances. All of the smart kids are underachievers who don't understand why I want to study and learn. Everybody else just says how smart I am or calls me a genius (which I am not), and I don't like that. If anyone would talk to me once in a while, they would find out that I am *not* just a quiet little freshman who reads all the time! I have a few true friends, outside of school. They understand me, don't think I'm a genius (because they are smart, too!), and we just have fun together!"

Teacher comments can either feed these comparisons or minimize them. For example, a teacher may decide that he needs to put a gifted child in his place with, "It doesn't matter that you go out twice a week to a special gifted class. You still have to do all the work in my class," or "This should be easy for you; you're gifted." Comments like these foster unhealthy comparisons. In other circumstances, some teachers unwittingly create disharmony and unhealthy competition simply because of the gifted label. "Wait until you see how hard this test is; I doubt any of you smart kids can pass it." Such negative messages and lack of respect are not only frustrating for a gifted child but can also create additional peer difficulties. Modeling healthy respect for all children, including gifted children, minimizes the stress that results from the gifted label.

Peer Pressure

Teenagers are particularly concerned with peer relations, and many of their actions deal with the fundamental question, "Who am I and where do I belong?" Gifted teens often have at least a vague sense that they are different from their classmates, and they are painfully aware of the stereotypes some peers hold about high ability and achievement. They struggle with myths and derogatory comments about their giftedness. Teens themselves write about the social challenges they face simply because they are gifted. These stories about growing up gifted, which are easily found in books and online, can help gifted students understand both themselves and others.

As gifted teens develop, they explore themselves. Don't be surprised if your gifted teenager temporarily camouflages her abilities or chooses friends that you think are not particularly desirable when they are struggling with difficult issues. This can be stressful when parents realize that they cannot necessarily select or limit their child's friendships. They will have apprehension about the child's associations while the child resolves these issues. Parents hope that they have planted the seeds of good judgment and self-worth so the child will decide that being one's own person is more important than indulging a dubious peer friendship. If a parent has reasonably good communications with a teenager, they may be able to raise questions about the value of a specific peer relationship, as well as what costs or disadvantages might be involved. Parents may also want to talk about their own issues with peers at various points in their life.

When peer pressures mount for some gifted children, underachievement can emerge as they struggle with fitting in and balancing that with their desire to achieve. Though they may be pleased and grateful that they are bright, they may also worry that their talents will alienate them from their friends. Our culture is one of conformity, and the farther the student is from the intellectual norm, the more he may have to give up of his "true self" to fit in. The influence of ever-present news and social media has made attitudes and expectations far more homogenized than in previous decades. Pressures to act certain ways or do certain things are always around, and the desire to belong and fit in is one of the biggest reasons for underachievement, both for smart boys and smart girls, because peer values often do not emphasize achievement.

The problem for bright girls was first noted many years ago by columnist Ann Landers, who wrote, "It's not too smart to be too smart—not if you're a girl and you want to fit in." To be popular, girls "should" be nice, sensitive, friendly, passive rather than aggressive, compliant, pretty, and not too bright. Notice how many of these qualifications are irrelevant to academic success or even run counter to characteristics of eminent women. Gifted boys have similar pressures. Some believe they must learn to be self-sufficient, engage in behaviors requiring courage and bravery, strive for dominance, and take care not to show too much warmth, empathy, or dependence on others.

Cultural factors can also be a part of pressures to underachieve. High achieving Hispanic or African American males, for example, may be seen by their peers as "acting too white" and betraying their culture. Being academically successful may mean rejection. If a gifted child is a high academic achiever, her accomplishments may be seen by peers as threatening, since they point out the relative weakness and inadequacy of those who do not achieve as highly. Classmates may criticize the brighter child, creating yet another barrier to gaining acceptance from peers.

It can be difficult for teenagers to develop a sense of self sufficiently strong to refuse to join a peer group that engages in negative, immoral, or destructive behaviors; ; the attraction of camaraderie and social acceptance may be too great to resist. This is especially true for a child with long-standing peer difficulties who yearns to fit in somewhere. In these cases, academics take a back seat. When schools, cultures, and societies value academic effort and achievement, gifted children are better able to show their true selves, gain personal validation, and find peer acceptance.

Bullying

Peer pressure and peer comparisons can fuel bullying. While the stereotype of the nerdy gifted kid (most likely wearing thick glasses and a pocket protector) getting shoved into lockers and having their lunch money stolen has existed for decades, bullying in today's world has evolved. We are much more aware of the subtle bullying by social exclusion, as well as the risk of cyberbullying over social media. But are gifted children and teens more at risk for victimization through bullying?

To have a conversation about bullying, we must consider what bullying actually is. Many behaviors are called bullying when they don't quite fit the definition. Bullying is not the same as an isolated physical aggression incident or an argument that devolves into name-calling between two peers. In order to be considered bullying, the behavior must fit three criteria:

1. It is one-directional, unwanted, aggressive behavior intended to inflict physical, psychological, social, or educational harm.

2. There is a real or perceived power imbalance between the people involved, with a powerful person acting aggressively toward a weaker one. The power imbalance can be characterized by greater physical strength, social status, or intellectual ability (either real or perceived) of the perpetrator than the victim.

3. The aggression is repetitive and occurs multiple times or is highly likely to be repeated.[1]

Bullying and Gifted Children

Are gifted children more likely to be victims of bullying? Gifted children are not exempt from bullying, but research is mixed. Some studies show that gifted students are bullied at the same rate as non-gifted age-mates, while others find that giftedness draws more negative attention, such as teasing and name-calling. [2,3] Still others show that gifted students are no more likely to be either perpetrators or victims of bullying behavior than their classmates.[4]

There are some important considerations related to bullying and gifted children because intelligence can affect how children they react to it. For example, because gifted children often have strong metacognitive and predictive skills, they may be able to hypothesize reasons that explain a bully's motivation, or understand what it feels like to be bullied. This awareness can lead to heightened empathy for everyone involved, intense emotions about the injustice of bullying, or anxiety that they may be the next target, even if they are only a bystander.[5]

Another factor that may influence gifted children's response to bullying is their willingness to advocate for support when bullying occurs. Students are often taught to report bullying behavior to a trusted adult, though many bullying incidents go unreported. Over half of gifted students in one study said they talked to someone about bullying situations *never* or *not often*.[6] Even so, gifted children reported incidents to an adult when they were the targets of bullying behavior at similar rates to their peers, but they *were more likely to disclose to their peers* that the bullying was occurring.[7] Gifted children may be fearful of retribution if they report bullying, or they may have seen that past reports were ignored. Confidence that their reports will be addressed, whether they or someone else is the target, is important, and a solid peer group that can be trusted is a key protective factor against bullying for gifted students.

For mild teasing and put-downs, teach gifted children to ignore or avoid reacting. Being able to "laugh off" or redirect mild teasing can help decrease negative behaviors. Making a joke or responding in an unexpected way can disrupt the pattern, though they will need to be careful not to do so in a negative way, which can perpetuate the cycle. Finding ways to avoid or distract peers who are showing negative behaviors can also help. However, be sure to teach your children how to report more serious incidents of bullying so that they are taken seriously.

Gifted children are not exempt from becoming the perpetrators of bullying behaviors. The gifted child with a quick wit and advanced verbal abilities may easily be able to come up with scathing remarks if they intend to hurt another child. Taking a strengths-based approach can be helpful in this situation. Leveraging the metacognitive skills, sense of fairness, and verbal abilities of a bright child who is tempted to bully will help them take another's perspective and understand the emotions they are experiencing. Some gifted children may not realize they are bullying another child; use explicit instruction to help them understand what bullying is and to realize their position of power in the situation.

Cyberbullying

With the rise of social media, cyberbullying has become a new method for students to target vulnerable peers. Absent the watchful eye of caring adults, it is easy for students to engage in cruel behavior through a text message or a comment on a post. Additionally, the targets of the bullies often feel helpless and uncertain of what to do if there are no bystanders to verify that the bullying took place.

The best protection we can give children from cyberbullying is to be involved with their social media use and educate them about what to watch for and when to share it with an adult. Being a friend, follower, or subscriber on your child's social media accounts gives you a window into their online interactions; it also provides a guardrail for their actions when they know that their parent is part of their online community.

Helping Parents Cope with Peer Pressure

Adults experience peer pressure as well. Parent shaming on social media has become all too frequent. Expectations of "good parenting" and how children "should" act are provided, even when not wanted or expected. Parents of gifted children often get peer pressure through judgmental looks or comments from other parents. "Why are you putting so much pressure on your child to learn to read?" The comment stings, because the parents of the gifted child are *not* teaching their daughter to read. The child is learning on her own from asking questions like, "What is this word?" Yet, parents feel peer pressure and judgment from other parents.

Traits that are normal for gifted children make them stand out when compared to other children their age. When parents of gifted children talk with others about their children, they are often met with disbelief, questions, or criticisms. "*My* child isn't that sensitive. What have you done to make your child so thin-skinned?" "Why do you let your child act in such a rude manner and ask adults so many questions?" "Why doesn't your child play with children her own age?" "Why is he so bossy?" "Don't you think you're spoiling him when you cut the tags out of the backs of all of his shirts and let him wear shorts all the time?" When other adults lack an understanding of the implications of giftedness, they may blame the parent for things that are inherent in the child's nature. Parents may be accused of being overly proud of their children or bragging. Others may comment that the gifted child would play better with other children if only the parent wouldn't talk about his abilities so much. Comments like these can hurt deeply.

Frequent encounters like these can make parenting gifted children a lonely experience. It can be hard to find other parents with whom they can share their child's unusual accomplishments or their own unique parenting experiences. Parents of gifted children often need their own parents for emotional support and encouragement. They need someone to listen and to believe and accept that this is the parent's true experience. Sometimes the peer pressure is so great that one or both parents find themselves wanting their children to be "normal" or "average," or at least not so different from other children. It can be difficult to resist peer pressure from others, and parents need courage—just as gifted children do—to continue to support their children's interests and intensities, whatever they may be.

Practical Solutions

○ *Provide structure.* Parents and teachers, particularly with younger children, can help promote peer relationships by offering structure as well as limits. "You can build LEGO® until lunchtime, and then you can all help make sandwiches." Or "Here are some supplies for your fort, but if it gets too noisy, you'll need to go outside to play." Semi-structured or structured play dates can set clear parameters and increase the likelihood of positive interactions. Making implicit rules explicit can help.

○ *Avoid overscheduling.* The interests of gifted children and their parents' wish to provide plenty of enrichment sometimes lead these children to become so overscheduled that they have little time to develop friendships. When you add up the hours involved each week with homework, music lessons, soccer, Scouts, religious school, and driving to and from each, there is little time left to simply play with friends. Your child might make friends at many of these activities, but what good is it to make friends if there is no time to get to know them?

○ *Change bossiness into leadership.* Some gifted children may not be liked by their peers because they are perceived as bossy or domineering. Gifted children usually don't irritate their peers intentionally. Typically, their new idea or the new game they just invented is so exciting that they blurt it out in a bossy tone without being aware of how the others feel or whether they understand. They may be so intensely involved that they don't notice the others' lack of interest or negative reactions. Others may have no clue about the game or the rules and walk away, saying, "We don't want to play that. We want to play what we played yesterday." Or worse, they say something like, "He's so weird!" to each other as they walk away.

Gifted children can learn to analyze situations and to appreciate the difference between leadership and bossiness. If this enthusiastic, bossy one is your child, you may be able to gently explain that other children may not always want to do the activity that he chooses, and that if he wants to have friends, he needs to listen to what *they* want to do before deciding what they will play. You can suggest that the other children probably don't like to be controlled and bossed around, and sometimes it's fun to let someone else be the leader. Tying in the child's interest to your explanation can increase understanding. Talk about team sports and about how different athletes take on different roles depending on what the team needs. One person leads for a while, then another.

Try to impart to your child that a good leader lets others have ideas and input, doesn't always make all the decisions, and understands that teamwork and alternating leadership roles have value. Delegating, assisting, and facilitating are all important aspects of leadership—the key is to understand when to do which behavior. A good leader usually has more ideas than the others, but she is not so visionary or complex that the others are left far behind.

Talk about the difference between bossiness and cooperation. To illustrate the difference, you can ask your child to give you an order with his bossy tone of voice, and then ask you to do something using a more cooperative, persuasive style. You can ask him to reflect on which style of request he would prefer and why. Help him compare styles.

It also helps to provide outlets for the leadership skills to emerge. At home, you can provide a bossy child a healthy and appropriate way to be in charge. *Super Saturdays*, described in the chapter on communication, can be a way for your child to practice leadership skills. Help your child find other options for leadership and initiative within the community.

○ *Consider special schools or programs.* Special schools or programs for gifted children typically group students by ability as well as by age, and it is more likely that a gifted child will find appropriate peers there. This is not a panacea; gifted children don't always relate well to other gifted children, though the likelihood of peer problems is reduced when one is surrounded by kindred spirits.

○ *Avoid too many comparisons.* Peer relations are not going to be helped if parents or teachers hold up a gifted child's achievement as a model to her peers. Some parents make comparisons to shame a child into changing behavior. Such an approach is probably not as helpful as asking the child how she feels about her behavior.

○ *Put peer pressure in perspective.* Peer pressure is most intense for children during those school years when they are forced into same-age groupings, and it diminishes during college and beyond. It is important to help a gifted child understand that, after graduation, virtually no one cares who was the most popular boy or girl in school. One way of communicating this is by using the following joke adapted from the writings of Dr. Sylvia Rimm:

> Parent: "What do people call a student who studies hard, does extra work, wants to do his schoolwork, and seriously tries to learn lessons from the teacher?"
>
> Child: "Nerd, brainiac, suck-up."
>
> Parent: "What do people call adults who put forth their best efforts, do extra work, enjoy their work, and try to learn new things?"
>
> Child: "Gee, I don't know?"
>
> Parent: "You call them 'boss.'"

Short vignettes like this can help your child understand that academic achievement and *independence from peer pressure* can open doors for the future.

○ *Use bibliotherapy and cinematherapy.* Gifted children can learn more about friendships, tolerating imperfection, accepting friendly pranks, sharing fears and sorrows, keeping secrets, forgiving mistakes, and tolerating idiosyncrasies from reading books and watching movies that address these topics. Seeing these topics through another's eyes can increase a child's insight and enhance peer relationships. Exploring and discussing the characters and their feelings is safely separate from the child's own feelings and can foster understanding in a non-threatening way. With the gifted adolescent and young adult, one effective technique involves using biographies of well-known persons. When selected wisely, these books and stories can send the desired message with less confrontation— increasing the likelihood that the message will be understood. These powerful techniques can help a child develop insight, allowing behavior to gradually change.

CHAPTER 10

Family Relationships:
Siblings and Only Children

Relationships in families with gifted children can be intense. Interactions within the family influence the way one learns to relate and communicate with others as an adult. Parenting styles, too, carry over from one generation to the next, affecting how one parents their own family. These styles tend to vary, depending on whether the adult was an only child or had siblings. While negotiating these relationships, some special issues can arise for gifted children, whether they are an only child or a child with siblings.

Only Children

In some ways, only children and first-born children are alike, perhaps because until a sibling is born, these first-born children *are* only children—sometimes for many years. Only children tend to be independent, often modeling themselves after adults and taking initiative to keep themselves busy. Because they don't have pressure from siblings, they don't have to accommodate themselves to other children, and so they may be nonconformist. Though they may be good leaders, they also are likely to be self-contained in their interests and engage in individual rather than group activities.

When there are two adults in the family, parenting an only child is often easier, and the child receives a great amount of adult attention. Parents can more easily take one child to concerts, libraries, or adult social functions where the child is exposed to sophisticated conversation and activities. The only child may also have easier access to educational opportunities, which helps explain why many high achievers are first-born or only children.

Sibling Competition and Cooperation

A gifted child's intensity naturally affects his relationships with siblings. Gifted children often compare themselves with other children in the household and may even measure their value by the extent of power, attention, and time that they get from their parents. Sibling rivalry and sibling closeness generate distinctly strong emotions. Some parents become quite frustrated with volatile sibling relationships; other parents indicate that sibling relationships are generally pleasant. All families experience periods of conflict and tension, and sibling relationships can certainly contribute to family distress. Fortunately, there are strategies parents can use to reduce stress and minimize bickering, competition, and fighting in the family, which can increase family enjoyment. In their book *Siblings Without Rivalry*, Adele Faber and Elaine Mazlish emphasize, "Our relationships with siblings can have a powerful impact upon our early lives, producing intense feelings, positive or negative.... [T]hese same feelings can persist into our adult relationships with our brothers and sisters [and]...can even be passed on to the next generation."[1] Developing positive sibling relationships early can have lasting beneficial effects throughout one's life.

Better awareness of common sibling behaviors and roles can help us guide our children to less argumentative ways of interacting and toward more and better cooperation. We can model ways for children to handle their differences so that the oldest isn't quite so "bossy" or the youngest quite so "helpless" or "needy" or "whining," and we can use other strategies to foster positive relationships. It helps if we understand some basic family roles, and how those change with the addition of each new family member.

Birth Order and Family Roles

Much has been written about birth order and the "roles" different children in the family take on. Some say the oldest child, the first-born, is usually the highest "achiever" often seen as "bossy" by the others. Some describe the youngest as the attention seeker who performs, is social, or takes the "baby of the family" role. A middle child (or middle children) may feel "squeezed" or neglected but may in the end turn out to be the best adjusted and the most able to get along well with others. While these family roles aren't strictly defined, they are trends that ring true for many families.

First-born children are more likely to be identified as academically gifted.[2] Parents spend more time with the first-born child. They talk to the child, take the child on outings, and generally have high expectations. When a second child comes along, parents have less time to play and interact with the baby and often expect the older child to assume some of the responsibilities, including looking after the younger one(s). Not surprisingly, research shows that most first-born children are serious, dependable, conscientious, and eager for adult approval. They tend to be better organized and more concerned with academic achievement than their younger siblings.

Observations from practicing clinicians suggest that second children are less likely to be identified as gifted, though research shows similar intellectual potential among siblings due to genetic factors and similarity of the family environment, even if a younger child's gifts may not be as obvious. Research indicates that second-born children are usually more focused on peer and sibling approval and are less likely to be concerned with pleasing parents or teachers. Reasons for this are not completely clear, but parents do seem more tolerant in their expectations and less demanding of younger children.

Middle children are often described as strong leaders with excellent interpersonal skills. They are the mediators who settle squabbles. Because they are not the oldest, a middle child does not get equal recognition, and are further displaced when a new baby sibling arrives. They may feel overlooked, and their giftedness may go unnoticed.

Regardless of birth position, competition for status and roles within a family is normal and to be expected. Of course, all children want to be recognized by their parents as special—and unique. They observe their parents carefully to ascertain what is valued, and they watch to see how parents react to their behaviors and those of their siblings. When one child gets a response for a certain behavior, whether appropriate or inappropriate, another may mimic it or try an alternative behavior. Children frequently compare their proficiency in various areas with that of their siblings. Are they equally able to make the parents laugh and smile? Can they play an instrument better? Do they know as much about cars or computers? Are they as athletic? Best in academics? Best at giving directions? These evaluations and comparisons are the beginnings of finding a role in the family and answering questions like, "What do I do well?" or "What do I add to this family?"

Through these comparisons and competitions, whether open or covert, siblings carve out their roles and status. If one child seems to have a firm hold on first place for academics, the next child will often try for first place in another area, such as being more social. Even though a child may have substantial potential in many areas, these roles often become hardened, sometimes quite early. One child becomes known as "the musician," another as "the smart one," another as "the clown," "the social one," or even "the troublemaker." If one child successfully carves out a role, the rest of the family often unknowingly reinforces it by giving special attention to those behaviors.

On the one hand, these differing roles can be good, because they give a child reassurance that he does have a special place. Sometimes special roles flow naturally from a child's own inborn talents, personality, interests, or temperament. Every child will have certain skills that come more easily. On the other hand, roles can be limiting if children mistakenly believe that their roles are "either-or" so that only one child in the family can be special in a particular area. This type of exclusionary thinking risks preventing development in an area, for fear of appearing less competent than a sibling. Because one child is talented in a certain area should not be a reason for other children to refrain from developing that skill as well. If a child enjoys music or gymnastics lessons even though she is not as talented as a sibling, a parent should allow and encourage the lessons to continue.

Roles and status also relate to academic underachievement. Many first-born children who are recognized as "special" within the family become underachievers if that "specialness" is at some point withdrawn, and the distinctive recognition is given to another child. This might occur because of a parent's remarriage and the introduction of step-siblings, or in cases where parents withdraw because they are angry or disappointed with a child, allowing a sibling to claim new status or distinction within the family.

Whatever roles children have, it is possible for a family to nurture a sense of status and importance for each child while simultaneously helping each child explore new skills and roles. Encourage cooperation and discourage fierce and destructive competition while reinforcing the importance of all children and all their talents. If you are a sibling yourself, you know that patterns developed in childhood can be long lasting. At family reunions, you know which sibling will dominate the conversation, which one will complain, which one is in charge and makes all the decisions, and which one is ignored. Family patterns seldom change because roles were well-established after being practiced for many years in many different settings. Although these roles may be uncomfortable for some, the predictability is reassuring for others. When all family members feel valued and accepted, relations are more likely pleasantly predictable, regardless of the roles. When issues and resentment from childhood linger, the relationships may be less pleasant but still predictable.

Understanding Sibling Rivalry

In their classic *Siblings without Rivalry*, Faber & Mazlish describe an interesting awareness exercise that can help parents understand the intensity of their children's feelings about siblings. Try to imagine that one day your partner comes home and says, "Honey, I love you so much, and you are so wonderful and absolutely delightful that

I've decided to get another partner just like you." The reaction could include everything from shock and denial to hurt and rage. The exercise continues with several new scenarios, including having to share clothes or other possessions with the new partner, who is receiving much attention and praise from others as to how cute and wonderful they are. Many adults doing this exercise react with strong feelings, which are no less intense for your children who, because they are children, have even fewer rational and "adult" thinking skills to help them understand family changes.

Sibling rivalry can occur in many ways, but is most often expressed through angry behaviors—selfish or spiteful words or actions, tattling, bullying, disturbing or destroying one another's possessions, criticizing, blaming, embarrassing others, or fighting. Though it is difficult in the moment, parents should try to focus on the underlying reasons for the behaviors rather than on the specific behaviors themselves. Children react strongly when they think a sibling is taking over their place in the family: you can more easily respond calmly to the need, rather than the behavior, if you understand the reasons. This doesn't mean that you should ignore the behavior, though sometimes that can be the best initial course of action; rather, try to ascertain the motivations behind the behavior to determine *how* best to intervene.

Children often compete for something they feel is important— attention, or recognition, or power. Although rivalry isn't accidental behavior, even the children may not be aware of the purpose behind their actions. Gifted children, like all children, need to be recognized as loved, valued, and competent. They compare themselves to their siblings, and sometimes the competition becomes extreme as they assess possible threats and react accordingly. If one sibling thrives in an activity, the other may give up that activity. If one hesitates and shows vulnerability, another sibling may plunge in to demonstrate his excellence. Rivalry can be intense and obnoxious when which children "tattle" or "report" on their siblings, with complaints like, "She's sitting in my chair," "He's looking at me," or "He's breathing my air." They may try to make themselves look better by pointing out the sibling's mistakes and flaws.

The less children feel valued and accepted for themselves and what they do, the more likely they are to be rivals, to compare themselves to one another, and to engage in dramatic measures to gain attention from their parents and power over their siblings. One bright seven-year-old used his advanced vocabulary to demean and torment his little brother, saying, "Ewww! You have 'garments' all over you! I don't want to play with you!" This boy took advantage of his younger brother's limited vocabulary, knowing his younger brother wouldn't understand that he was taunting with empty words.

When a gifted child feels that she is not getting enough attention, for whatever reason, she can be quite skilled at calling attention to herself. She may do this through positive actions, such as acting particularly mature in conversations with adults. Or, she may gain attention in less positive ways, such as asking a stream of questions to keep the adult focused on her. Because most gifted children are very verbal, perceptive, and even shrewd, they may be able to engage adult attention so that a parent spends more time with them and less with the siblings.

Even gifted children who are well-adjusted and feel accepted and valued can be very demanding of adult time and attention. After all, they have many interests and are curious about many things. It is easy for a parent to find herself giving more time and attention to a particular child, especially if the child is exceptionally gifted. Of course, siblings are keenly aware when more attention is given to one child, and it can be quite a challenge for a parent to give equal time. Sometimes one child, because of unusual talent or perhaps a disability, truly does need extraordinary school opportunities, private lessons, or some sort of advanced instruction or tutoring. When a parent finds herself giving extra hours to these specialized but necessary activities, maintaining a balance of attention for all children becomes even more difficult. When imbalance occurs, children will typically inform the parent, sometimes subtly or nicely, and sometimes clearly or harshly. Do not be surprised if the other children complain or engage in disobedient behaviors to get their fair share of attention.

In addition to seeking power through rivalry, gifted children sometimes gain power due to family circumstances. For example, older gifted children can be particularly influential in the family, and some parents—particularly single parents—drift into letting the gifted child be the *de facto* head of the family. The child seems so capable, knowledgeable, and demanding that it is easy to hand over control about what the family will talk about, where to vacation, and even how much money is spent for certain activities. Siblings, though they may acquiesce, are likely to harbor resentment and may withdraw in such cases.

There can be many other reasons for sibling squabbling and rivalry, such as attention-seeking, jealousy or frustration about perceived inequities, discouragement with self or others, or underlying depression. When a child feels left out, lonely, unappreciated, or unfairly treated, you will be able to respond more effectively if you know the motivation and feelings that prompted the behavior. Responding to the underlying motivation helps a parent reaffirm the child's value and place in the family.

A different, though usually less obvious, manifestation of sibling rivalry appears in children who are more passive and dependent. They may mimic the behavior of another sibling if they think that sibling is the favorite. This can be especially true of the older sibling of an infant or toddler who is just learning many new skills. Although the older sibling is also learning many skills, she doesn't get the same kind of praise as the baby learning to crawl or pull himself up, or the toddler learning to talk, run, or climb. The older sibling may revert to behaviors like those the younger child is displaying to get praise, even though she mastered those skills years before. In the reverse, a younger child may try to mimic an older child if he sees those behaviors as more valued. Sometimes a child may even imitate parent behaviors as a way of seeking attention, esteem, and value.

On the one hand, such imitation is desirable; it can be a normal, appropriate developmental phase that helps children learn new behaviors. However, some children who are extreme in their modeling can become almost copies of the other person, stifling their own development. These children are usually insecure in their identity and do not feel accepted or valued for who they are within the family. It is as though they dare not be themselves and must assume another role. For example, an athletic father is proud of the child who does well in sports. Seeing the positive attention athletics brings, the younger sibling tries sports even though they prefer other activities, like playing the clarinet.

Unequal Abilities among Siblings

In most families, the general ability level among siblings will probably be similar. In some families, one or more siblings may have distinctly less overall ability, or they may be gifted but also have a learning disability or other limiting condition. Even when overall ability level among siblings is similar, children may differ dramatically in areas of competence and approach to tasks. These differences are factors in sibling relations, and they also have implications for parent behaviors.

Family history, traditions, or values influence a parent's behavior. Sometimes families value one kind of ability, such as music or math or athletics, above another. Messages about these values can be overt or subtle, but the words, body language, or lifestyle of the family can make a child feel that his unique talent is undervalued. How the parents spend their time, energy, and resources sends a message to the family. The lead author of the first edition of this book, Dr. James Webb, would frequently say, "What a society values, it supports." The same is true for a family. Be aware of your support because you can inadvertently indicate that one talent is more valued than another, if, for example, the family spends hundreds of dollars on one child's activity and barely anything on another's.

Obviously, we do not want children who are less capable in an area to feel less worthy of our attention and love. If children doubt that we value them, they are likely to feel resentful and to express those feelings directly or indirectly. Yet with all the demands of a gifted child, it can be easy to neglect less able children, and gifted children themselves can sometimes be hypercritical of siblings, saying hurtful things like, "She's just stupid!"

Although children may be similar in abilities, they may be quite different in types of intelligence or talent. Parents can highlight strengths as well as weaknesses for all children, raising awareness of differences between siblings while not judging. Strengths, weaknesses, and the asynchronous development of bright children are appropriate topics for discussions about unequal abilities among siblings. Are the abilities unequal in only some areas? Is the "less gifted" child actually *more* able in certain areas? Could the child be a "late bloomer" or one who has not yet had appropriate opportunities to demonstrate talent? It is easy for a parent or teacher to have a narrow view of giftedness and miss a child's special talents. Cast your net wide and look for strengths to foster in many areas. Remember, if your oldest child is gifted, chances are there are others in the family who are also gifted, even if their abilities and talents aren't as obvious, don't fit a specific type of giftedness, or aren't at the same level of giftedness as another child.

If a child does not excel in academic areas and does not qualify as "gifted" academically, perhaps he is especially kind and compassionate toward others, or perhaps he is good leader, talented at soccer, or great at making friends. Look for each child's unique abilities and gifts, and reinforce those strengths by stating your belief that the child is worthy and capable and that you are proud of his abilities. It is important for children's self-esteem that they feel loved, accepted, and capable and that they believe that each child is equally valued within the family.

Role Models

Believe it or not, parents are major role models for sibling behaviors. Think back to your own sibling relationships and how your parents handled them. How do you portray your siblings when you talk to your children? Are you repeating patterns that you learned in your family of origin? Are they ones that you want in your family now? If we want to be effective role models to our children, we should look at our own childhoods to see how they have influenced our adulthood. We may gain insight into the way we currently handle not only our sibling relationships but also our relationships with others. This insight affords us a better chance to be better role models by modifying our beliefs and behaviors to ones that are more helpful to us and our families.

As parents, we want to promote cooperation and teamwork within the family. We don't want children to feel that they need to struggle for power, that they have to act out to get our attention, that they can never be good enough to please us, or that one is valued more than another. By modeling cooperation and positive conflict resolution in our adult relationships with family members and coworkers, we teach cooperation to our children. Perhaps you have friends whose interactions you would like to model. Get to know more about them and their interactions and look for things you can copy and use in your own.

Practical Solutions

○ *Use special time.* Earlier in this book, special time was explained and encouraged; you give each child your undivided attention for at least a few minutes each day. This strategy is particularly useful in preventing or diminishing sibling rivalry when one child feels that she is getting less attention than the others. It lets the child know that she is personally valued. By giving each child special time, you show that you appreciate each child as a unique person.

○ *Set limits.* Make clear to your children any behaviors that will not be tolerated among siblings. No name calling or covert hurtful pranks. Some limits, like no hurting, will be universal and non-negotiable. Others will be more subjective, and your values will determine the limits appropriate for your family. Once limits are set and family rules are clear, intervention is easier and may even be expected.

○ *Foster a comfortable environment.* As a parent, you have a right to enforce the type of atmosphere you want in your home. Setting limits will certainly be the first step. You also have the right to protect your eardrums and your own peace and quiet. For example, "All that noise is hurting my ears. Please use your quiet voices," sends a clear message about expectations for the home.

Take a firm stand against unacceptable behavior but avoid being overly critical and punitive. As we have said earlier, severe and harsh punishment damages your relationship with your child and usually prompts even greater sibling rivalry, ruining your chances of creating a pleasant and comfortable environment. Harsh reactions may induce children to compete even more strongly to reassure themselves that they are at least equal to their siblings, and they often look for more devious methods of sibling rivalry in an attempt to avoid punishment for themselves and induce it for siblings, which then elevates their status. A parent's overreaction can also make children feel guilty, insecure, or less confident that they are accepted in the family.

○ *Avoid (or at least minimize) comparisons.* Many adults still compare themselves with their siblings. "My sisters were smarter and got better grades than I, but I was more social, and I think I get along with people better." "I was the 'nerd' of the family, and I still am." "My brother was a real hellion. I saw the problems he had because he was so stubborn, so I made sure I didn't do the same things." We define ourselves compared to others in the family. How then, can we hope to avoid comparing our children?

Perhaps we cannot completely avoid comparisons, but we can lessen their frequency and become more sensitive to how comparisons affect our children. In addition to not comparing children openly to each other, parents should try to not compare their children when talking with friends, especially when the conversation might be overheard by the children. When you talk about your children with others, please be sure to do it in private. Parents may not realize, for example, that they are evaluating, comparing, and assigning or defining roles by saying things like, "Well, my oldest is 'the student.' She gets A's in everything. My second is 'the social one.' She spends every spare minute with her friends." That parent may have felt they were simply noting differences between the girls, but the child overhearing such talk may interpret it in the worst possible way. "Mom likes [my older sister] better because she gets the good grades." Since the gifted child is already comparing herself with her sibling, when the parent also does it, it may be too much to handle.

When one parent unintentionally identifies more with one child than with another and conveys a sense of favoritism, other children in the family are likely to be distressed. A father might say, "Hannah is so talented in art, just like her grandmother," communicating a not-so-subtle message that Hannah is preferred in some way. Comparing achievements is particularly likely to have negative effects—sometimes on the siblings, sometimes on the gifted child—because it implies an underlying evaluation of personal worth. The important message for parents to convey is that each child is an individual, that they want each child to try to do their best, and that they are not interested in comparisons.

○ *Describe, rather than compare.* Gifted children, like all children, want to be evaluated on *their* actions, not the actions of others, and making this implicit belief very explicit is important. Instead of comparing, simply *describe* what is happening—the behavior you don't like—or *describe* what needs to be done without bringing in another child for comparison. Describe what you *see.* Describe what you *feel.* Describe *what needs to be done.* When the child succeeds, again describe what you see and feel. This states the problem without involving a sibling, deals with it directly, and allows the child to respond directly. Instead of criticizing or comparing the child, you redirected her to the behavior you would prefer, gave her a chance to succeed on her own, and avoided any hurtful comparisons.

○ *When others make comparisons.* Sometimes relatives, neighbors, teachers, or others make careless comments comparing siblings in ways that stir up rivalry. Ask them to avoid measuring one child against another wherever possible, and to do so in private, out of the child's hearing, if they must. Remind them that each child is an individual with unique strengths and weaknesses, and that differences are natural. Of course, you can't always control what others say, and detrimental comparisons will occur. You can counterbalance any harm by again letting the child know that you value his special strengths and abilities. Let him know he is one-of-a-kind and that you appreciate his uniqueness.

○ *Minimize your involvement.* All siblings quarrel, bicker, argue, and fight. We recommend that you ignore bickering unless it escalates to a point where adult intervention is needed because harm or danger might ensue. Children often fight or argue just to get parents' attention, to draw you in, or to get the other sibling in trouble so one child can come out looking better. When you allow yourself to get involved, you are reinforcing the fighting, because you are now giving them the attention they want. If you simply ignore the noise and go about your business, you communicate your belief that this is their issue to solve, not yours, and they are competent to resolve their own issues. You can even say, "I think the two of you can solve this on your own, so I'm not going to get involved." An important part of growing up is learning how to settle disputes and problems, and children can't learn these skills if we always intervene. Younger children may need some modeling or guidance in solving disputes, but even young gifted children can learn to resolve conflicts on their own.

In the earlier chapter on discipline, we described "taking the sail out of the wind." This technique can also be used when siblings are squabbling and trying to draw you into their arguments. When the audience goes away, the bickering usually stops. Take yourself out of proximity of the argument or run the vacuum cleaner to drown out the argument, and you will be better able to ignore it and still be able to keep an eye on the situation in case intervention becomes necessary.

○ *Acknowledge the feelings.* Even when you prohibit a certain behavior, you can recognize and accept the feelings that prompted it. Squabbling and fighting are forms of communication, and feelings are an important part of all communication. If a child can describe the feelings associated with the conflict, or a parent can help the child express the feelings in words, the child gets some immediate relief from the pain and hurt. Observe, identify, and validate the feelings so that the child can then focus better on finding a solution.

○ *Don't take sides.* Generally, it is more effective if you do not attempt to ascertain which child is the instigator or the one primarily at fault. Gifted children can be very adept at quibbling, manipulation, rationalizing, and arguing. It is better to provide a consequence to both children and/or tell them that you are confident they can come up with a reasonable solution. Unless you witnessed the entire scenario, searching for the troublemaker only leads to more conflict, as each child tries to avoid blame or explain a litany of reasons dating back several years. Providing a consequence for each child may decrease future instigation because they learn that it is difficult to get the other into trouble, and regardless, both will have the same consequence.

○ *Teach sharing and problem solving.* Fairness issues arise when siblings share a toy or divide an item. When there is a cookie or pizza slice to be split, have one child divide and give the other first choice. Or if the item is a toy that cannot be split, ask the children to devise a fair way of sharing it. Conveying the expectation that children can solve things themselves is to say, "Boy, the two of you sound really mad at each other!" (Notice and acknowledge their feelings.) "Wow! Two children and only one screen. That's a problem, isn't it?" (Describe the problem.) "Well, I'm sure you can figure something out so you can each have a turn." (Encourage them to solve it themselves.) Then you walk away. Disengaging yourself not only encourages them to solve the problem on their own but also removes your attention, which may be part of what they want.

○ *Expand and highlight the child's roles.* If a child's identity seems strongly linked to a particular role (or roles), expanding the roles can help. For example, parents might gently encourage new interests, or they can simply highlight the different functions and responsibilities the child has during a typical day and how their behaviors add value to the family. Perhaps you may wish to invent new roles or find opportunities for role-reversals. The child who is generally the follower may be assigned the role of the leader for the day. The family "Super Saturday" idea described in Chapter 4 is one easy way to give each child a chance for a leadership role. Parents of a young, introverted gifted child may need to work harder to engage the child in new and different interests. When these role expansions occur, it helps to emphasize your appreciation of them.

In the child's eyes, some roles convey less status than others. Being a talented musician or dancer may not seem as valued as being a star athlete. In such cases, it may be helpful to point out the specific skills involved to show the child that her role has more prestige than she realized.

○ *Treating children fairly does not always mean identically.* "He got more" is a frequent theme at the computer or kitchen table, among other places. For the gifted child, it is an issue of fairness and personal worth. The child who is complaining wants to know that he is valued as much as his sibling, and he therefore deserves the exact same amount of time on the tablet. Asking for a larger portion than a sibling is, in a way, asking the parent to validate some difference the child feels—for example, I am older; therefore, I should get more. When this relates to food, parents are wise to respond the feelings and simply ask, "Are you saying you're still hungry? If so, we have plenty of food." When it relates to computer time or other privileges, having clear limits will help, as some privileges will differ based on age.

In many instances, children need to be treated uniquely and not equally. Suppose you have some chocolate cake, and to be "fair," you divide it into four equal parts for your four children. While this is equal, it isn't fair if one child is on a diet and shouldn't have it, a second is allergic to chocolate, a third doesn't like chocolate, and the fourth is thrilled to have a piece of chocolate cake. We need to respond individually to the four children rather than treating them alike.

As children get older, do they all get the same lessons or other resources? If one is talented in music and wants guitar lessons, we can offer that. Suppose another child has no interest in music lessons of any sort. We wouldn't offer piano lessons "just to be fair." We would we seek other options more consistent with the child's interests.

These examples illustrate the point that in some circumstances, we must treat each child individually because equal treatment is not always appropriate. Look for each child's unique needs based on talents, interests, and abilities. When out shopping, if a parent sees something of particular interest and needed by one child, that parent need not buy something similar or of equal value for the child's sibling. Being clear and consistent with a purposeful approach sends the message to both children that when they need something, the parent will provide it. Instead of giving equally with evenly measured amounts, we encourage parents to think about giving uniquely according to each child's individual needs. Equal treatment means that we give each child what that child needs, not that we give identical items or resources to each child.

○ *Encourage sibling cooperation.* Find ways for the family to work together toward a common goal. Perhaps make a game of saving money for something the family wants. Everyone can invest in both the process and the outcome. Children will learn the value of cooperation, hard work, and a job well done. Each child had an important role, and each role was valuable. Cooperative board games can also be used toward this end, helping each member feel valued, fairly treated, encouraged, and confident, diminishing the likelihood of negative sibling rivalry. Fostering closeness in this way can lead to more periods of cooperation. Respectful cooperation may not change the basic family roles, but the anger, jealousy, and resentment may lessen.

Sibling cooperation is a healthy goal, and wherever possible, encourage your children to appreciate it as vastly superior to rivalry. Some families work hard to recognize and value the importance of not only their own activities and roles, but others' as well, which is certainly more desirable than a family in which children are competitively vying for the parents' attention and the household is in constant chaos. Although people tend to keep the same general behavior patterns throughout life, change *is* possible. But it is easier to change patterns earlier in life rather than as adults, and parental management of early sibling interactions is certainly key.

CHAPTER 11
Gifted Children and School

Since much of a child's life is related to school and schoolwork, it is important to find appropriate educational opportunities for gifted children. There are many factors to consider when determining what type of schooling best fits a gifted child, such as how gifted students are identified and served. Informed parents who know local and state regulations related to gifted students can work with schools in ways that will benefit their child, and they can make better decisions when they understand how schools to identify gifted learners and what services are available.

Identification processes and gifted programs vary considerably in different school districts and in different states. Some schools are mandated to identify and serve gifted students; others are not. There is a myth that gifted children are easily identified because of their talents, and some gifted children do stand out because of their unusual abilities. Others may not be as noticeable, or they may hide their talents to ensure that they don't stand out, and some schools miss gifted children in the identification process. Schools should have specific testing procedures to identify all gifted students, especially those who are traditionally underrepresented in gifted education programs, like twice-exceptional children and children from culturally and linguistically diverse backgrounds. These students may need alternative identification processes to capture their ability and make sure they aren't overlooked.

Once students are identified, it is essential that gifted programs are matched to the identification procedures because there are many different types and levels of giftedness, including academic skill, intellectual ability, visual arts, and creativity. Even though giftedness is not always related to academics, many school-based gifted programs focus on academic skills that can challenge and engage students whose needs are not being met in the general education classroom. This can be problematic, for example, when a student qualifies for a gifted education program based largely on visual arts or creativity, as they may struggle when placed in a program that requires strong reading and writing skills.

Processes Used for Identifying Gifted Students in Schools

Many parents are aware of intelligence tests (colloquially called IQ tests), which are often used to identify giftedness, but there are many other measures used to objectively identify gifted children. Schools use additional information, including checklists, rating scales, work samples, and academic achievement tests in the process. Generally, schools cast a wide net and filter candidates using some combination of the above measures to determine who is eligible.

Group Administered Ability Tests

Historically, students had to be nominated or referred for gifted education testing by a teacher or parent who noticed characteristics of giftedness in their behaviors. However, many school districts have moved away from this model because of implicit biases toward nomination of students who are compliant and verbal, for example. Additionally, parents who do not have the educational or cultural capital to realize they can nominate a student for gifted education services are also at a disadvantage.

Many schools have come to prefer what is called *universal screening*. *All* students are tested at least once to decrease the likelihood that students are overlooked. Universal screening tools, which might include measures of general ability like the Cognitive Abilities Test

(CogAT) and the Naglieri Nonverbal Ability Test (NNAT), are group administered assessments of problem solving and cognitive abilities. Students either qualify for gifted education services or move on to another round of testing based on the results. The cost for universal screening prevents some districts from adopting it, leaving gifted students to rely on parent or teacher nominations or other less equitable practices.[1]

Academic Achievement Tests

Many schools will consider standardized reading or math achievement scores, either in addition to or instead of ability tests, to identify gifted learners. Achievement tests measure what has been learned so far in various academic skill areas. There are statewide tests given annually, along with other benchmark assessments used locally throughout the school year.

Achievement tests, particularly in the early grades, have limitations. Young children may score very high on achievement tests if they have had excellent learning opportunities in the home and are highly motivated; they may earn high scores even when their intellectual ability is only somewhat above average. On the other hand, achievement measures can miss those children who have not had enrichment opportunities before going to school, even though the potential is there.

In some schools, educators are reluctant to identify gifted children before third grade, preferring to wait to see the child's response to the intellectual and academic stimulation that school provides. Some educators believe that, by third grade, children's abilities will "even out," and many of those former high scorers will perform closer to average. Such a delay in recognizing advanced abilities is not beneficial for gifted children who are ready for extra stimulation and who, if appropriately challenged, will remain in the gifted range on achievement tests. If a child enters kindergarten reading at the second-grade level and their scores "even out" by the end of second grade (after *three* years of schooling), it should raise concerns about whether the child was challenged to grow academically. Every child should gain knowledge and show at least one grade level of academic progress and skill development each year, but gifted students will often advance further in a year.

Some gifted children will score well below their actual ability on school achievement tests because: (1) they are not motivated to answer questions in a standardized multiple-choice format, (2) they are too "creative" with the test and are looking for answers with more complexity and originality, (3) the tests emphasize verbal abilities, but the child's skills are in other areas, or (4) the student has limited English proficiency. Some gifted children acknowledge inattentively rushing through group tests to get to a preferred activity (like reading or extra recess) promised upon completion. This often goes unnoticed because testing students in groups prevents individual analysis, resulting in some students not getting services they need.

Another concern about achievement testing for gifted children is the "ceiling" effect. On one commonly used group test, the highest score possible, even if all items are answered correctly, yields a score below typical cutoffs for giftedness at certain age levels. Missing just one item decreases the score markedly because there are simply not enough difficult test items to allow gifted children to show how much they know. Such ceiling effects penalize gifted children, and an "above-level test" that is designed for children who are older is needed to assess skills accurately. Above-level testing can minimize, but not eliminate, ceiling effects, as it compares students to those at higher grade levels to show achievement. For example, a third-grade student might take an achievement test created for fifth graders to measure reading and math abilities compared to students two years above them. High scores on such tests show advanced achievement, indicate the need for above grade level work, and provide data for gifted service planning.

Creativity Assessments

Creativity is more elusive than intelligence. They are of course related, but creativity involves *divergent* thinking, whereas intelligence, especially as measured by current tests, involves *convergent*, traditional thinking and problem solving. Creativity, which is easily spotted in products like paintings or music, is difficult to measure objectively, though some tests attempt to quantify it.

Two early creativity theorists, Guilford and Torrance,[2] described four cognitive creative abilities: fluency, flexibility, originality, and elaboration, which form the basic components of *The Torrance Tests of Creative Thinking*.[3] Test items require students to create *many* ideas (*fluency*), ideas that go *beyond* (*flexibility*), ideas that are *novel and unique* (*originality*), and ideas that *build* on earlier ideas (*elaboration*). The test responses are awarded points based on how well they demonstrate the four creativity markers. The scoring is time-consuming, partly subjective, and usually done by someone professionally trained in the scoring methodology. Due to the time and training needed for test administration and scoring, this test is not commonly used in schools.

Gifted Characteristics Inventories
Schools frequently include teacher or parent ratings of gifted traits when assessing for gifted services. These rating scales describe whether students exhibit characteristics like advanced vocabulary, rapid learning, or abstract problem-solving skills. Making accurate judgments is difficult for both teachers and parents. Limited understanding of giftedness, whether due to lack of training or bias, can affect who is selected. When a student shows inappropriate behavior as a reaction to a mismatched educational placement, characteristics of giftedness may not be observed. Training about giftedness is needed to ensure these measures accurately identify gifted students so they can receive the services they require and deserve.

Individually Administered Intelligence Tests
Intelligence differs from achievement, and tests for them are different as well. Intelligence or IQ tests measure overall cognitive ability and intellectual potential. Individual intelligence tests consist of subtests that assess verbal and nonverbal reasoning, memory, processing speed, abstract thinking, and numerical ability with novel and engaging tasks

that do not allow a child to "guess" their way to high scores. It may take a bright child two or more hours to complete a comprehensive test (although there are abbreviated versions of some tests), and a gifted child's subtest scores frequently show significant peaks and valleys, with scores ranging from average (or even below average) levels to "off the chart" scores that exceed the standard scoring tables. These score variations highlight a gifted child's asynchronous development and may reflect developmental lags or a learning disability, even though the lowest scores are average. Significant differences should not be ignored as they can help parents and teachers engage strengths, accommodate deficits, and manage expectations.

Although overall intelligence scores generally become stable after about age 10 .[4], they may vary from test to test. Tests of intelligence are a snapshot at a given time, and scores can be negatively affected by fatigue, emotional upset, illness, fear of testing, lack of rapport with the test administrator, lack of intellectual stimulation, or other factors. Individual testing allows the examiner to observe and factor any concerns into the process of making an accurate assessment. Intelligence tests provide a wealth of data about strengths, weaknesses, and educational needs to help parents and teachers estimate what can reasonably be expected in academic performance. They are only one measure, but the data they provide can guide academic planning to meet a student's needs. However, a child should not be defined or limited by his IQ score, just as a professional quarterback is not defined only by his completion percentage, or a baseball player by his on-base percentage.

The individual intelligence tests most frequently used by psychologists are the Wechsler series—the *Wechsler Intelligence Scale for Children-Fifth Edition* (WISC-V), designed for ages six and up, and the *Wechsler Preschool and Primary Scale of Intelligence-Fourth Edition* (WPPSI-IV), designed for ages three through seven. The *Stanford-Binet Intelligence Scale-Fifth Edition* (SB-5) and the *Kaufman Assessment Battery for Children-Second Edition* (KABC-2) are among other that are used. Each of these assessments provides a Full Scale IQ score and various composite scores related to verbal ability, visual-spatial reasoning, and abstract reasoning.

Schools should not rely solely on a child's Full Scale IQ to identify giftedness, especially if they are twice exceptional. For example, on the WISC-V, there are subtests that measure working memory and processing speed, and individuals who are neurodivergent may show significantly weaker skills in these areas than others, which can pull down a child's Full Scale IQ score. In these cases, the General Ability Index (GAI) supplemental score, which eliminates the effects of working memory and processing speed, can be calculated from the other WISC-V subtest scores. The National Association for Gifted Children recognizes that the GAI score (or other composite scores) may give a better picture of a child's overall ability, and their position statement on the WISC-V outlines best practices for identification of gifted and twice-exceptional students.

Using Multiple Data Points to Find Giftedness

Use of multiple criteria—teacher ratings, grades, achievement and ability test scores, creativity measures, portfolios of a student's work—is certainly appropriate in searching for gifted children, as is particularly important for finding gifted children who also have other educational needs, like twice-exceptional or culturally or linguistically different students. Unfortunately, the use of multiple criteria has sometimes been misinterpreted as "multiple hurdles," where students are required to meet *all* of the criteria in order to be considered gifted. Using multiple criteria correctly means using various sources of data to provide alternative pathways to identification, [5] not having to cross multiple barriers, thus ensuring that more gifted students are identified and served.

Should You Seek Testing Outside of the School?

After reviewing the entire situation of your child's well-being and behavior both at home and at school, you may decide to seek a qualified private psychologist to conduct a comprehensive assessment of your child. Outside testing by an evaluator knowledgeable about giftedness can be very helpful in determining educational needs and finding gifted resources in your area. Individualized assessment data for a gifted, highly gifted, or twice-exceptional child shows just *how* bright he is in particular areas, and which areas may be problematic. This process highlights unusual abilities, and such evaluations are sometimes needed to convince school personnel that specialized educational services are required, though parents should be aware that some schools don't accept outside tests. Finding qualified gifted examiners can be difficult, and state and national gifted organizations can help.

How Early Can You Do IQ Testing?

While some testing can be done as early as age two, individual intelligence testing is usually more helpful when done around age five, and then again around age 10. By age five, test scores become reasonably predictive and relevant for educational planning. Early identification helps schools create appropriate academic engagement and challenge during this crucial period of learning. Accuracy of test scores increases as children age, and is quite accurate by around age 10.[6], which justifies a second testing that can help plan for middle and high school years. The second test can identify changing needs and additional necessary accommodations like the need for a grade skip or single-subject acceleration. For example, if a fifth-grader scores at the eleventh-grade level in reading and language, the child can be offered single-subject acceleration or other advanced options.

Trust Your Own Observations

As we have noted, identification can be difficult, and some gifted children are overlooked in school. Even when parents obtain testing outside of the school, they may meet administrative resistance. Parents report schools saying, "The only score we accept for entry into our gifted program is our own." It is frustrating to advocate for your child and run into such roadblocks, and parents should remember that their own observations and judgments are also valuable. Parents know their child more intimately than a test score can describe. Some gifted children will not always demonstrate their abilities through school achievement, and the NAGC definition of giftedness allows for the *capability* to perform at high levels, regardless of achievement. As a parent, you do not need to depend solely on school personnel to determine whether your child is gifted. Trust your observations, and if necessary, seek outside assessment to determine what is best so that you can advocate for your child's special needs.

School Provisions for Gifted Children

Most classroom teachers receive little to no training about gifted children—their traits, their needs, how they differ from others, how they learn, or how to organize classroom experiences for them. Most states don't require giftedness training to earn a teaching certificate. Even trained teachers find barriers to adequately challenging gifted children. They may be so busy with the demanding needs of struggling students or those with behavior problems that the brighter students just "slide."

Gifted children need challenging work, just like their peers. We all need to struggle, ask for help, and get things wrong to learn persistence and develop confidence. Being in an environment where everything comes easily can create unhealthy beliefs about what it means to have to work to achieve, earn the approval of others, and when it is okay to self-advocate. Gifted students who are now adults report that they *never* had to study until they reached high school and took advanced classes like geometry, chemistry, or calculus. Some "slid through" until college, graduate school, law school, or medical school. When they finally reached a class in which they had to study, they had trouble because they were so accustomed to breezing through without opening a book. Overcoming these habits in college can be a difficult task.

Fortunately, there are well-trained and dedicated teachers who work effectively with gifted students and seem to have an intuitive understanding of gifted children, probably because they are gifted too. While most schools resist allowing parents to request a specific teacher, many consider a specific child's needs when placing them (especially in the younger grades). Parents can let administrators know what type of teacher will help their child flourish, and perhaps they can enlist the help of a current teacher to describe a child's educational needs to future teachers.

Programming Options for Gifted Children

Differentiation of curriculum and instruction. Teachers plan, organize, and provide different content, methods, and materials for the different levels of learners in their mixed-ability classrooms. A teacher who modifies the content, process, or product of the curriculum for students is "differentiating" instruction to meet the different student needs within the classroom. Careful thought and planning allow each of the various groups to be engaged while the teacher works with one group or another. A designated gifted program allows more appropriate accommodation because the range of differentiation is not as large as in a regular classroom with a wider range of student abilities.

Enrichment. Enrichment is modified instruction that can include exposure to new ideas, an extension of topics in the regular curriculum, or exploring a concept in more depth. Horizontal enrichment explores material related to the standard curriculum, and vertical enrichment involves more advanced work. Enrichment means adding breadth or depth to the curriculum being studied, not just extra work. If children are learning about medieval castles in Europe, they might also learn about gradual changes in the construction of castles as new weapons were developed to attack castle walls. A broad concept like "change" will add breadth and depth to any unit of study, because change occurs in all areas. How did castles change over time? What brought about these changes? What things in today's society have changed as a result of new developments? Questions like these involve students in higher-level thinking and make learning more interesting for gifted children.

Some enrichment may be offered as a supplement to regular classroom experiences. For example, following an assembly dance performance given for the whole school, a few gifted students might explore the area in greater depth by studying choreography or dancer training methods, or by choreographing their own dance.[7] Enrichment also happens at special Saturday classes, summer programs, intersession exploratory topics, or special interest clubs.

In some schools, the gifted program is primarily enrichment through a "pull-out" or "send-out" program. Students leave their regular classes and meet with other gifted students and a specially trained teacher. These programs extend what is taught in the regular classroom; the gifted specialist may collaborate with the regular teacher to develop challenging work for the students in their regular classroom as well. In this model, the gifted child spends most of the time in the regular classroom.

Pull-out programs work best when the regular teacher is supportive and does not insist that students complete all work missed. Some classroom teachers avoid introducing new concepts during the time that students are attending the gifted education program and use the time to review concepts with the remaining students. Twice-exceptional students might have additional difficulties if they miss instruction or work time while attending the gifted program.

Despite limitations, pull-out programs are still popular and are the most widely used educational option for gifted students. They offer at least a once-a-week opportunity to interact with other gifted children and provide emotional and interpersonal support. Though pull-out programs may be just a few hours per week, they are better than nothing. Gifted students often enjoy them, describing these days as their favorite part of the week.

Cluster grouping. Cluster grouping refers to placing a small group of gifted students within a single general education classroom. It is cost-effective for schools, since no "additional" teacher needs to be hired. If there are four second-grade classes in a school and each class containing 25 students is sprinkled with a few gifted students, then the gifted students can be placed in a "cluster group" with the second-grade teacher who has the most training in working with gifted children. The benefit of clustering for teachers is that it allows them to differentiate for a group of students, making planning more efficient for all teachers on the team. The students can interact with one another and feel free to be themselves. When placed in a class with no other students who are like them, they may feel isolated and camouflage their abilities.

Whole-Grade Acceleration (Grade Skipping). The term "acceleration" describes the practice of moving a student ahead one or more grade levels to be in a more advanced and appropriate curriculum. According to the National Association for Gifted Children, acceleration strives to match the pace of instruction to the student's ability by providing appropriately challenging material while also reducing the time students spend completing traditional schooling.

Whole-grade acceleration includes early entrance to kindergarten, skipping a grade (being promoted from second to fourth grade), or moving mid-year to the grade above. Although research shows acceleration to be beneficial for gifted students, many educators have a personal bias against all forms of acceleration, convinced that students should stay with their age group. But research from the Belin-Blank Center at the University of Iowa shows that acceleration of gifted students can be an inexpensive, easy-to-implement, and an equitable option to ensure that bright students are challenged.[8] Studies show that students who were accelerated, whether through early entrance, grade skipping, telescoping of the curriculum, or early entrance to college, enjoyed and benefited from their experiences.[9] Acceleration has more research support than many academic interventions, even though it is implemented less frequently.

Many schools use the *Iowa Acceleration Scale* to help educators and parents determine when acceleration is appropriate. It includes specific conditions when acceleration should never be used, and its question-and-answer format allows families and educators to systematically consider factors that research has shown to be important in successful early entrance or whole grade skipping.[10] This tool considers ability, achievement, social, and emotional components of a student's development to determine if they are a candidate for grade acceleration.

Subject Acceleration. Subject acceleration benefits students in their area of special strength. Math, for example, lends itself well to subject acceleration because the progression through the topics is linear, at least through middle school. Math can be difficult to differentiate within a regular classroom for a student who has already mastered grade level content. Subject acceleration allows the student to attend an advanced class to learn new material. Subject acceleration creates a logistical challenge when a gifted student misses instruction in one class while attending an advanced class, but this obstacle can be overcome with supportive teachers or alternative solutions like online learning courses.

Advanced Placement classes. Bright high school students who plan to attend college can participate in Advanced Placement (AP) program offered through the American College Board. More than 30 specific course areas are available, including History, Physics, Chemistry, English Literature, Calculus, Art History, Spanish, and Music Theory. These classes are designed for students in need of academic challenge and offer an opportunity to study college material while still in high school. The students sit for standardized nationwide exams in May. They might receive college credit, advanced standing, or both, with many colleges and universities. Some students earn college credit for as much as one or two semesters.

International Baccalaureate. The International Baccalaureate (IB) diploma program is a rigorous program for high ability students in grades 10 through 12. The IB diploma is highly regarded by elite colleges and universities throughout the world. Initially, the program served children of ambassadors and others living abroad. Now, many schools are authorized to participate, and different programs are offered in elementary and middle schools as well. In high school, students are required to complete an extensive original research project; write a 4,000-word Extended Essay; take a Theory of Knowledge course; complete a project based on creativity, action, and service; and meet international achievement standards in six subject areas to receive an IB diploma. High level achievement is expected, including mastery of a second language. Schools and districts that offer the IB program must agree to the rigorous course standards and may need additional equipment for the required hands-on experiments in biology, chemistry, and physics.

Other Schooling Options

Charter schools. Charter schools developed in some states to provide parents with a non-parochial alternative to public education. They are state funded and nearly always smaller than public schools. Parents who believe their child's needs are not being met in public school appreciate the smaller classes and increased teacher interaction promised in these schools.

Private and parochial schools. Although private and parochial schools face some of the same problems as public schools, they may have smaller classes and a larger per-student budget because tuition is paid by families. Parents should be aware that these schools can be selective about which children they accept and can refuse to serve students with special psychological or cognitive needs. Many of these schools pride themselves on their rigorous curriculum; however, parents should do their homework when searching for the right school. Smaller schools may have fewer resources available for twice-exceptional students. Also, unless the school specifically provides service for gifted students, bright children may find themselves with few opportunities to learn with other children of their same ability-level.

Special schools for gifted students. Medical schools, law schools, and other graduate schools are specialized schools with specific entrance requirements for young adults. To serve school-age gifted students, there are similar independent, private schools specialized to serve the needs of gifted learners. Magnet schools, for example, have been created to focus on a specialty area or to try to attract children who are motivated or talented in a specific area. Such schools offer individualized work or advanced work in small classes with other gifted students, and teachers who understand giftedness and its implications for learning. Most have strict entrance requirements or criteria, and some have extensive waiting lists as well.

Homeschooling. There are increasing numbers of families educating their gifted and talented children at home because their child's unique needs do not match the education offered in public or private schools. There are various models of homeschooling, and it is important to find the fit that is right for your child. Gather as much information as you can so you know what to expect and how to plan; it is important to know the local and state requirements for homeschooling. Homeschooling is a full-time job and can be difficult. Consider the changing parent-child relationship and explore how to ensure social interaction opportunities as you determine whether homeschooling is a fit for you. Documentation is important, especially with so many more colleges using more personalized, test-optional admissions procedures. Colleges report great success with homeschool students, finding them to be self-motivated, disciplined learners with good social skills. Some college planning services provide specialized help for homeschoolers to prepare for success at the college level.

Advocating for Your Child

Parents are often frustrated or angry that their child's educational needs are not being met and that their child is becoming discouraged about school. If you are such a parent, you will need to be well-informed, positive, and persistent when dealing with schools. Know local and state regulations, understand your child's needs, and be prepared to provide evidence for their abilities. You will achieve far better results if you approach the school in a collaborative spirit rather than with anger.

When you negotiate an education plan for your child, be aware of the proper "chain of command" and protocol for talking to school staff. A parent should initially talk to the child's teacher to resolve the problem at the local school level. If necessary, the parent should then go to the principal, then perhaps to the gifted educational coordinator for the district, or perhaps also the school psychologist. Do not complain to the school superintendent or a school board member unless you have tried to resolve the issue at each of the lower levels first. You don't want to "go around" the teacher or the principal; you want them on your side. Go to higher authorities only if you don't get help from the teacher and the principal. If you do go to a higher authority, the first question they will ask is whether you have already talked to the teacher or the principal about your concern.

Trying to change school attitudes, policies, procedures, or funding is a difficult and lengthy process. Several years of planning are usually necessary to implement a gifted program. However, there are communities where parent advocates have succeeded in making these kinds of changes. But it takes more than one parent; it takes a group of parents working together. In states where there is a mandate for gifted education, parents can initiate legal action or request mediation, but this is time-consuming and tedious. By the time the school changes, your child may have experienced several years of insufficient progress.

CHAPTER 12
Finding Support and Help

Because your child is different, you will probably feel like you have to rely on yourself—more than most parents—to decide what parenting actions are most appropriate. You cannot always depend on common practices of child-rearing or even guidance from professionals such as educators, psychologists, or physicians, since so few of them have had any training related to the characteristics and needs of gifted children, or how to deal with issues that affect their families. You should consider their advice, but sometimes you will need to make decisions for your child that others may question. As we have discussed earlier, your child may show uneven development, may be sensitive to sounds, or may need to be accelerated in mathematics. As the parent of an exceptional child—a child with special needs—you may have to expend more energy and time attending to your child's needs. You are also likely to get unsolicited advice from many sources, including your child, suggesting how you could do a better job of parenting.

Even your daily experiences may be quite different from those of your friends and neighbors. One parent of a gifted boy complained that she was tired of her child's continual questioning and verbal challenges. She said it seemed as if he was already a skilled attorney, noting every loophole and exception. With keen powers of observation, intensity, and strong personalities, these children often have a big impact on their families. As one mother said, "I'm not a pushy parent; he's a pushy child!"

Parents can't always easily talk to other parents or professionals. It is hard for people who don't have experience with giftedness to comprehend the complex issues involved. If you discuss examples with others, they may think you are exaggerating. They simply cannot believe that gifted children could do and say the things that their parents describe. It is understandable why parents of gifted children say they tell very few friends about their child's accomplishments, and often feel it necessary to downplay their child's abilities. Families with gifted children may even find it hard to socialize with other couples or families if the children in those other families don't share the same interests.

Former President of the American Psychological Association (APA), the late Dr. Ronald Fox, once said, "There are two kinds of people—those with problems, and those you don't know well enough yet to know what their problems are." Each of us finds ourselves struggling at some point. Some parents, like their gifted children, are hesitant to ask for help, but finding appropriate support and guidance is necessary.

Gifted children often need counseling and guidance in three areas: academic planning and career opportunities; personal and social concerns with their families, peers, or teachers; and specialized outside-of-school experiences. While parents and teachers can provide some guidance to gifted children, they may need professional help, though when and how to find it can be challenging. It is important to find a psychologist or counselor who understands giftedness and its implications, someone who can discern atypical behaviors that can be explained by giftedness from those indicating a behavioral disorder.

Consult with Other Parents

Preventive guidance is certainly the best, whether it is from professionals during routine office visits or from other sources. Sometimes the most helpful advice comes from other parents of gifted children. You may worry about whether your child's experiences are normal, whether you are providing adequate stimulation, how you should react to the exhausting intensity that your child shows, or how you might avoid power struggles. Conversations with other parents of gifted children can provide you with new perspective on a child's behaviors and a variety of coping strategies that they may have tried. Parents are often amazed at how similar the issues are, at home and at school, for all gifted children. They can help reassure one another that things may not be as "strange" or "bad" as they seem. There is often a sense of relief in finding other parents who have had the same issues and concerns and who may be able to recommend an appropriate professional.

Parenting a gifted child is far less lonely when one finds another parent with whom to share concerns and successes. While it can be difficult, parents can find other parents of gifted children through their child's school, through their state gifted association, or by contacting organizations like the National Association for Gifted Children (NAGC) and Supporting Emotional Needs of Gifted (SENG). Online resources are growing, and there are discussion and support groups specifically developed for parents of gifted children, such as the SENG Model Parent Groups.

Find Mental Health Professionals

Parents of gifted children might choose to seek mental health guidance. Consultation, assessment, preventive maintenance, and/or therapy can all be useful in managing the challenges that come with giftedness. Parents might seek therapy for themselves to be more effective parents; they may have unexplained issues related to their own unsupported gifted traits. Counseling can help them accept and understand themselves better, improve their relationships, and make them better parents for their gifted child.

Parenting gifted children involves challenging interpersonal interactions and intense, constantly changing emotions. How does one know when to seek professional help? Watch for changes in behavior or sleep patterns, decreases in motivation or curiosity, or fluctuations in school performance. Emotional withdrawal, abrupt secrecy, a loss of interest in a previously enjoyed activity, or an unusual reluctance to try new things are other signs of concern. Find gentle ways to communicate about such things. If communication fails and problems persist for more than a few weeks, or if you detect anxiety or depression, it would be wise to find a professional for clarity, reassurance, and guidance.

Introducing young gifted children to the counseling process early can normalize the experience and reduce the perceived stigma of mental health services. Counseling can help gifted children understand their behaviors and reactions and learn to modify them when needed. With a positive therapeutic experience, you normalize seeking help, increasing the likelihood that your child will seek support and assistance when needed as an older child or adult. Counseling should involve clear questions and goals, as well as an understanding that parents will be an active part of the process, especially with younger children. Consider the cost an investment in making things better for everyone. An appropriate early intervention will increase the likelihood of a positive outcome for all.

While many behaviors can be changed with counseling, medication is sometimes appropriate as well. A child should not be given medication unless it is needed, and thorough evaluation is essential to determining whether medication is truly needed. Medication should not be prescribed to "treat" gifted behaviors such as intensity, curiosity, divergent thinking, or boredom with an educationally inappropriate placement. If medication is used, parents should be aware of possible side effects.

The benefits of effective counseling are often worth the effort and cost of arranging it. Parents appreciate the professional guidance and recommendations offered by experts. You may find a professional who not only understands the needs of gifted children, but who also learns the needs of your family. A good therapist is a resource that doesn't end. This professional can become a guide, advocate, and anchor point for you and your family well into the future.

Seek Psychological Evaluation

Earlier, we discussed the utility of individual assessment for giftedness, such as intelligence and achievement testing, in advocating for educational services. When gifted children are struggling with possible mental health concerns, formal psychological evaluation can provide additional data to help clarify the situation, whatever may be occurring. There are many good reasons for testing a gifted child—evaluation of depression or anxiety, diagnosis of a learning problem such as dyslexia, intellectual and achievement testing for school placement issues, or assessment for possible problems such as ADHD or autism. When needed, testing should be done by a specialist who has experience with gifted children. Inexperienced professionals, though they may be quite skilled in testing generally, will not be aware of the many issues that can confound test results of gifted children or will not know the implications of the results. Accurate test results, clear interpretation, and appropriate recommendations are important for access to special programs and appropriate educational services.

A good assessment should answer the parents' questions and provide specific recommendations to address the concerns. It should also direct parents toward appropriate resources. For example, individual intelligence and/or achievement testing can help determine whether a child is gifted; assist in educational planning for children already identified; reveal information about strengths, weaknesses, and preferred learning styles; and clarify what is appropriate for others to expect from the child. If requested, evaluations should provide information about any diagnosable conditions. Following assessment, results and recommendations will be explained to the parents.

After assessment by a knowledgeable professional, most parents feel that they have a better understanding of their child, and they find the evaluation well worth the cost. With new and improved understanding and data, parents are better able to get their children appropriate and needed interventions. It is a good idea to have a re-evaluation in two or three years to monitor progress.

Find the Right Professional

Along with understanding giftedness, the relationship between a child and a mental health professional is paramount. Organizations like SENG and NAGC have resources to help parents ask potential clinicians the right questions about their background and experience with gifted children and families to facilitate a connection. Local gifted organizations may also have resources. Online counseling is expanding, and some states have agreements to allow clinicians in other states to provide video teletherapy, which can greatly expand the list of appropriate professionals. If you have difficulty finding a qualified counselor or healthcare professional who is knowledgeable about gifted children, you may be able to find a well-trained counselor or psychologist who is at least receptive to learning about gifted children and adults, and that is usually sufficient. The counselor, psychologist, psychiatrist, or pediatrician might be willing to learn about gifted individuals through continuing education courses for mental health professionals, like those offered though the American Psychological Association and SENG.

Too often, well-meaning but uninformed professionals believe that giftedness can only be an asset, never a liability. Unfortunately, some parents have found clinicians who have little interest in giftedness or insist on "taking giftedness out of the equation" while addressing the other or "real" problems. This approach is not only inadequate but potentially damaging. Although a child's giftedness is rarely the entire issue that prompts professional intervention, it must be factored into the process. Without doing so, issues are less likely to be completely resolved. Giftedness is a fundamental part of a child's development and is as important as knowing about the child's general health. Just like you can't buy pants without knowing how tall a child is, you can't work well with a gifted child without acknowledging and understanding giftedness.

When undertaking counseling, start on a trial basis to see if the counselor's approach and style fit with your family's needs because a good relationship contributes to a positive outcome. Clinicians have different approaches, and a very competent psychologist may have a personal or professional style that simply doesn't match. Mental health clinicians who work well with gifted children and adults tend to be flexible, open to questions, smart, creative, resilient, and skilled in avoiding power struggles. If you are uncomfortable with the initial meeting, findings, or recommendations of a professional, or if the professional has not considered the influence of giftedness, consider getting a second opinion.

Second opinions have been accepted for a long time in medicine, and they are also appropriate in both psychology and education.

Expect Growth

Not all parents of gifted children will need professional help. Not all gifted children will struggle, but some will and finding caring others who can help them understand themselves is necessary for growth and development. The most immediate and important assistance comes from family and from a sense of support and belonging. As a parent, you will strive to create that environment from the moment your first child arrives. As they grow, you will seek educational experiences for your child that are appropriately challenging and enriching. Your relationship with your child and the relationships both within the family and outside of it will be significant in helping your gifted child grow and mature into a healthy adult. Giftedness can be an asset toward growth, but when not understood or addressed, it can cause problems with family, education, and social relationships. Finding support from family and professionals, when necessary, will help your relationship with your gifted child grow, thrive, and last a lifetime.

Endnotes

Preface

1 Strip, C. A., & Hirsch, G. (2000). *Helping gifted children soar: A practical resource for parents and teachers.* Scottsdale, AZ: Great Potential Press.

2 Betts, G. (2018). *Whole Gifted Child Task Force: National Association for Gifted Children.*

3 George, C. (2019). *10 Challenges You May Not Know Your Gifted Child is Facing:* National Association for Gifted Children Blog.

4 Stanley, T. (2018). *10 Myths of Gifted Children: GED Circuit.*

5 Gottfried, A. W., Gottfried, A. E., Bathurst, K., & Guerin, D. W. (1994). *Gifted IQ: Early developmental aspects.* (The Fullerton Longitudinal study). New York: Plenum Press.

Rinn, A. N. (2020). The social, emotional, and psychosocial development of gifted and talented individuals. Routledge.

Ruf, D. A. (2005). *Losing our minds: Gifted children left behind.* Scottsdale, AZ: Great Potential Press.

Silverman, L. K. (1993). *Counseling the gifted and talented.* Denver, CO: Love.

Webb, J. T., & Kleine, P. A. (1993). Assessing gifted and talented children. In J. L. Culbertson & D. J. Willis (Eds.), *Testing young children: A reference guide for developmental, psychoeducational and psychosocial assessments* (pp. 383-407). Austin, TX: Pro-Ed.

Webb, J. T., Meckstroth, E. A., & Tolan, S. S. (1982). *Guiding the gifted child: A practical source for parents and teachers.* Scottsdale, AZ: Great Potential Press.

6   Peters, D. (2016). *The Art of Parenting:* Dr. Dan's Blog.

Introduction

1   Roeper, A. M. (1995). *Selected writings and speeches.* Page 142. Minneapolis, MN: Free Spirit Press.

2   Haydon, Kathryn. (2016). *The Importance of Parent Intuition and Observation in Recognizing Highly Creative Children.* NAGC's Parenting for High Potential magazine.

3   Glynn, Jennifer. (2020). *Cooke-ing Excellence Through Research.* Jack Kent Cooke Foundation, National Asssociation for Gifted Children Blog.

Chapter 1

1   Johnson, S., Makel, M., Bilash, M., Breedlove, L., Foley-Nicpon, M., Peters, S., Rinn, A., Shah-Coltrane, S., Trotman-Scott, M. F., Webb, J., & Worrell, F. (2019). Key considerations in identifying and supporting gifted and talented learners: A report from the 2018 NAGC definition task force. https://doi.org/https://www.nagc.org/sites/default/files/Position%20Statement/NAGC%20Gifted%20Definition%20Task%20Force%20Report%20(3-2019)(2).pdf

2   Plomin, R., & Deary, I. J. (2014). Genetics and intelligence differences: Five special findings. *Molecular Psychiatry, 20*(1), 98–108. https://doi.org/10.1038/mp.2014.105

3   Krapohl, E., Rimfeld, K., Shakeshaft, N. G., Trzaskowski, M., McMillan, A., Pingault, J.-B., Asbury, K., Harlaar, N., Kovas, Y., Dale, P. S., & Plomin, R. (2014). The high heritability of educational achievement reflects many genetically influenced traits, not just intelligence. *Proceedings of the National Academy of Sciences, 111*(42), 15273–15278. https://doi.org/10.1073/pnas.1408777111

4   Nisbett, R. E., Aronson, J., Blair, C., Dickens, W., Flynn, J., Halpern, D. F., & Turkheimer, E. (2012). Intelligence: New findings and theoretical developments. *American Psychologist, 67*(2), 130–159. https://doi.org/10.1037/a0026699

5   Miller, E. M., Matthews, M. S., Dixson, D. D., & Mammadov, S. (2022). In *The development of the high ability child: Psychological perspectives on giftedness* (pp. 130–150). essay, Routledge, Taylor & Francis Group.

6   DeYoung, C. G., Quilty, L. C., Peterson, J. B., & Gray, J. R. (2013). Openness to experience, intellect, and Cognitive ability. *Journal of Personality Assessment, 96*(1), 46–52. https://doi.org/10.1080/00223 891.2013.806327

7   Piechowski, M. M., Silverman, L. K., & Falk, R. F. (1985). Comparison of intellectually and artistically gifted on five dimensions of mental functioning. *Perceptual and Motor Skills, 60*(2), 539–549. https://doi. org/10.2466/pms.1985.60.2.539

8   Winkler, D. (n.d.). Giftedness and overexcitability: investigating the evidence. https://doi.org/10.31390/gradschool_dissertations.3543

9   Adapted from Clark, B. (2002). *Growing up gifted* (6ᵗʰ ed.). Upper Saddle River, NJ: Merrill Prentice Hall and Seagoe, M. (1974). Some learning characteristics of gifted children. In R. Martinson (Ed.), *The identification of the gifted and talented* (pp. 20-21). Ventura, CA: Office of the Ventura County Superintendent of Schools.

10 KenVinton, personal communication (1999).

Chapter 2

1   Seale, C. (2019, September 3). Equity Does Not Mean Everyone Gets Nothing: There's a Better Way to Address New York City's Gifted Gap. *The 74 Million*. Retrieved October 1, 2022, from https:// www.the74million.org/article/equity-does-not-mean-everyone-gets-nothing-theres-a-better-way-to-address-new-york-citys-gifted-gap/.

2   Grissom, J. A., & Redding, C. (2016). Discretion and disproportionality. *AERA Open, 2*(1), 233285841562217. https://doi. org/10.1177/2332858415622175.

3   Davis, J. L. (2010). *Bright, talented, & black: A guide for families of black gifted learners*. Gifted Unlimited.

4   Ford, D. Y., Grantham, T. C., & Whiting, G. W. (2008). Another look at the Achievement Gap. *Urban Education, 43*(2), 216–239. https:// doi.org/10.1177/0042085907312344

5   Davis, J. L. (2010). *Bright, talented, & black: A guide for families of black gifted learners*. Gifted Unlimited.

6   Bonner, L., Hicks, J., & Pennie, G. (2019). Recreating community among gifted African American students through Group Counseling. *The Journal for Specialists in Group Work, 44*(4), 271–285. https://doi.org/10.1080/01933922.2019.1669752

7   Grantham, T. C., & Ford, D. Y. (2003). Beyond self-concept and self-esteem for African American students: Improving racial identity improves achievement. *The High School Journal, 87*(1), 18–29. https://doi.org/10.1353/hsj.2003.0016

8   Allen, M. S., & Walter, E. E. (2018). Linking big five personality traits to sexuality and sexual health: A meta-analytic review. *Psychological Bulletin, 144*(10), 1081–1110. https://doi.org/10.1037/bul0000157

9   Warrier, V., Greenberg, D. M., Weir, E., Buckingham, C., Smith, P., Lai, M.-C., Allison, C., & Baron-Cohen, S. (2020). Elevated rates of autism, other neurodevelopmental and psychiatric diagnoses, and autistic traits in transgender and gender-diverse individuals. *Nature Communications, 11*(1). https://doi.org/10.1038/s41467-020-17794-1

10   Sedillo, P. J., & Chandler, K. (2022). The Why, Who, What, Where, and How for this Under-identified Underserved Population. In J. Castellano (Ed.), *Identifying and Serving Diverse Gifted Learners Meeting the Needs of Special Populations in Gifted Education* (pp. 68–90). essay, Routledge Taylor & Francis Group.

11   Shapiro, E. (2021, October 15). De Blasio to Phase Out N.Y.C. Gifted and Talented Program. *New York Times.*

12   Kircher-Morris, E. (2022). *Raising twice-exceptional children: A handbook for Parents of Neurodivergent Gifted Kids.* Routledge, Taylor & Francis Group.

13   Webb, J. T., Amend, E. R., Beljan, P, Webb, Kuzujanakis, M., Olenchak, F. R., & N. E., Goerss, J., (2016). *Misdiagnosis and Dual Diagnoses of Gifted Children and Adults: ADHD, Bipolar, OCD, Asperger's, Depression, and Other Disorders* (2nd Edition). Scottsdale, AZ: Great Potential Press.

     Kaufman, S. B. (2018). Twice Exceptional: Supporting and Educating Bright and Creative Students with Learning Difficulties. Oxford University Press.

14   Silverman, L. (2019). *General Resources.* Gifted Development Center. Retrieved July 31, 2022, from https://www.gifteddevelopment.org/general

15   See, for example, Robinson, N. M., & Olszewski-Kubilius, P. A. (1996). Gifted and talented child: Issues for pediatricians. *Pediatrics in Review, 17(12)*, 427-434.

Silverman, L. K. (1997a). The construct of asynchronous development. *Peabody Journal of Education, 72(3-4)*, 36-58.

16   See Silver, S. J., & Clampit, M. K. (1990). WISC-R profiles of high ability children: Interpretation of verbal-performance discrepancies. *Gifted Child Quarterly, 34*, 76-79; Sweetland, J. D., Reina, J. M., & Tatti, A. F. (2006, Winter). WISC-III Verbal/Performance discrepancies among a sample of gifted children. *Gifted Child Quarterly, 40(1)*, 7-10; Gilman B. & Peters, D. (2018). Finding and Serving Twice Exceptional Students: Using Triaged Comprehensive Assessment and Protections of the Law in Kaufman, S. B. (Ed.) *Twice Exceptional: Supporting and Educating Bright and Creative Students with Learning Difficulties.* Oxford University Press; Amend, E. R. (2018). Finding Hidden Potential: Toward Best Practices in Identifying Gifted Students with Disabilities in Kaufman, S. B. (Ed.) *Twice Exceptional: Supporting and Educating Bright and Creative Students with Learning Difficulties.* Oxford University Press.

17   Maddocks, D. L. S. (2018). The Identification of Students Who Are Gifted and Have a Learning Disability: A Comparison of Different Diagnostic Criteria. Gifted Child Quarterly, 62(2), 175–192. https://doi.org/10.1177/0016986217752096

18   Kircher-Morris, E. (2021) *Teaching twice-exceptional learners in today's classroom.* Free Spirit Publishing Inc. Kaufman, S.B. (2018). Twice Exceptional: Supporting and Educating Bright and Creative Students with Learning Difficulties. Oxford University Press.

19   Rinn, A. N. (2020). *Social, emotional, and psychosocial development of gifted and talented individuals.* Routledge.

20   Kaufman, S.B. (2015) *Ungifted: Intelligence redefined.* New York: Basic Books.

21   Centers for Disease Control and Prevention. (2021, September 23). *Data and statistics about ADHD.* Centers for Disease Control and Prevention. Retrieved July 31, 2022, from https://www.cdc.gov/ncbddd/adhd/data.html

22 American Psychiatric Association (2000). American Psychiatric Association. (2000). *Diagnostic and statistical manual of mental disorders* (4ᵗʰ ed., text revision). Page 91. Washington, DC: Author.

23 Barkley, R. A. (2014). Attention-Deficit/Hyperactivity Disorder: A handbook for diagnosis and treatment, 4ᵗʰ edition. New York: Guilford Press.

24 Gomez, R., Stavropoulos, V., Vance, A., & Griffiths, M. D. (2019). Gifted children with ADHD: How are they different from non-gifted children with ADHD? *International Journal of Mental Health and Addiction, 18*(6), 1467–1481. https://doi.org/10.1007/s11469-019-00125-x

25 Bishop, J.C. & Rinn, A.N. (2019). The potential of misdiagnosis of high IQ youth by practicing mental health professionals: A mixed methods study. High Ability Studies.

Hartnett, D.N., Nelson, J.M., & Rinn, A.N. (2004). Gifted or ADHD? The possibilities of misdiagnosis. Roeper Review, 26(2), 73-76.

26 Moon, S. M. (2002). Gifted children with Attention-Deficit/Hyperactivity Disorder. In M. Neihart, S. Reis, N. Robinson, & S. Moon (Eds.), *The social and emotional development of gifted children: What do we know?* (pp 193-201). Washington, DC: National Association for Gifted Children.

Webb, J. T., Amend, E. R., Beljan, P, Webb, N. E., Kuzujanakis, M., Olenchak, F. R., & Goerss, J., (2016). *Misdiagnosis and Dual Diagnoses of Gifted Children and Adults: ADHD, Bipolar, OCD, Asperger's, Depression, and Other Disorders* (2nd Edition). Scottsdale, AZ: Great Potential Press.

27 Kaufmann, F. A., Kalbfleisch, M. L., & Castellanos, F. X. (2000). *Attention-Deficit Disorders and gifted students: What do we really know?* Storrs, CT: National Research Center on the Gifted and Talented.

28 Crespi, B. J. (2016). Autism as a disorder of high intelligence. *Frontiers in Neuroscience, 10.* https://doi.org/10.3389/fnins.2016.00300

29 Billeiter, K. B., & Froiland, J. M. (2022). Diversity of intelligence is the norm within the autism spectrum: Full scale intelligence scores among children with ASD. *Child Psychiatry & Human Development.* https://doi.org/10.1007/s10578-021-01300-9

30 Michaelson, J. J., Doobay, A., Casten, L., Schabilion, K., Foley-Nicpon, M., Nickl-Jockschat, T., Abel, T., & Assouline, S. (2021). Autism in

gifted youth is associated with low processing speed and high verbal ability. https://doi.org/10.1101/2021.11.02.21265802

31 American Psychiatric Association. (2013). Diagnostic and statistical manual of mental disorders (5th ed.). https://doi.org/10.1176/appi. books.9780890425596

32 Neihart, M. (2000). Gifted children with Asperger's Syndrome. *Gifted Child Quarterly, 44(4)*, 222-230.

Chapter 4

1   The technique of using I-statements was developed by Dr. Thomas Gordon. Gordon, T. (2000). *Parent effectiveness training: The proven program for raising responsible children*. New York: Three Rivers Press.

2   This term was coined by Satir, V. (1988). *The new peoplemaking*. Palo Alto, CA: Science & Behavior Books.

    Betts, G. T., & Neihart, M. F. (1985). Eight effective activities to enhance the emotional and social development of the gifted and talented. *Roeper Review, 8*, 18-21 discuss the use of this technique with gifted children.

3   Delisle, J. R. (2006). *Parenting gifted kids: Tips for raising happy and successful children*. Page 131. Waco, TX: Prufrock Press.

Chapter 5

1   Whitney, C. S., & Hirsch, G. (2007). *Motivating the gifted child*. Scottsdale, AZ: Great Potential Press.

2   Peters, S. J., Rambo-Hernandez, K., Makel, M. C., Matthews, M. S., & Plucker, J. A. (2017). Should millions of students take a gap year? large numbers of students start the school year above grade level. *Gifted Child Quarterly, 61*(3), 229–238. https://doi. org/10.1177/0016986217701834

3   Whitney, C. S., & Hirsch, G. (2007). *A love for Learning: Motivation and the gifted child*. Great Potential Press, Inc.

4   Kerr, B. A., & Multon, K. D. (2015). The development of gender identity, gender roles, and Gender Relations in Gifted Students. *Journal of Counseling & Development, 93*(2), 183–191. https://doi. org/10.1002/j.1556-6676.2015.00194.x

5   Kerr, B. A., & Cohn, S. J. (2001). *Smart boys: Talent, masculinity, and the search for meaning.* Gifted Psychology Press.

6   Davis, J. L. (2010). *Bright, talented, & black: A guide for families of black gifted learners.* Gifted Unlimited.

7   Kanevsky, L. (2011). Deferential differentiation. *Gifted Child Quarterly,* 55(4), 279–299. https://doi.org/10.1177/0016986211422098

8   Kohn, A. (2018). *Punished by rewards: The trouble with gold stars, incentive plans, A's, praise, and other bribes.* Houghton Mifflin Company.

Chapter 6

1   Afifi, T., Mota, N., Dasiewicz, P., MacMillan, H., & Sareen, J. (2012). Physical punishment and mental disorders: Results from a nationally representative us sample. *Pediatrics, 130*(2). https://doi.org/10.1542/peds.2011-2947d

2   Betts, G. T., & Kercher, J. (1999). *Autonomous learner model: Optimizing potential.* Greeley, CO: Alps.

3   Rimm, S. B., & Lowe, B. (1998, Fall II). Family environments of underachieving gifted students. *Gifted Child Quarterly, 32(4),* 353-359.

4   Adapted from Rimm, S. B. (1996). *Dr. Sylvia Rimm's smart parenting.* New York: Crown.

5   Cornell, D. (1983). Gifted children: The impact of positive labeling on the family system. *American Journal of Orthopsychiatry, 53,* 322-335.

Dweck, C. S. (2007) Mindset: *The New Psychology of Success.* Ballantine Books.

Rimm, S. B. (2007). *Keys to parenting the gifted child* (3rd ed.). Great Potential Press.

Chapter 7

1   Neihart, M., Pfeiffer, S. I., & Cross, T. L. (2016). *The social and emotional development of gifted children what do we know?* Prufrock Press Inc.

2   Shaunessy-Dedrick, E., Foley-Nicpon, M., & Rinn, A. N. (2018). Social and emotional considerations for gifted students. In *APA handbook of giftedness and talent* (pp. 453–464). essay, American Psychological Association.

3   Hoge, R. D., & Renzulli, J. S. (1991). *Self-concept and the gifted child.* Storrs, CT: National Research Center on the Gifted and Talented; see Rinn, A. N. (2020). The social, emotional, and psychosocial development of gifted and talented individuals. Routledge for an overview.

4   Neihart, M., Reis, S. M., Robinson, N. M., & Moon, S. M. (Eds.). (2002). *The social and emotional development of gifted children: What do we know?* Waco, TX: Prufrock Press.

     Reynolds, C. R., & Bradley, M. (1983). Emotional stability of intellectually superior children versus nongifted peers as estimated by chronic anxiety levels. *School Psychology Review, 12,* 190-194.

     Scholwinski, E., & Reynolds, C. M. (1985). Dimensions of anxiety among high IQ children. *Gifted Child Quarterly, 29(3),* 125-130.

5   Neihart, M. (1999). The impact of giftedness on psychological well-being: What does the empirical literature say? *Roeper Review, 22(1),* 10-17.

6   Hollingworth, L. S. (1975). *Children above 180 IQ.* Page 13. New York: Arno Press. (Original work published 1942)

7   Baum, S. M., & Owen, S. V. (2004). *To be gifted and learning disabled.* Mansfield Center, CT: Creative Learning Press.

8   Schultz, R. A. (2018). Recognizing the Outliers: Behaviors and Tendencies of the Profoundly Gifted Learner in Mixed-Ability Classrooms. *Roeper Review, 40*(3), 191–196. https://doi.org/10.1080/02783193. 2018.1469068

9   Schuler, P. (2002). Perfectionism in gifted children and adults. In M. Neihart, S. Ries, N. Robinson, & S. Moon (Eds.), *The social and emotional development of gifted children: What do we know?* (pp. 71-79). Waco, TX: Prufrock Press has eloquently described the differences between healthy and unhealthy perfectionism.

10   Neihart, M. (2006) used this analogy at the Montana AGATE conference.

11   Adelson, J., & Wilson, H. (2021). *Letting go of perfect: Empower children to overcome perfectionism. Prufrock Press.*

12   Hewitt, P. L., & Flett, G. L. (1991). Perfectionism in the self and social contexts: Conceptualization, assessment, and association with

psychopathology. *Journal of Personality and Social Psychology, 60(3), 456–470.* https://doi.org/10.1037/0022-3514.60.3.456

13 In the 1950s, psychologist Albert Ellis developed "Rational-Emotive Therapy," in which he articulated the concept of "self-talk" as being the key aspect of faulty thinking that then resulted in distressed feelings. His theory is explained in Ellis, A., & Harper, R. A. (1979). *A new guide to rational living* (3rd ed.). Los Angeles: Wilshire.

14 Whitney, C. S., & Hirsch, G. (2007). *Motivating the gifted child.* Scottsdale, AZ: Great Potential Press.

15 Adapted from Delisle, J. R. (1992). *Guiding the social and emotional development of gifted youth: A practical guide for educators and counselors.* New York: Longman. and Ellis, A., & Harper, R. A. (1979). *A new guide to rational living* (3rd ed.). Los Angeles: Wilshire.

16 Sharp, J. E., Niemiec, R. M., & Lawrence, C. (2016). Using Mindfulness-Based Strengths Practices with gifted populations. *Gifted Education International, 33(2), 131–144.* https://doi.org/10.1177/0261429416641009

17 Steadman, J. L., & Feeney, M. E. (2018). *Playing with biofeedback: A practical, playful approach to using biofeedback in pediatric health.* In L. C. Rubin (Ed.), *Handbook of medical play therapy and child life: Interventions in clinical and medical settings* (p. 329–350). Routledge/Taylor & Francis Group.

Chapter 8

1 U.S. Department of Health and Human Services. (n.d.). *Major depression.* National Institute of Mental Health. Retrieved August 2, 2022, from https://www.nimh.nih.gov/health/statistics/major-depression

2 Cross, T. L., & Cross, J. R. (2018). *Suicide among gifted children and adolescents: Understanding the suicidal mind.* Routledge, Taylor et Francis Group.

3 Selph, S. S., & Montgomery, M. S. (2019). Depression in Children and Adolescents: Evaluation and Treatment. *American Family Physician, 100(10), 609–617.*

4 Pawlowska, D. K., Westerman, J. W., Bergman, S. M., & Huelsman, T. J. (2014). Student personality, classroom environment, and student outcomes: A person–environment fit analysis. *Learning and Individual Differences, 36,* 180–193. https://doi.org/10.1016/j.lindif.2014.10.005

5   Mueller, C. E., & Winsor, D. L. (2018). Depression, suicide, and gift-edness: Disentangling risk factors, protective factors, and implications for optimal growth. *Handbook of Giftedness in Children*, 255–284. https://doi.org/10.1007/978-3-319-77004-8_15

6   Johnson, J., Panagioti, M., Bass, J., Ramsey, L., & Harrison, R. (2017). Resilience to emotional distress in response to failure, error or mistakes: A systematic review. *Clinical Psychology Review, 52*, 19–42. https://doi.org/10.1016/j.cpr.2016.11.007

7   Leigh-Hunt, N., Bagguley, D., Bash, K., Turner, V., Turnbull, S., Valtorta, N., & Caan, W. (2017). An overview of systematic reviews on the public health consequences of social isolation and loneliness. *Public Health, 152*, 157–171. https://doi.org/10.1016/j.puhe.2017.07.035

8   Pfeiffer, S. I., Shaunessy-Dedrick, E., Megan, F.-N., Niehart, M., & Yeo, L. S. (2018). Psychological issues unique to the gifted student. In *APA handbook of giftedness and talent* (pp. 497–510). essay, American Psychological Association.

9   Koutsimani, P., Montgomery, A., & Georganta, K. (2019). The relationship between burnout, depression, and anxiety: A systematic review and meta-analysis. *Frontiers in Psychology, 10.* https://doi.org/10.3389/fpsyg.2019.00284

10 Delisle, J. R. (2006). *Parenting gifted kids: Tips for raising happy and successful children*. Page 88. Waco, TX: Prufrock Press.

11 Delisle, J. R. (2006). *Parenting gifted kids: Tips for raising happy and successful children*. Page 124. Waco, TX: Prufrock Press.

12 Berman, S. L., Weems, C. F., & Stickle, T. R. (2006). Existential anxiety in adolescents: Prevalence, structure, association with psychological symptoms and identity development. *Journal of Youth and Adolescence, 35*(3), 285–292. https://doi.org/10.1007/s10964-006-9032-y

13 Vötter, B., & Schnell, T. (2019). Cross-lagged analyses between life meaning, self-compassion, and subjective well-being among gifted adults. *Mindfulness, 10*(7), 1294–1303. https://doi.org/10.1007/s12671-018-1078-x

14 American Psychiatric Association Publishing. (2022). *Diagnostic and statistical manual of mental disorders: DSM-5-TR.*

15 Swannell, S. V., Martin, G. E., Page, A., Hasking, P., & St John, N. J. (2014). Prevalence of nonsuicidal self-injury in nonclinical samples: Systematic Review, meta-analysis and meta-regression. *Suicide and*

Life-Threatening Behavior, 44(3), 273–303. https://doi.org/10.1111/sltb.12070

16 Aacap. (n.d.). *Suicide in Children and Teens.* Suicide in children and teens. Retrieved August 2, 2022, from https://www.aacap.org/AACAP/Families_and_Youth/Facts_for_Families/FFF-Guide/Teen-Suicide-010.aspx

17 Delisle, J. R. (1986). Death with honors: Suicide among gifted adolescents. Page 560. *Journal of Counseling and Development, 64,* 558-560.

18 These principles are adapted from Hayes, M. L., & Sloat, R. S. (1990). Suicide and the gifted adolescent. *Journal for the Education of the Gifted, 13*(3), 229-244.

Chapter 9

1 Gladden, R. M., Vivolo-Kantor, A. M., Hamburger, M. E., & Lumpkin, C. D. (2014). Bullying surveillance among youths: Uniform definitions for public health and recommended data elements. *National Center for Injury Prevention and Control, Centers for Disease Control and Prevention, and U.S. Department of Education.*

2 Shaunessy-Dedrick, E., Foley-Nicpon, M., Espelage, D. L., & King, M. T. (2018). In *APA handbook of giftedness and talent (pp. 659–669).* American Psychological Association.

3 Pfeiffer, S. I. (2013). *Serving the gifted evidence-based clinical and psychoeducational practice. Routledge.*

4 Peterson, J.S. (2015). Gifted children and bullying. In M Neihart, S. I. Pfeiffer, & T. Cross (Eds.) *The social and emotional development of gifted children: What do we know?* (2ⁿᵈ ed., pp. 131-142). Waco, TX: Prufrock Press.

5 Pfeiffer, S. I., Shaunessy-Dedrick, E., Megan, F.-N., Espelage, D. L., & King, M. T. (2018). Bullying and the Gifted. In *Apa Handbook of giftedness and talent* (pp. 659–669). essay, American Psychological Association.

6 Peterson, J. S., & Ray, K. E. (2006). Bullying and the Gifted: Victims, Perpetrators, Prevalence, and Effects. *Gifted Child Quarterly, 50(2), 148–168.* https://doi.org/10.1177/001698620605000206

7 Jumper, R. L. (2019). Communicating about bullying: Examining disclosure among gifted students. *Gifted Education International, 35*(2), 110–120. https://doi.org/10.1177/0261429418824113

Chapter 10

1   Faber, A., & Mazlish, E. (1988). *Siblings without rivalry: How to help your children live together so you can live, too.* Page 29. New York: Avon Books.

2   Gross, M. U. M. (1993). *Exceptionally gifted children.* London: Routledge.

Chapter 11

1   Peters, S. J. (2021). The challenges of achieving equity within public school gifted and talented programs. *Gifted Child Quarterly, 66*(2), 82–94. https://doi.org/10.1177/00169862211002535

2   Guilford, J. P. (1967). *The nature of human intelligence.* New York: McGraw-Hill.

     Torrance, E. P. (1966). *Torrance tests of creative thinking.* Bensenville, IL: Scholastic Testing Service.

3   Torrance, E. P. (1974). *Torrance tests for creative thinking: Grades K-graduate school.* Los Angeles: Western Psychological Services.

4   Sattler (2001) reports that IQ test scores obtained at age three correlate .60 with adult IQ scores.

5   Callahan et al. (1995).

6   Sattler, J. M. (2001). *Assessment of children: Cognitive applications* (4th ed.). San Diego, CA: J. M. Sattler reports that IQ test scores obtained at age three correlate .60 with adult IQ scores.

7   This Renzulli model uses Type I, Type II, and Type III activities that a student selects based on interest and competency level. For more information, see Davis (2006). Davis, G. A. (2006). *Gifted children and gifted education.* Scottsdale, AZ: Great Potential Press.

8   Assouline, S. G., Assouline, S. G., Colangelo, N., & M., G. M. U. (2015). *A nation empowered: Evidence trumps the excuses holding back America's brightest students.* Connie Belin & Jacqueline N. Blank International Center for Gifted Education and Talent Development, University of Iowa.

9   Assouline, S. G., Colangelo, N., & Van Tassel-Baska, J. (2015). *A Nation Empowered, Volume 1: Evidence Trumps the Excuses Holding Back America's Brightest Students.* Belin Blank.

Colangelo, N., Assouline, S. G., & Gross, M. U. M. (2004). A nation deceived: How schools hold back America's students. *The Templeton National Report on Acceleration* (Vols. 1 & 2). Iowa City, IA: Belin-Blank Center.

Gross, M. U. M., & van Vliet, H. E. (2005). Radical acceleration and early entry to college: A review of the research. *Gifted Child Quarterly, 49(2)*, 154-171.

10   Assouline, S. G., Colangelo, N., Lupowski-Shoplik, A., Lipscomb, J., & Forstadt, L. (2009). *Iowa Acceleration Scale (3rd Edition)*. Gifted Unlimited.

About the Authors

Edward R. Amend, Psy.D. is a clinical psychologist at The Amend Group in Lexington, KY, where he focuses on the social, emotional, and educational needs of gifted, twice-exceptional, and neurodivergent youth, adults, and their families. Dr. Amend has authored articles, book chapters, columns, and award-winning books about gifted children. He presents nationally and internationally, and his service has included various roles with the Kentucky Association for Gifted Education, the National Association for Gifted Children, SENG (Supporting Emotional Needs of the Gifted), and The G-WORD film's Advisory Board. Ed is grateful for the enduring love and support of his wife Heidi Carman and their two children, who have shared his journey and enlightened him along the way.

Emily Kircher-Morris, LPC is the host of The Neurodiversity Podcast, which explores the psychological, educational, and social needs of neurodivergent people. After working as a gifted education teacher and school counselor, Emily pursued her passion of supporting the affective needs of gifted and twice-exceptional children as a clinical mental health counselor. She currently works in private practice near St. Louis, Missouri. She is also the author of several books related to the development and education of twice-exceptional children. Her three neurodivergent children provide an unending supply of content for her podcast and books.

Janet L. Gore has over 30 years experience with gifted and talented students and their families, first as a teacher and later as a school administrator, guidance counselor, policy maker, state director and parent. She is co author of two award winning books, *A Parent's Guide to Gifted Children*, and *Grandparents' Guide to Gifted Children*. For five years she worked as a designated counselor/advocate for gifted high school students in Tucson, Arizona, and for three years served as State Director of Gifted Education in Arizona where she helped to draft legislation and create funding for gifted programs across the state. In that role she traveled across the state to provide training and technical assistance to school personnel to help them meet the legislative mandate.

She is a former member of the Board of AAGT, the Arizona Association for Gifted and Talented, serving one year as conference chair. Her administrative experience includes being an Assistant Principal in a district that included a high percentage of Native American students.

She has taught middle school, high school and college students and has coached Academic Decathlon and Future Problem Solving programs. She has taught graduate level courses in gifted education and creativity. She graduated from Carleton College, received an M.A. in English from the University of Iowa and an M.Ed. in Guidance and Counseling from the University of Arizona. She lives in Tucson, Arizona.

CPSIA information can be obtained
at www.ICGtesting.com
Printed in the USA
JSHW010829240323
39394JS00003B/4